Tracks of the Bear

OTHER BOOKS BY EDGAR O'BALLANCE

The Arab-Israeli War, 1948-49
The Sinai Campaign, 1956
The Third Arab-Israeli War, 1967
Arab Guerrilla Power
The Electronic War in the Middle East, 1968-70
War in the Yemen
The Kurdish Revolt, 1961-72
Korea, 1950-53
The Algerian Insurrection, 1954-62
Malaya: The Communist Insurgent War, 1948-60
The Greek Civil War, 1944-49
The Indo-China War, 1945-54: Study in Guerrilla Warfare
The Red Army of China
The Story of the French Foreign Legion
The Red Army (of Russia)
The Wars in Vietnam
No Victor, No Vanquished
Language of Violence: The Blood Politics of Terrorism
Terror in Ireland: The Heritage of Hate

Tracks of the Bear

Soviet Imprints in the Seventies

Edgar O'Ballance

★
PRESIDIO

Published by Presidio Press,
31 Pamaron Way, Novato, CA 94947

Library of Congress Cataloging in Publication Data

O'Ballance, Edgar.
　Tracks of the bear.

　Bibliography: p.
　Includes index.
　1. Soviet Union—Military policy.　2. Soviet Union—
Foreign relations—1953-1975.　3. Soviet Union—Foreign
relations—1975- .　4. World politics—1965-1975.
5. World politics—1975-1985.　I. Title.
UA770.02　1982　　　355'.0335'47　　　82-9819
ISBN 0-89141-133-X　　　　　　　　AACR2

Cover design by Kathleen Jaeger
Illustration by Allyson Ward-Pirenian

Printed in the United States of America

Contents

List of Maps

Abbreviations

ABM	Antiballistic missile
ALCM	Air launched cruise missile
ANC	African National Council, Rhodesia
ARVN	Army of the Republic of Vietnam
ASEAN	Association of Southeast Asian Nations
ASW	Antisubmarine warfare
BENELUX	The Belgium, Netherlands, and Luxembourg Economic Union
BPLM	Baluchistan People's Liberation Movement
BTR	Soviet armored vehicle
CENTO	Central Treaty Organization
CIA	Central Intelligence Agency, U.S.
CIDG	Civilian Irregular Defense Group
COMECON (CMEA)	Council for Mutual Economic Assistance
COREO	Guerrilla group, Mozambique
CPI	Communist Party of India
CSCE	Conference on Security and Cooperation in Europe
DEFCON	U.S. defensive condition ("Red Alert")
DOSAAF	Soviet part-time military training organization
DRG	Democratic Republic of Germany (East Germany)
ECM	Electronic countermeasures
EDU	Guerrilla group, Eritrea
EEC	European Economic Community
ELF	Guerrilla group, Eritrea
ELF–PLF	Guerrilla group, Eritrea
ELF–RC	Guerrilla group, Eritrea
EPLF	Guerrilla group, Eritrea
ERW	Enhanced radiation weapon (neutron bomb)

FNLA	Guerrilla movement, Angola
FRELIMO	Guerrilla movement, Mozambique
FRG	Federal Republic of Germany (West Germany)
FROG	Soviet ground-to-ground rocket
FROLIZI	Guerrilla coalition, Rhodesia
FUMO	Guerrilla group, Mozambique
GRAE	Angolan government-in-exile
GRU	Soviet military intelligence
ICBM	Intercontinental Ballistic missile
IISS	International Institute for Strategic Studies (London)
JVP	Political Party, Sri Lanka
KGB	Committee of State Security (Secret Service), USSR
MAAG	Military Assistance and Advisory Group, U.S.
MACV	Military Advisory Command, Vietnam
MBFR	Mutual Balanced Forces Reduction Talks
MIRV	Multiple independently targetable reentry vehicle
MPA	Main Political Administration, USSR
MPLA	Guerrilla movement, Angola
MVD	Minister of Internal Affairs, USSR
NATO	North Atlantic Treaty Organization
NIF	National Iranian Front
OAU	Organization of African Unity
OPEC	Organization of Petroleum Exporting Countries
OTRAG	Orbital Transport and Rocket Company
PAIGC	Guerrilla movement, Portuguese Guinea
PDP	People's Democratic Party, Afghanistan
PDRY	People's Democratic Republic of Yemen (South Yemen)
PFLO	Guerrilla group, South Yemen
PFLOAG	Guerrilla group, South Yemen
PFLP	Popular Front for the Liberation of Palestine

PLO	Palestine Liberation Organization
POLISARIO	Guerrilla movement in former Spanish colonial territory
PPP	Pakistan People's Party
PRG	Provisional Republican Government, South Vietnam
RDF	Rapid Deployment Force, U.S.
SALT	Strategic Arms Limitation Talks
SAM	Surface-to-air missile
SAVAK	Secret police, Iran
SCP	Soviet Communist Party
SEATO	Southeast Asia Treaty Organization
SHAPE	Supreme Headquarters Allied Powers, Europe
SLMB	Submarine-launched ballistic missile
SWAPO	Guerrilla movement, Namibia
UANC	United African National Council, Rhodesia
UNIFIL	United Nations Interim Force in Lebanon
UNITA	Guerrilla movement, Angola
VTOL	Vertical take-off and landing
WSLF	Guerrilla movement, Somalia
ZANLA	Guerrilla army, Rhodesia
ZANU	Guerrilla movement, Rhodesia
ZAPU	Guerrilla movement, Rhodesia
ZIPRA	Guerrilla army, Rhodesia
ZSU	Soviet antiaircraft gun

Preface

ON 31 DECEMBER 1979, Soviet leaders must have sat back to congratulate themselves on a successful and satisfying ten years of strategic expansion and increased global influence. This is a study of that period, in which Soviet "peace strategy" operated with success to the detriment of the United States, especially in Southeast Asia, Africa, and the Middle East. The seventies was not one of America's finest and most glorious decades, but one of milestones of miscalculation and misjudgment in strategic matters. It will long be remembered for its Watergate affair, its uncharacteristic Vietnam experience, its lack of self-confidence and resolute leadership, and its constant appeasement of the Kremlin. The latter years of the decade were somewhat reminiscent of the period of the British Chamberlain administration, just prior to World War II, which concentrated on appeasing Hitler.

The outstanding lesson of the seventies is that the Soviets do not react to gestures of goodwill, kindness, or consideration. Negotiations between the United States and the USSR should be more realistic, and a little practical horse-trading would not come amiss. For example, the Soviets quite openly sent weapons into Vietnam to be used against American soldiers; so why should the U.S. not send arms to resistance fighters opposing the Soviets in Afghanistan? If it had, the U.S. administration could have told the Kremlin, "We will give you a free hand in Afghanistan if you will give us one in Cuba." Sometimes the United States will have to choose the lesser of two evils, as in El Salvador, or lose out by defeat, as in Angola.

The Soviets are bully boys who need to be taken down a peg or two, who despise and take advantage of good nature and weakness, and they have to be dealt with as such. American negotiators must play them at their own game and win; to do so at times may mean taking the gloves off. The Soviets respect only force and the will to use it, as their "peace strategy" demonstrated in the seventies. The Soviet brand of communism will never sell, as few would volunteer to live under it for any length of time. The Soviets know they will have to force their political philosophy on the world, but the Kremlin will not start a world war it did not think it could win. However, the Soviet Union will go right to the brink of war in its "peace strategy" operations.

World War III can be avoided if the United States is strong and resolute. A peaceful future depends not on such impractical gestures as unilateral nuclear disarmament, but on a relaxation of existing tension that will lead to multilateral arms limitation talks. The Soviets have no intention of abandoning their nuclear weapons, or their biological, chemical, or germ warfare ones, for that matter, but would like the United States and its NATO allies to do just that. Nations, especially the European NATO allies, should have the moral courage to stand up and be counted, and not to give way to Soviet threats and pressures. Long-term hope for a peaceful future lies in a pentagonal economic balance in the world between the United States, Western Europe, the USSR, China, and Japan linked with the Association of Southeast Asian Nations and Australasia, in which each would counterbalance the other, and none would be militarily strong enough to dominate or attack and defeat the others.

Meanwhile, the United States must negotiate with the Soviets from a position of strength and have plenty of bargaining counters on the table, and a few underneath it as well. In the seventies, all the American cards were placed on the negotiating table face up, while all the Soviet ones were face down, or up their sleeves: the United States sat naked in the negotiating chamber. Reflections on the misjudgments, miscalculations, and ineffective "mirror-imaging" negotiations of the seventies may produce positive changes for dealing with the Kremlin in the eighties.

—Edgar O'Ballance

Tracks of the Bear

1  Soviet Leadership in the Seventies

We should remember Lenin's words that in our society everything which serves to build Communism is moral. We can paraphrase this by saying, that for us everything which serves the interests of the people and the building up of communism is democratic.
—Leonid Brezhnev, 25th Congress, 24 February 1976

WESTERN LEADERS HAVE long been mesmerized into believing that Soviet leaders think and react much as they themselves do, are primarily concerned with good government and cordial relations between nations, and above all will do almost anything to avoid a Third World War, which would inevitably be a nuclear one. Regarding Soviet statesmen as replicas of their Western counterparts has come to be known as "mirror-imaging"; it is, in short, expecting the Soviets to observe the rule of law and to respect accepted international usages, as would any responsible (American) statesman. Unfortunately, Soviets think and react very differently from Americans and West Europeans.

During the seventies Western leaders were painfully anxious to believe, and frequently to accept without question, Soviet propaganda that their huge nuclear and conventional arsenals existed only because of disastrous Soviet experiences in World War II, in which they lost well over 20 million dead. Remembering that Hitler's troops came within sight of Moscow in 1941, Western statesmen thought they understood the deep-felt Soviet delusion that the USSR was hemmed in by a deliberate military enforcement. They realized that this anxiety neurosis and persecution mania caused the Soviets to carry their need for national security to an extreme, but it was hoped these neuroses would gradually fade away. American statesmen thought the Soviets merely wanted to

1

gain military parity with the United States, so as to be able to shake off their hallucinations. The acquisitive colonial and imperialistic character of Soviet leadership was not yet fully appreciated. It was not realized that Soviet leaders were following a long-term aim to achieve global hegemony, and that nothing else was acceptable. This basic misunderstanding meant that the United States was always at a disadvantage when dealing with the Soviets.

The Soviets have no wish to be "equal" to any other nation, and "parity" is not in their vocabulary either, as that would mean a continuing stalemate, a prolongation of the existing status quo of the strategic balance of their armed forces against those of the United States. This would be of no benefit to them in their global ambitions as it would simply prevent progress towards their desired world socialist order.

Strategic expansion is a Soviet hallmark. Peter the Great, a clever and ambitious czar (1672–1725), considerably enlarged the Russian Empire, and in the eighteenth and nineteenth centuries, he was succeeded by other like-minded expansionist czars. Largely balked in eastern Europe, they marched into Asia, adding large tracts of Asian territory and millions of non-Russian peoples to their domain. After the Communists seized power in Russia in the Revolution of 1917, their leaders simply continued the work begun by Peter the Great. In the civil war that continued until 1924, they consolidated their hold on the former Imperial Russian Empire outside Europe[1] and successfully repulsed allied intervention. After World War II, Stalin annexed almost 400,000 square miles in eastern Europe, bringing another 87 million non-Russian peoples under the hammer and sickle emblem. Soviet ideology and terminology may differ from that of the Orthodox Russian Church and the czar's Imperial government, but their dual long-term material aims and empirical ambitions do not.

Many years ago Lenin enunciated his doctrine of the "Universal Dictatorship of the Proletariat." Stripped of its pompous communist jargon, this means a determination to work unceasingly to bring about a world socialist (meaning communist) order, dominated and directed from the Kremlin. That is, and always has been, the long-term aim of the Soviet governments led by Stalin, Krushchev, and now Brezhnev, from which they have never deviated. They have only paused in their expansionist efforts because of lack of sufficient means and capability, but never longer than necessary. Soviet leaders have always taken full advantage of any opportunity to expand their influence beyond their borders.

[1]See Edgar O'Ballance, *The Red Army* (London: Faber).

They do not set a rigid timetable for this progression to global domination, but they do occasionally set short-term or medium-term objectives. Such a socialist order would give the Soviets access to the world's resources, both human and material. It would also remove all external challenges and enable them to eliminate all alternative political and social systems. The main obstacle to Soviet global hegemony is the United States of America, which the Soviet government regards as the center and rallying point of the "enemy capitalistic camp." The Soviet government is, and has been for years, constantly working to reduce and undermine the power, influence, and prestige of the United States, and to isolate it from the rest of the world. In particular, the USSR has worked to divorce the United States from countries that provide it with natural resources, so as to reduce it to economic as well as political impotence.

The Soviets remain in a continual state of ideological warfare with nations that do not accept the Moscow brand of communism and its leadership. This type of Soviet warfare can be waged by violent or non-violent means, whichever is more suitable, opportune, and advantageous at the moment. Violent means include open warfare, but the Soviet Union will not deliberately enter such a conflict unless it is sure it will win and no lesser alternative is available. When the enemy has superior military strength and capability, the Soviet Union invokes its policy of "prevention of war," which really means avoiding war until it is absolutely compelled to fight one, or until it is convenient to do so.

Short of waging open war to achieve their global aim, the Soviets continually operate what they refer to as their "peace strategy," which utilizes nonviolent means such as fighting proxy wars with the United States (as in Vietnam), supporting and supplying arms to liberation movements, and giving selective aid to international and national terrorist groups through its secret service, the KGB.[2] The KGB thinks of itself as the fighting wing of the Soviet Communist Party and has over 110,000 full-time operatives and a large army of agents.[3] Nonviolent means also embrace negotiation, propaganda, misinformation, trade agreements, espionage, and aid to local Communist parties. For example, Lenin once wrote: "Negotiations are one tool among many others in the conduct of the international class struggle, to be judged by its utility in advancing Soviet objectives, but without any inherent value in itself."[4]

[2]Komitet Gosudarsivennoy Bezopasnosti, meaning Committee of State Security.
[3]H. Chapman-Pincher, *Inside Story* (London: Sidgwick and Jackson, 1978).
[4]Vladimir Ilyich Lenin, *Collected Works,* 4th ed. (Progress Pubs., Russia) 1975.

Communist parties of all countries are considered by the Kremlin leaders to be legitimate tools in the struggle for global hegemony. Moscow encourages these Communist parties to make themselves viable and powerful within the existing political framework of their own countries, to build a power base that can be expanded, and to spread tentacles of subversion into government services, the armed forces, and other institutions. The presence of an indigenous Communist Party, together with the sight of Soviet warships on the horizon, has a deeply unsettling psychological effect on governments of some Third World countries, especially weak ones and those feeling in need of a superpower as protector against regional rivals. This is the age-old criminal protection racket expanded into an international dimension.

The Kremlin gives a varying degree of support, either moral or practical or both, to the almost worldwide network of Communist parties, especially those that have a commitment to the Moscow-based Marxist-Leninist brand of communism. The Soviets especially encourage and help, while at times disclaiming such contact, those Communist parties in states where political freedom, or a fair degree of it, allows them to operate openly. In countries where the Communist Party has to operate underground because of lack of political freedom, the KGB sometimes helps. Weaker parties are kept in existence wherever possible, even if a small core has to be in exile in the USSR.

One of the "other means" the Soviets use in their constant ideological struggle with the West is that of "peaceful coexistence." To Americans this expression generally means "live and let live," and not to interfere in domestic affairs of other nations; in short, to be a good neighbor. The Soviets see it differently. Both Lenin and Stalin pursued a policy of peaceful coexistence when they considered it to be of value or an interim necessity. To them it simply meant a breathing space in which "the situation is enabled to be improved, so that the Soviet Union can steadily increase its power position in the world without danger of global war."[5]

Soviet interpretation of peaceful coexistence was put bluntly by Brezhnev: "We Communists have got to string along with the Capitalists for a while. We need their credits, their agriculture, and their technology. But we are going to continue massive military programmes, and by the middle of the 'Eighties' we will be in a position to return to a much more aggressive foreign policy, designed to gain the upper-hand in our rela-

[5]Joseph D. Douglass, Jr., *Soviet Military Strategy in Europe* (New York: Pergamon Press, 1980).

tionship with the West.''[6] This policy was followed consistently in the seventies as the USSR strove to manipulate arms control talks, extend its influence farther afield, deepen its influence in certain regions of the world, dominate the world's oceans, and impose new Soviet imprints where none had been before.

The Soviets believe that a kind of World War III is now in progress, characterized by proxy and subversive warfare as well as ''all other means,'' the object being to prepare the way for a possible World War IV, which could be the ultimate one that would bring total victory to Moscow and establish its brand of communism throughout the world. However, the Soviets do hope that their ''peace strategy'' will eventually bring about the collapse or fragmentation of the United States, NATO, and other pro-Western alliances, in which case a World War IV may not be necessary.

Global hegemony remains the distant prize, but in the interim the Soviets devised a medium-term strategy, which they began in the sixties and operated well into the seventies. Apart from avoiding open nuclear war with the United States, the first Soviet priority was to strengthen and modernize the Soviet economy, which was antiquated, weak, and badly in need of modern technology. As an essential requisite to improving overall military strength and capability, this was to be achieved by obtaining advanced technology, economic aid, and as much hard Western currency and exchange credits as possible from America and the Western world.

The next priority was to try to divide Western Europe from the United States—in other words, to split the Atlantic Alliance wide open and thus eliminate NATO as a major military power bloc barring Soviet aggression in Europe. This was to be done by improving and manipulating existing Soviet-European links, such as those formed by national Communist parties and Communist front organizations; to establish others; and also to seek to convert the growing European concept of a national communism that would be completely independent of Moscow leadership and influence.

The third priority was to try to sever Western, and in particular American, trade links with certain Third World countries, especially those in Black Africa, which were the producers or potential producers of huge quantities of natural resources, oil, and minerals essential to Western economies. China was to be isolated and contained for the time being, but action was to be taken to prevent the Chinese from

[6]Ibid.

ganging up with either the United States, Japan, or NATO against the Soviet Union. In the seventies Soviet effort and attention were largely focused subversively on American and the NATO European nations.

Unlike America, which in the seventies had three administrations—those of Richard Nixon, Gerald Ford, and Jimmy Carter—each of which made several switches in foreign policy, the Soviets were fortunate that throughout almost the whole decade their government consisted of the powerful triumvirate of Leonid Brezhnev, general secretary of the Central Committee of the Soviet Communist Party; Nikolai Podgorny, president of the Supreme Soviets Presidium; and Alexei Kosygin, the prime minister. Their policies were firm and consistent; they presented a "collective leadership" to their people and to the world at large; they were able to plan ahead; and they did their best to stay in office to implement their plans.

The cold, despotic Stalin died in bed in 1953, to be succeeded by the flamboyant and abrasive Nikita Khrushchev, who gained notoriety for, among other things, taking his shoe off and banging it on the table to emphasize a point in the United Nations forum. Khrushchev obtained autocratic powers equal almost to those of Stalin, but he fell from office in October 1964. He presided over a period referred to as the Soviet "quantity race" in armaments, wherein the USSR strove to build up an inventory equal at least to that of the United States. It was a time when the Soviet armed forces were definitely on the defensive against the United States, as they lagged behind in nuclear arms, means of delivery, and technology.

Under Khrushchev's direction, discussions within the Soviet leadership took place on how to take full advantage of the rapid Western decolonization process that was taking place in the world, especially in Africa. Khrushchev was of the opinion that local Communist parties in decolonizing countries should be supported, encouraged, and secretly helped, whenever necessary, to force their way to power in their respective states. This policy was adopted.

The Khrushchev period (1953–1964) was one of "peaceful coexistence," which he explained at the Twentieth Congress of the Soviet Communist Party, in 1956, as "War is not inevitable, nor is revolution, but the victory of Soviet Socialism is inevitable." In 1960, Khrushchev boasted that within a decade the Soviet economy would overtake that of the United States; but while some big strides were taken, this was not accomplished. In 1970, the gross national product of the United States was about $932 billion, and that of the USSR only $600 billion.

Brezhnev, Podgorny, and Kosygin worked together closely. All major decisions, and at times less important ones, too, had to have the agreement of all three men, but from the beginning Brezhnev was the "first among equals." The son of a Ukrainian steel worker, Brezhnev was always the orthodox political organizational man, a protege of Khrushchev, but forever maneuvering within the Party for his own personal advancement. The West became so used to seeing Brezhnev's huge, unsmiling, dour, expressionless face in the media that it was assumed he might simply be the "front man" of the Politburo. This was not so. He admired power, coveted it, and enjoyed using it; he appreciated strength and was contemptuous of weakness. In many ways he epitomized the character of the Soviet top leadership, which Westerners hoped was really only a stern exterior.

Brezhnev had a private side to his personality as well as the carefully cultivated public one. He possessed an extremely good flair for public relations, considerable political skill and acumen, and a good sense of political timing, all of which he used to climb to the top of the Party hierarchy. Behind the scenes he could be affable and smiling, giving effusive handshakes and bear hugs, pats on the back, and verbal praise —all very selectively and with a scheming purpose. In this way, not only did he climb to the top, but he also gained a large personal following within both the party and the leadership. Brezhnev, who claimed he pursued a "more considered policy on a scientific basis," had been the main protagonist of the Soviet military intervention in Czechoslovakia in 1968, while his two "equal colleagues" had been only lukewarm on this issue, to say the least.

Podgorny, a quieter, less colorful man, was also from the Ukraine. After holding a number of local Party posts, he became a member of the Politburo in 1960, having been a candidate (i.e., nonvoting) member two years previously. Considered to be unassuming, solid, and reliable, Podgorny was in 1965 appointed president of the Supreme Soviets Presidium, a position equal to that of head of state in other nations. Podgorny was associated with the succeeding Five Year Plans and presented them to the congresses in 1971 and 1976.

An engineer and technologist, Kosygin was a survivor of the Stalin era and had been a member of the ruling Politburo since 1948 (he had been a candidate member since 1946). He spent most of his career in administrative jobs rather than purely political ones, was appointed deputy prime minister in 1940, and in 1964 succeeded Khrushchev as prime minister. During the sixties, Kosygin advocated avoiding confrontation with both the United States and China; at the Twenty-Third Congress, in 1966, he emphasized the importance of buying Western technology because, as he said, "It is simpler to buy 'start-up capability' than develop it" from scratch.

The year 1970 was one of celebration in the USSR as the centennial of the birth of Lenin, and there were many ceremonies across the length and breadth of the country. Unexpectedly, Brezhnev thrust himself into the limelight, shedding his deliberately acquired publicity-avoiding image to take prominent part in as many of these ceremonies as possible. He simply hogged all the media coverage; as the media is, of course, state-controlled in the USSR, he must have deliberately stage-managed his many public appearances himself. Such blatant junketing had not been seen in the Soviet Union since the days of Khrushchev. Brezhnev played to his audience, telling them things they wanted to hear and having tactful and soothing words for all factions. To the watching and wondering Soviet generals, suspicious of this unusual, almost Tammany Hall type political electioneering, he said, "If anyone tries to gain military superiority over the Soviet Union, we will reply with the necessary increase in military might." The generals relaxed and purred: this was just what they wanted to hear. The spotlight of Soviet media coverage has since remained primarily on Brezhnev.

As general secretary of the Soviet Communist Party, Brezhnev somewhat naturally dominated the Twenty-Fourth Congress, held in Moscow in April 1971, which produced an overwhelming show of leadership solidarity. The congress elected its new Central Committee, which in turn elected the Political Bureau and the Party Secretariat. The new Central Committee was enlarged to 241 full members (from 195) and 165 candidate members (from 155). There were some dual elections, but with three exceptions due to deaths and one resignation, the twenty-five men elected to the Politburo and the Secretariat were exactly the same as those who had sat on those bodies since the 1966 congress. In the customary Soviet manner, names were announced in their accepted order of importance. The list began with Brezhnev, Podgorny, and Kosygin.

Brezhnev plugged the peaceful coexistence policy, and put forward a so-called peace plan that called for the abolition of both NATO and the Warsaw Pact, arms control negotiations and treaties, and nuclear weapon free zones. He also stated that all "foreign bases" should be dismantled, meaning the American ones in Europe. Tongue in cheek, Brezhnev appealed for the normalization of Soviet relations with China and for efforts "to eliminate the hotbeds of war in the Middle East and South East Asia." This barb was directed at the U.S. administration, which was supporting Israel against Soviet-armed Arab forces and was involved in fighting communist insurgent forces in South Vietnam.

Brezhnev also called for "definite recognition of the territorial changes that have taken place as the result of World War II," which has been a Soviet nagging demand ever since the Stalin era. In plain language, the Soviets wanted universal recognition of the "legality" of their sovereignty over the territory in east and central Europe annexed by them. Brezhnev also stated that the Soviet Communist Party had over 14.4 million members.

In May 1973, Brezhnev removed two men from the Politburo and brought in four new ones, further increasing his personal following in that body. This brought the strength of the Politburo up to twenty-two members; and of the sixteen who had full voting rights, at least seven were now dedicated Brezhnev men. The two men relieved from duty were Pyotr Shelest and Gennady Voronov, both of whom had opposed some of Brezhnev's initiatives. The four newcomers were Andrei Gromyko, the foreign minister; Yuro Andpopov, head of the KGB; Grigory Romanov, the Leningrad party secretary; and Marshal Andrei Grechko. Grechko, the first serving soldier in the Politburo since 1957, had been the Soviet Defense minister since 1967; before that, he had been commander in chief of the Warsaw Pact Joint Armed Forces for seven years. Grechko was in favor of easing East-West tensions, even if it meant marginally reducing Soviet arms, but Brezhnev needed his expertise for the arms control talks.

The Khrushchev policy of supporting local Communist parties in the hope they would be able to claw their way to power in newly emergent Third World countries had not proved successful, so when the Brezhnev Trio came to power in 1964, this was changed and supplanted by another policy, which became known as "power projection." In practice this meant supporting any "progressive forces sympathetic to the Soviet Union, struggling for power," especially in Africa, and marked the Soviet switch from the defensive to the offensive in the Third World.

A resolution of the Central Committee of the Soviet Communist Party in August 1967 had decided on "measures for further developing the Social Sciences, and heightening their role in Communist construction"; these measures were designed to "ensure Socialism's victory over Capitalism." The Soviets began giving all aid and support possible, short of provoking World War III with NATO, to "officially approved movements of liberation." Money, weapons, training facilities, and sanctuary were provided for "freedom fighters" practically anywhere in the world. The KGB secretly aided selected terrorist groups, especially small Middle Eastern ones, which the Soviet government wanted to keep active for their trouble-making capability.

In short, from the mid-sixties through the seventies, the Soviet peace strategy was outward-looking and far ranging. It was also assisted by the rapidly expanding Soviet Navy. A more scientific approach to target countries was adopted, but studies were made to determine local tactics. Existing but moribund institutes for the study of special areas such as Africa, Latin America, the Middle East, and the Far East were revived, and high-ranking Soviet military officers were appointed to the command, teaching, and administrative posts in these institutes. In 1972, the Soviet Institute for the Study of the United States of America was established.

The Soviets piously alleged that their assistance to liberation movements was confined strictly to moral, educational, and cultural activities, such as free scholarships to the Patrice Lumumba University in Moscow and similar establishments. They firmly denied they were financing or arming freedom fighters, a denial that was more than partially believed by some American statesmen until "military artifacts" proved the falseness of these Soviet claims. These military artifacts, littered around the world, included such items as Soviet AK-47 automatic rifles, rocket launchers, mortars, and even SAM-7 missiles, and were found in the possession of irregular armies and various liberation movements.

As the AK-47 achieved such worldwide revolutionary notoriety, a few words can be written about it. First produced in 1947, it was designed by Mikhail Timfeevich Kalashnikov, a Soviet inventor now laden with Soviet honors for his other inventions and innovations in weaponry. Having a 7.62 mm caliber, a prominent curved magazine holding thirty rounds of ammunition, a fairly short barrel, a comparatively short range, and the ability to fire 100 rounds a minute, it is simple to operate. Little can go wrong with it mechanically, as has been proved over the years, and it functions ably in all weathers and climates, including ice, snow, mud, and sand. Like the old Model T Ford, it is rough and ready and keeps firing when more sophisticated weapons fail.

Over 30 million AK-47s have been distributed outside the Soviet Union, mainly to Third World countries and liberation movements.[7] The Communist Omnipol armaments factory near Prague, in Czechoslovakia, where almost any amount of certain types of Soviet pattern weapons can be obtained for hard Western currency without too many questions being asked, has turned them out by the thousands each month for years. Many find their way into arms bazaars and black markets of the world.

Additionally, the Soviet ground forces in the sixties and seventies

---

[7] According to *Jane's Infantry Weapons* (London: Jane's Publishing Company).

were armed with AK-47s. In an economy measure as the seventies drew to a close, the Soviets replaced their AK-47s with an improved AK-74 of 5.45 mm caliber, whose bullets use less copper and lead. These bullets also have a "tumbling" effect that causes tearing wounds. The AK-47 was first seen at the Moscow military parade, in November 1978; the following year, all the Soviet troops in that annual parade were armed with them. By 1979, about 1.8 million Soviet soldiers had been rearmed with AK-74s. Most of the withdrawn AK-47s will go to reserve formations and to reserve inventories, but some perhaps will find their way into the hands of freedom fighters elsewhere in the world.

In the early seventies, other Soviet weapons began to appear in the hands of freedom fighters and terrorists, including SAM-7s. The SAM-7 is a surface-to-air, heat-seeking missile that is shoulder-held and operated by one man. With an infrared optical aiming device, it has a range of over three miles. In the Yom Kippur War of 1973, it proved to be very effective against helicopters and low- or slow-flying aircraft.

In the seventies, as part of their peace strategy, the Soviet government selectively, and at a political price or as a political gift, supplied weapons and military equipment openly to several Third World countries. Unlike most Western countries, the USSR does not completely discard or destroy its weapons as they become obsolete or are superseded by more modern ones. They are passed over to reserve or shadow formations, put into mobilization stores, or doled out to Third World nations, liberation movements, and even terrorist groups. At first they are made as a gift to any target Third World country, much as a salesman's sample; then come offers to sell more, either at specially low prices or in exchange for facilities, resources, or political influence.

In some instances Soviet second-hand arms are unwanted commodities that have to be forced on reluctant target countries, perhaps because those countries cannot afford to buy them and any money they do have would be better spent on food and development projects. Soviet policy is to persuade newly emergent nations, and even established ones, that they simply must have arms as they are the prestige symbols of a fully independent state. The result is that Soviet weapons, often in the form of T-34 tanks, older armored vehicles, guns, and military vehicles, and even MiG-15 and MiG-17 aircraft, are seen in small numbers in a great many countries. These Soviet arms are substitutes for the lowered flag of the former colonial power. Countries with money to spend, or some commodity the Soviets want, are persuaded to buy more modern arms (such as T-54, T-55 or T-62 tanks, missiles, antiaircraft guns, artillery, and even MiG-21 aircraft) in greater quantities, whether they really need them or not. However, the Soviets strictly control and regulate the supply of ammunition and spare parts as a means of political blackmail to ensure good "socialist" behavior and loyalty to the Marxist-Leninist brand of communism.

In summary, the Soviet objective is to persuade Third World countries to adopt Soviet arms systems and reject those left behind by the former colonial powers, and to deprive those powers of further lucrative arms sales and the influence that goes with supplying arms. More important, it is to make newly emergent states militarily dependent on the USSR for ammunition, spares, and follow-up replacements and progressions. Having changed over from a Western arms system to a Soviet one, the target nation becomes a "client" one.

When the Twenty-fifth Congress of the Soviet Communist Party (SCP) commenced in Moscow on 24 February 1976, Brezhnev again presented the Central Committee's report in a major opening speech. He reaffirmed the Soviet government's intention to continue a policy of detente, while continuing to support national liberation movements. He also said, "As long as the NATO bloc continues to exist . . . our country, and the other signatories of the Warsaw Pact, will continue to strengthen this political-military alliance." Brezhnev mentioned that the Soviet Communist Party had a membership of over 15.5 million, and emphasized that members must "set an example of Communist principles in action, wherever they worked." Party members were urged to be organizers and activists.

On 26 April 1976, Marshal Grechko died and was replaced as defense minister by Dmitri Ustinov, who was made a full member of the Politburo and given the rank of general. Ustinov was the first civilian to hold this office since Trotsky in 1918. It had been widely expected that Marshal Viktor Kulikov, commander in chief of the Warsaw Pact Joint Armed Forces, would have become the defense minister. Ustinov was not the complete civilian, however, as he had served in the army as a commissar from 1943–53 and had also held the appointments of minister of armaments and minister of defense industries before becoming secretary to the Central Committee of the SCP in 1965, when he became a candidate member of the Politburo.

As the Kremlin leadership was elderly by Western standards, it was predicted that perhaps General Secretary Brezhnev, then seventy years old and seemingly in poor health for some time, would step down. Precisely the opposite happened. On 24 May 1977, Podgorny was suddenly removed from the Politburo without explanation; on 16 June, he formally resigned as president of the Supreme Soviets Presidium, again without explanation. Aged seventy-four, Podgorny departed from the scene of Soviet power in silence, which under Soviet custom meant he had been pushed out. Instead of stepping down, Brezhnev took Podgorny's appointment.

Retaining his post as general secretary of the Soviet Communist Party, Brezhnev now additionally became president of the Supreme Soviets Presidium, and so Soviet head of state. He now held a massive slice of Soviet power and was the undisputed master in the Kremlin. One of his first duties as president was to approve the text and music of the new Soviet national anthem, which was similar to the previous one but omitted all references to Stalin. Kosygin retained his post as prime minister, but he had become a subdued figure beside Brezhnev and was in a subordinate role. Kosygin's health was failing, and he formally resigned his office of prime minister in October 1980, only to die three months later.

The Soviet leadership, now clearly personified in Brezhnev, became supremely confident, in comparison with that of President Carter of the United States, and Brezhnev was emboldened to indulge in a massive step of brinkmanship which might have plunged both superpowers into war against each other. Just a few days before the end of the seventies, Soviet armed forces invaded Afghanistan. Brezhnev had assessed the situation and American reaction correctly, calculating that Carter would make no military riposte in 1980, which was a presidential election year. Carter's almost pathetic response of calling for a boycott of the Moscow Olympic Games left his NATO allies flabbergasted and speechless. This indication of American hesitation and weakness, of course, delighted the Soviet leadership, which sat back to congratulate itself on the successful and satisfying manner in which its peace strategy had unfolded during the seventies.

2  The Soviet Political-Military Mind

The detente process should be kept separate from the continuing ideological struggle.

— Leonid Brezhnev, 24th Congress, 1971

AMERICAN STATESMEN DEDICATED to mirror-imaging do not understand Russian mentality, although they are convinced they do. Likewise, the Soviets have their own vision partly obscured by seeing everyone else, the Americans in particular, as they see themselves. For example, the West regards NATO as a defensive pact, but the Soviets do not believe that for one moment, as that is the sort of description they would use to deceive the enemy, knowing it to be untrue. Neither do they believe that NATO forces would not fire the first shot in any World War III.

Mirror-imaging obliterates the fact that the Soviet political-military mind works in a very different way from that of a Western one. If an American, a British, and a Soviet general were each given the same set of objective facts and scientific data to analyze, it is possible that the American and British generals may come to much the same conclusion, but the Soviet general would arrive at a radically different one because he would start from a completely different set of basic premises and preconceived ideas. The logical process of his mind, unlike that of his Western counterparts, would follow Marxist dialectics, instead of some form of deductive reasoning. A different set of moral laws governs and restricts the Soviet general's behavior because his aim would be radically different from the Western ones.[1]

Ignorance of these differences should not be excused. Plenty of evidence exists in books and articles produced for the education and

---

[1] Douglass, *Soviet Strategy.*

conditioning of Soviet officers, although many of these are in Russian and would need translating into English. Written by Politburo members, senior Party members, ministers, serving marshals and generals, military strategists, thinkers, and historians, many are declassified and easily obtainable. They manifest collective Soviet military thought, and as such should be translated and distributed to Western generals, senior government officers, war and staff colleges, and be available for sale to the American people to read for themselves.

At the Twentieth Congress of the SCP, in 1956, Khrushchev called for reassessment of Soviet military policy. This resulted eventually in the "Special Collection" of military papers, compiled by armed services chiefs to guide the USSR in preparing its armed forces for war. They were published in *Military Thought,* the classified journal of the Soviet general staff; extracts later appeared in the so-called Penkovsky Papers.

A series of at least thirteen books has been published for Soviet officers, with such titles as *The Officer's Handbook (A Soviet View); Marxism-Leninism War and Army (A Soviet View);* and *Scientific-Technical Progress and the Revolution in Military Affairs (A Soviet View).* At least five of the titles were translated and published under the auspices of the U.S. Air Force, owing to the foresight of Maj. Gen. George Keegan, when he was chief of intelligence. Another valuable work is *Soviet Military Strategy,* a compendium of articles by distinguished Soviet authors, compiled and edited by Marshal Sokolovsky.

Soviet military expressions and methods of strategic analysis differ from those of the West. For example, Soviet "military doctrine" is equivalent to Western "national security policy"; both provide guidance to the military establishment on the type of war they are to prepare for. There is no argument about the Soviet military doctrine, and none is allowed: it is not open for discussion. However, all else in the Soviet military sphere is embraced in the expression "military science," about which guided arguments and controlled criticism are allowed and even encouraged in some instances.

Military science includes general military theory, the theory of war or "military art," the theory of training and education, military-historical science, military administration, military geography, and all other military matters.[2] The most important branch of military science is military art, which comprises general theory, strategy, operational art, and tactics. In the Soviet Union there is only one integrated school of military theory and knowledge, and not one for each service. There is also only

[2]Douglass, *Soviet Strategy.*

one military strategy in the USSR, to which all five of the armed services conform. The five Soviet armed services are the Strategic Missile Force, the Ground Force, the Air Force, the Naval Force, and the National Air Defense Force. Certain special troops, including those involved in chemical warfare, civil defense, and rear areas, come directly under the Ministry of Defense.

The Sokolovsky book states that "military strategy is governed by the Marxist-Leninist definition of war as the continuation of political policy by states, and classes, by violent means." This is almost a straight crib from Clausewitz. Sokolovsky places special emphasis on nuclear war, political and psychological factors in war, and the importance of political indoctrination of Soviet youth. He states clearly that the first priority is to maintain firm political control over the armed forces; accordingly, every serviceman must receive intensive and continuous indoctrination in Party dogma.

At the Twenty-Second Congress of the SCP in 1961, Defense Minister Marshal Malinovsky outlined the new Soviet doctrine, which became known as the "Revolution in Military Affairs." It was based on the inevitability of nuclear war between forces of diametrically opposed social systems and envisioned employing missiles to achieve preemptive strikes against deep rear areas of enemy territory, concurrently with highly mobile combat operations involving special covert units. These principles continued to be reiterated long after the fall of Khrushchev in 1964.

The vital difference between the Soviet armed forces and those of noncommunist states is that a separate political organization controls and monitors them. This is the Main Political Administration (MPA), a political-military structure through which the Party controls the armed forces. While appearing to be simply an offshoot of the Ministry of Defense, the MPA is directly responsible to the Central Committee of the Soviet Communist Party. MPA directives on Party political work are jointly signed by the defense minister and the MPA chief. The MPA is in charge of the political indoctrination of the country's youth and also of all military publishing and broadcasting.

Soviet officers are in two categories, usually referred to as line officers and political officers. Line officers are the counterparts of Western military officers, with much the same responsibilities and duties and with a similar chain of command. They are in command of and provide staffs for formations and units; they also command operations and exercises. Political officers have no counterpart in noncommunist armies; they are responsible for political indoctrination, morale, and loyalty of the Soviet armed forces to the Party. They have their own separate chain of command, and report through it to the MPA. Both Khrushchev and Brezhnev were political officers, or commissars, in World War II, and not combat ones, as was Marshal Ustinov, who became defense minister in 1977.

Some Soviet troops are not under control of the Ministry of Defense. These are the border troops, which in 1970 numbered about 175,000[3] and came directly under the KGB; and the internal security troops, which numbered about 125,000 and were the responsibility of the minister of internal affairs. There were also about 1.5 million members of the part-time military training organization known as DOSAFF,[4] whose instruction in shooting, parachuting, outdoor pursuits, and "adventure training" is given through colleges, schools, and workers' centers for those under sixteen years of age.

The Soviets hold two firm concepts on war that differ from those held by the West. The first is that any war is automatically a "total war" that must be fought until it is won, with a clear Soviet victory as the only acceptable ultimate outcome. Western expressions such as flexible response, limited nuclear war, nuclear options, and conflict control have no place in the Soviet military vocabulary, or indeed in Soviet military thought. For example, in January 1974, when U.S. Defense Secretary James Schlesinger defined his doctrine of conflict control as "stopping a war at the lowest possible level," he said nothing about winning a war. To the Soviets, a war must be fought to be won or not fought at all; when winning is not possible, their prevention of war tactics would be employed instead.

The other Soviet concept not copied by the West is that of an "all-arms strategy" which embraces nuclear, chemical, biological, conventional, and all other weapons available. Either singly or in conjunction with one another, they are all ready to be employed as required to bring about speedy victory. The Western idea, or false hope, that any future world war would begin with a conventional phase and then only slowly escalate to a "nuclear threshold" is not echoed by the Soviets, who believe that if—and only if—there happens to be an initial conventional phase for some unplanned reason, it would be one of "convenience" for them, in which preparation for the vital massive victory strike could be made more adequately.

---

[3]Figures quoted are generally those given by the London-based International Institute for Strategic Studies (IISS), the U.S. Defense Department, the Pentagon, or the CIA.
[4]Initials meaning the Voluntary Society for Assisting the Army, Air Force, and Navy.

The West seeks to divorce nuclear weapons from conventional ones, while the Soviets think of them as being interoperative. The Soviet military mind is conditioned to think of a preemptive attack in which both nuclear and chemical weapons would be instantly used to avoid being taken by surprise. An examination of Soviet weaponry and field exercises confirms this. This is the military philosophy on which Soviet officers are nurtured, and is confirmed in writings by senior Soviet statesmen, marshals, and generals.

Soviet attitudes towards war differ from those in the West, where the motivation is defensive. Lenin accepted completely the Clausewitz theory that war is the continuation of politics by other means, and the Soviets are conditioned to accept war as one of these means, although perhaps only as the ultimate one. The Soviets believe that given the correct strategy, adequate training, and preparation, they can survive, fight, and win a nuclear war with the West. The West relies on its nuclear strategic weapons to be the deterrent to a World War III. The Soviet Union relies largely on the same premise, but in a somewhat different way: Soviet nuclear strike weapons are simply part of its "all-arms" concept, and their deterrent aspect is almost a spinoff. The Soviets concentrate on survival measures far more than does the West.

The Soviets have distinct views on the value of military strength, which they consider makes them superior, enabling them to dominate and bully (whereas inferior military strength makes them feel weak and vulnerable). This is the frame of mind in which the Soviets approached the negotiation tables during the seventies.

Before going into the various salient negotiations between the Americans and Soviets, it will serve well to comment briefly on "detente," a much bandied-about French word (there is no exact equivalent in either English or Russian) that had become fashionable jargon by 1970. It had been introduced into international linguistic currency by President Charles de Gaulle of France. Appalled by the rigid Cold War stalemate and the terrifying nuclear arms race between the two superpowers, he actively tried to break down some of the barriers and proposed a gradual easing of tension by a process he described as "Detente—Entente—Cooperation."

De Gaulle had withdrawn French forces from the NATO military framework in 1966, largely because he felt that under American leadership, the nuclear arms race was getting out of control, and that unless something was done to ease the mounting fear and tension, it would inevitably end in a catastrophic nuclear conflict. Western Europe would certainly suffer terribly in any nuclear exchange—more so perhaps than the United States, as it would probably become a conventional battle-field as well. De Gaulle was not satisfied that the NATO European allies were being taken sufficiently into account by the U.S. Administration, or consulted sufficiently on certain matters of vital importance to them, such as nuclear strategy. In his stilted way he did his best to put his detente policy to work.

To the American people detente meant the easing of tension, but to the Soviets it was a diplomatic tool to help them achieve military superiority. Brezhnev made the Soviet attitude towards detente abundantly clear at the Twenty-Fourth Congress, in 1971, when he said, "The detente process should be separate from the continuing ideological struggle."

3 The Soviet Imprint on East-West Negotiations

Marshal Konev in Vienna was laughing and telling me that if I accepted all his preposterous demands one day, he would have ten new ones to hit me with the next.
— Gen. Mark W. Clark, *From the Danube to the Yalu*
(London: Harrap, 1954)

WHEN ONE THINKS of Soviet imprints one tends automatically to think of areas in the world where the Soviets have penetrated, but in the seventies one of the most important Soviet imprints lay heavily on the East-West negotiating tables, especially when arms control, SALT, and related subjects were being discussed. The Soviets knew the Americans would respect any agreement they signed, while they themselves had little intention of honoring any conditions unfavorable to their aims. Americans gave away much, while the Soviets conceded not an inch and, moreover, blatantly lied and cheated when it suited their purpose.

Negotiation is one of the "other means," a main tool of the Soviet peace strategy, one which was exploited to the full in the seventies. Gen. Mark W. Clark, who from mid-1945 to mid-1947 was American high commissioner for Austria, had a harrowing first-hand insight into the minds of Soviet negotiators and claims to have taken "a full course in Soviet duplicity."[1] He also wrote that "Marshal Konev in Vienna was laughing and telling me that if I accepted all his preposterous demands one day, he would have ten new ones to hit me with the next."[2] Similar comments have since been frequently repeated by many American diplomats and negotiators when speaking of their dealings with the Russians.

[1] In *Calculated Risks* (London: Harrap, 1951).
[2] In *From the Danube to the Yalu* (London: Harrap, 1954).

21

It seems that such lessons are never learned and handed on; Americans seem to start with the conviction that they will be able to get along with the Russians, just as they have been able to get along with other nationalities. Why should the Soviets be different? They soon became disillusioned.

Gen. Mark Clark also wrote: "Having seen the Red Army and Russian diplomacy in action, my own belief is that there is nothing the Soviet Union would not do to achieve world domination. But I am convinced they always respect force."[3] This is certainly true: the Russians respect force and despise weakness and hesitation. They stood in awe of President Harry S. Truman, who had demonstrated his will to use nuclear weapons; this was a large factor in retarding Stalin's aggressive moves in Europe after World War II. Stalin again drew back from the brink in 1950, during the Korean War, because he was still facing Truman, who had demonstrated his resolution to act defensively.

John Foster Dulles is often credited with inventing political brinkmanship, but Stalin was an arch exponent of it. In 1954, when the French were being defeated in Indochina by Ho Chi Minh's Communist Viet Minh forces, it appeared that President Dwight D. Eisenhower, supported by Secretary of State Dulles, who early realized the immensity of the Soviet Communist threat, was on the point of authorizing the use of American nuclear weapons. This made a deep impression on the Soviets. Presidents Truman and Eisenhower made the American nuclear deterrent a very credible one. The USSR would then have lost out badly in any nuclear exchange with the United States, so the Soviet leadership, under Khrushchev, remained on the peevish, prickly defensive, practicing their prevention of war policy.

During 1970, it was American belief that if sufficient concessions were made, Soviet hearts would be softened, and the Soviets would reciprocate in a like generous manner. Then, both the United States and the USSR would be well on the way to arms control, then disarmament, and eventually to peace. The Soviet response to this general policy was negative. In March 1970 the Soviets held their largest military exercise for several years in western Russia, under the personal direction of Defense Minister Grechko, and in the course of the year they forged ahead with their weapon improvement program. Having already deployed more land-based missiles than the United States, they concentrated on improving their missile accuracy and nuclear warheads, and on achieving success with the MIRV (multiple independently-targetable reentry

[3]Ibid.

vehicles).[4] The Soviets had already begun to move away from static land-based missiles to a mobile concept and were improving their SLBMs (submarine-launched ballistic missiles). They test-fired a larger-headed "multiple" system for their SS-18 ICBM, the largest missile constructed in the world, which had a range of over 6,250 nautical miles. They also test-fired the smaller "orbital" SS-9.

The USSR suffered two disappointments during 1971. The first was on 15 July, when President Nixon announced he would be visiting China the following year; the second was on 25 October, when Communist China wrested the U.N. seat from Taiwan. Meanwhile, little progress was being made on the Strategic Arms Limitation Talks (SALT I), even though on 13 July, the U.S. defense secretary stated that the American program for improving the accuracy of MIRV warheads was being deliberately retarded as a gesture of good faith.

However, two byproduct agreements came out of the SALT I talks between the United States and the USSR. Both were distinctly to the advantage of the Soviets. One was an agreement to reduce the risk of accidental nuclear war, under which each country agreed to maintain and improve "existing organizational and technical arrangements to guard against the accidental or unauthorized use of nuclear weapons under its control." The other agreement was to modernize the hot line between Washington and Moscow, which had been established in 1963, and to replace existing cable and radio teleprinter links with a satellite communications sytem.

The year 1972 was called the "Year of Detente" in America. To be more precise, it was one of the "euphoria of detente," being a period of hope for the American people and those in the West generally. It was also the year in which the United States reluctantly recognized Soviet strategic parity, and one in which Richard Nixon was reelected for a second presidential term.

On 3 January, Nixon expressed his view on the new balance of economic power evolving in the world. Accepting that the United States could no longer act as the world's policeman, he called it a "pentagonal balance" of five major economic units, two of which were superpowers in the military sense. He said, "I think it will be a safer world, and a better world if we have a strong, healthy United States, Europe, the USSR, China and Japan, each balancing the other, not playing one off

---

[4]On release, the MIRV warheads could be directed to separate individual targets, instead of merely "free-falling."

against the other: an even balance."[5] This did not amuse the Kremlin leadership, which wanted world hegemony, and not a pentagonal balance.

Nixon visited China in February 1972 and commenced the process of establishing diplomatic relations with that country after a breach of over twenty-two years. The Soviet fear has always been that one day the United States and China might gang-up against the USSR. In May, Nixon also visited Moscow, where, fueled by the euphoria of detente, two main treaties were signed. One was the Antiballistic Missile Treaty, and the other was the SALT I agreement.

The Treaty on Limitation of Antiballistic Missile Systems, usually referred to as the ABM Treaty, to be of unlimited duration, was signed by Nixon and Brezhnev on 26 May. Each side agreed to limit ABM systems to no more than 100 launchers and 100 missiles centered on each other's capitals, and not to develop, test or deploy any more. Each promised not to use deliberate concealment measures, and each promised not to interfere with national technical means of verification (meaning surveillance satellites, mainly). U.S. intelligence agencies soon discovered, however, that the Soviets were working hard on their "killer-satellite" project.

Moscow was already protected by an ABM system, referred to by the Pentagon as the AB-1 but code-named by NATO as the "Galosh." It had sixty-four missiles with nuclear warheads, with a range of about two hundred miles, in four sites around the city. This missile had first been seen in 1964 on the annual parade in Red Square. The Pentagon also had plans to deploy a similar ABM system, the "Safeguard," which had been approved by the U.S. Senate in 1969. The Pentagon proposal was to have fourteen sites across the country to protect certain ICBMs against a possible Soviet preemptive strike.

However, in September 1970, Congress gave permission for the establishment of only two Safeguard sites, withholding approval for the others until the system proved to work effectively. The Safeguard system was to have two missiles, the long-range Spartan and the short-range Sprint, both of which were test-fired in August and December. Later, on 9 March 1971, Defense Secretary Melvin Laird said that the deployment of the Safeguard depended on the evolution of the Soviet and Chinese threats and the outcome of the SALT process.

The SALT I agreement, which was to be in force for five years, was to be a relative first step in arms reduction between the two superpowers,

[5] *Time* Magazine, 3 January 1972.

reached on the principle of balancing American technological advantages in missile accuracy and MIRVs against the greater number of Soviet land-based missiles (which could deliver much larger warheads). Owing to the difficulty in differentiating between nuclear weapons with only one warhead and those with several, Nixon's plan had been for parity in systems delivery; so SALT I was concluded on a launcher count of strategic offensive weapons able to strike at each other's home territory, meaning those with a range of over 2,500 miles. The final figures, being virtually what each actually possessed, were that the United States could have 1,054 ICBMs and up to 710 SLBMs while the Soviet Union could have 1,618 ICBMs and 950 SLBMs. The United States was to have no more than 44 modern SLBM submarines and 656 launchers on them, and the Soviet Union no more than 62 SLBM submarines and 950 launchers on them. The Soviets came out by far the best in this agreement. Both sides agreed not to interfere with the other's means of verification.

In Moscow, Nixon and Brezhnev also signed an "Interim Agreement on Certain Measures with Respect to the Limitation of Strategic Arms," designed to continue the SALT process and to outline the basic principles. This became known as SALT II. Brezhnev, who had obtained a good bargain and was anxious to improve his advantages, wanted these talks to commence as soon as possible. After some indecision as to location, they began in November at Geneva, Switzerland. The U.S. administration saw that the Soviets were rapidly catching up in missile technology, and SALT II, from the American point of view at least, was to be aimed at achieving a "qualitative balance" in strategic offensive missiles, which it was hoped would be a further step towards an eventual reduction of such weapons.

Throughout the two and a half years of SALT I negotiations, the Soviet peace strategy had been hard at work: the Americans had been deliberately misled into thinking that the Soviet degree of technical capability was much less than in fact it was. The Soviets had been secretly developing four new missiles, of which the U.S. intelligence organizations had little or no prior knowledge. These were the SS-17, the SS-19, the mobile SS-20, and the naval SS-N-8. Almost immediately after signing the SALT I agreement, the Soviets began encoding the electronic signals normally given out on launch and flight by missiles; this deceived and confused the Americans. This Soviet avoidance tactic had been somehow overlooked by the mirror-imaging American negotiators, who neglected to insist on the inclusion of a clause forbidding this form of deception in telemetry.

The year 1973 opened hopefully for the American people. On 27

January, the peace agreement ending the war in Vietnam was signed in Paris. On the same day, the U.S. defense secretary announced the end of the draft. Joy faded as the country was smeared by the Watergate affair, while in Vietnam the fighting continued with ferocity. Commencing on 17 June, Brezhnev paid a nine-day visit to the United States, during which, on the 22nd, he signed the "Agreement on the Prevention of Nuclear War." Both sides declared they would avoid military confrontations and refrain from the use of threats and force against each other. In the event of difficulties, they would "immediately enter into urgent consultations with each other to make every effort to avert this risk" of nuclear war.

The treaty's six articles were couched in soothing prose, vague in detail, but high-sounding in moral declaration. On the 24th, in a long televised speech designed to lull American audiences into complacency, Brezhnev emphasized the importance of detente. He said that the Soviet people were prepared to work hard "to win the peace," then a much used American expression. The Soviet peace strategy operated quietly in the background: an additional four agreements were signed on this visit, all of which were to the Soviets' advantage. These were on transportation, studies of the world ocean, agriculture, and cultural and scientific exchanges.

On 17 August 1973, U.S. Defense Secretary James Schlesinger warned that the Soviets were not adhering to the spirit of detente, as they had just made successful test flights of MIRVs, which were to be fitted to their SS-17 and SS-18 missiles. The huge SS-18 was to have six MIRVs, each one megaton yield. Schlesinger also stated that the Soviets were developing other missiles that would completely upset the agreed SALT I balance of strategic offensive arms. On 12 September, the Soviets exploded a five-megaton-yield nuclear device underground.

Another set of arms control talks began on 30 October in Vienna. These were negotiations on the "Mutual Reduction of Forces and Armaments and Associated Measures in Central Europe" (which came to be known as the Mutual and Balanced Force Reductions, or MBFR), in which twelve NATO countries and five Warsaw Pact ones took part. America and the Soviet Union were represented. Although invited, France had declined to attend. One of the first tasks was to define "Central Europe," the anticipated ground-battle area in any World War III, in which there would be large concentrations of troops, tanks, and other arms. It was agreed the area should include, to the east of the Iron Curtain, Czechoslovakia, East Germany, and Poland; while to its west, West Germany, Belgium, Holland, and Luxembourg. This became known as the "guidelines area." NATO had wanted to include Hungary in the guidelines area, but the Soviet Union successfully objected, and so that country, with its quota of Soviet occupying troops, some 40,000 men, in four divisions, was not included. The Soviets had quickly moved an extra 1,200 tanks into Hungary just before the talks began.

The issue of mutual reduction of forces faced even tougher opposition. Talks and sessions followed one another without any agreement being reached. The Soviets were not interested in any sort of parity, and during the followng year (1974) they moved large numbers of their new T-72 main battle banks into the guidelines area.

On 5 December 1973, U.S. Sen. Henry Jackson alleged that the SALT II talks had reached an impasse because of the "completely unacceptable" Soviet proposals. On the 11th, Congress refused to grant the USSR the "most favored nation" status (which had been withdrawn in 1954) unless it allowed free emigration. Over three million Jews lived in the USSR, many of whom wanted to emigrate but were not allowed to do so. American doubts about the real intentions of the Soviets were growing, but eventually the trade agreement, with "most favored nation" status included, was agreed on by the Senate. Several conditions, known as the Jackson-Vanik Amendments, were attached. One was that the USSR relax its emigration controls. Others were that the "most favored nation" privileges would initially extend for only eighteen months, and that the amount of trade and credits would be limited to $300 million. However, on 10 January 1974 the Soviet Union suddenly cancelled this trade agreement. The political price was far too high: the Soviet government had no intention of allowing a mass exodus of its Jews.

On 8 June 1974, Nixon began a three-day visit to Moscow to meet Brezhnev. Two agreements resulted from this summit meeting. One was that the antiballistic missile systems be limited to one site per side. The Soviets already had their Galosh ABM system in place in four sites around Moscow, and the Americans had begun to install their first one at Grand Forks, North Dakota. The other agreement limited underground nuclear test explosions to yields of not more than 150 kilotons.

Meanwhile, during 1974, the Soviets continued with an intensive program of missile development, testing, and deployment. On 19 February, they test-fired their big SS-18, now with three MIRVs; and on the 27th, they test-fired their new SS-17 missile which carried four MIRVs. On 14 June, after these tests were completed, Brezhnev called for an agreement with the United States to halt the development of new strategic offensive weapons systems.

This was only a Brezhnev ploy to maintain the fiction of detente. In October the Soviets resumed their missile-testing program, firing two naval SS-N-8 missiles, each with a single warhead, from a submerged submarine. These missiles reportedly out-ranged the U.S. Poseidon C-3 missile by 1,500 miles. Next, Brezhnev called for the withdrawal from the Mediterranean Sea of both Soviet and American warships carrying nuclear weapons. This was just before the Soviets commenced another series of missile tests in the Pacific Ocean in December. Thus, Brezhnev's tactics were to carry out periodic missile and nuclear tests, and when they were completed to call for agreements to ban such weapons, hoping that the U.S. would suspend its missile development and testing to show its good faith in detente.

The Soviet peace strategy had an unexpected and considerable windfall in July 1974, when Turkish armed forces invaded Cyprus in furtherance of a long-running dispute involving Greeks, Turks, and displaced Greek Cypriots. Greece and Turkey were both NATO members. The Greeks lobbied Washington to persuade the president to stop sending arms to Turkey and to pressure the Turks into withdrawing from Cyprus. When nothing was done, Greece withdrew its assigned forces from the NATO military framework. Washington then belatedly stopped arms supplies to Turkey. Turkey responded by closing down twenty-five of the twenty-six U.S.-NATO bases on Turkish soil, which were mainly used to monitor Soviet missile activity in adjacent central USSR. This was a severe handicap to the United States and to NATO generally, as it enabled the Soviets to engage in considerable missile activity which the Americans were not able to monitor or verify.

The SALT I agreement was due to be superseded on 30 September 1977 by SALT II, which was to be operative until 31 December 1985, but the Soviets constantly stalled negotiations. In an effort to hammer out some mutually acceptable guidelines to reactivate the talks, President Gerald Ford went to Vladivostok, USSR, to meet Brezhnev on 23 November 1974. By this time, the SALT II talks had attracted a lot of American criticism, it being thought that the Soviets were demanding—and receiving—far too much. In the American hope and expectation that the USSR would be content with parity, the object had been to try to obtain a balance of strategic offensive weapons. The Americans had not yet realized that this was not what the Soviets wanted: the Soviets wanted strategic superiority.

However, the Soviets did not want the U.S. administration to lose all patience and break off the talks, as they eventually expected to extract considerable gains. In an interim agreement which became known as the Vladivostok Accords, Ford and Brezhnev agreed that each side would be allowed up to 2,400 intercontinental weapons, and that all should be counted as single launchers. Using satellite and other surveillance means, it was still difficult to distinguish MIRVs from other types of warheads, which in deployment were intermixed. A subceiling of 1,320 MIRVs was set for each side.

The Vladivostok Accords simply represented actual holdings. The Soviets retained their "throw-weight" advantage, and American critics feared that a Soviet preemptive attack might be instantly capable of destroying about 90 percent of the U.S. land-based missiles.

To the American people the main event of 1975 was the formal ending of the war in South Vietnam. By April the last American serviceman had been withdrawn from that country. The relief was dulled by the surrender of the South Vietnamese government to the North Vietnamese armed forces, and the uniting of the two parts of Vietnam under the Communist government at Hanoi. This was regarded by Communists everywhere as a victory for their superior ideology. American efforts to keep communism at bay in this part of Southeast Asia were denigrated and belittled.

On 22 January 1975, Ford signed the Geneva Conventions prohibiting the manufacture, stockpiling, and use of biological weapons. Belatedly (on 17 December 1974), the U.S. government had formally signed the Geneva Protocol of 1925, banning the use of poisonous gases and chemicals, which had already been ratified by 103 other nations. On 26 March, the Biological Weapons Convention, signed by both the United States and the USSR in 1972, calling for the destruction of existing weapon stocks, came into force. The U.S. Defense Department openly destroyed its biological weapons, but there is now considerable doubt as to whether the USSR carried out its part of this agreement; in fact, evidence seems to point to the contrary.[6] On 8 April, Ford made an executive order renouncing as a matter of national policy the first use in war of herbicides and lethal gases.

Otherwise, 1975 was notable as the year in which detente came to a thudding halt. Soon it was reputed that Ford was forbidding the use of that word in his Cabinet circles. Soviet negotiators continued to pro-

---

[6]On 18 March 1980, a Geneva Conference reviewing committee refused to endorse the USSR claim that the treaty had been effectively implemented because there had been no complaints or violations of it. The Soviet government stated it did not possess any germ weapons, but would not say whether it had any in the first place, nor would it confirm or deny whether it had destroyed its stocks of germ weapons five years previously as it had agreed to do.

crastinate in the SALT II talks, while in Vienna, at the MBFR talks, the Soviets were refusing to provide figures for the military strengths of the Warsaw Pact armed forces in the guidelines area. Soviet tank production had risen to over nine hundred units a year, almost twice that of the United States. In June, Helmut Sonnefeld, a Kissinger aide, said, "The Soviet Union is just beginning its truly imperial phase."

At the Twenty-Fifth Congress of the SCP, on 24 February 1976, Brezhnev put forward proposals for banning new destructive weapons in space. He obviously had in mind "killer satellites," which use the atomic particle principle of projection and on which the Soviets had been working for some time without satisfactory results. The Americans were also experimenting to produce a similar sort of weapon, on the laser-beam projection principle, and Brezhnev feared that American technology was still superior in this field.

Despite the uncompromising Soviet attitude, consignments of grain were still sent to Russia. On 20 October 1976, a five-year agreement was made to sell the USSR at least 6 million tons of grain annually; in return, the United States was given the option to purchase up to 10 million tons of Soviet oil.

Probably because 1976 was a presidential election year in the United States, it was a comparatively quiet one in the arms control field. Nothing moved at the MBFR talks in Vienna, and SALT II bogged down on such issues as whether the Soviet TU-26B bomber (its NATO code-name was Backfire) and the American cruise missiles were strategic offensive weapons within the Vladivostok Accords guidelines. On 10 February 1976, Ford gave up the U.S. option under the ABM Treaty of 1972 and the agreement of July 1974, and announced the closure of the solitary American Safeguard ABM site at Grand Forks, North Dakota. The Soviets, however, still retained their Galosh ABM system around Moscow.

In January 1977, Jimmy Carter assumed office as president of the United States of America. In the aftermath of the Watergate affair, he was a breath of fresh air and brought a seeming honesty of purpose with him. He was determined to reactivate detente; in his naivete, as he had little experience in foreign affairs, Carter felt, like many American statesmen before him, that if he made generous concessions to the Soviets, they would be shamed into doing likewise. Suspicions that the Soviets were manipulating detente for their own devious purposes, and were cheating, lying, and generally fooling the Americans, by this time had become rife within the United States. Even so, there was initial hope that Carter could deal with the Soviet leaders in a realistic manner to achieve a relaxation of tension and halt the nuclear arms race that was getting so wildly out of hand.

In May 1977, Andrei Gromyko, the Soviet foreign minister, and the new U.S. secretary of state, Cyrus Vance, agreed on a formula to reactivate the SALT II talks. The Soviets were now even more anxious than the Americans to conclude SALT II—but for opposite reasons. SALT I was to expire on 30 September, but it was agreed that its conditions should obtain until SALT II was finalized.

During 1977, the MBFR talks in Vienna ground on fruitlessly. The previous year the Warsaw Pact nations had produced figures for their armed forces in the guidelines area, and this year was mainly taken up with disputes over them. The Soviets stated there were only 805,000 men in the guidelines area, while NATO negotiators insisted they had at least 955,000—a difference of 150,000, equal in theory to some fourteen Soviet-type divisions, which were suspected to be somewhere in Poland. The other main dispute was that the Soviets wanted ceilings on troops and tanks on a national basis (that is, separately in each country) while the West wanted total or overall ceilings. No progress was made.

On 19 April 1978, the United States proposed a withdrawal from Europe of 1,000 tactical nuclear warheads, 54 F-4 Phantom aircraft (which had a nuclear carrying capability), 36 Pershing I missiles; and 29,000 troops as a first stage of force reductions, if the Soviets would withdraw 68,000 men and 1,700 tanks from the guidelines area. This was to be followed by Britain, Canada, West Germany and the Benelux countries[7] making force reductions at the same time as Czechoslovakia, East Germany, and Poland, in a second stage after the American and Soviet withdrawals had been completed. Like several previous Western proposals at the MBFR talks, this one came to nothing also.

On 30 June 1977, as a gesture of trust and goodwill, Carter announced he had decided to cancel production of the new B-1 military aircraft. On 12 July, he stated he was also delaying production of the neutron bomb (which had been tested on 7 July), but that the final decision on its production and ultimate deployment had not been made. In return, Carter had expected the Soviets to suspend deployment of their new SS-20 mobile missile and production of the new strategic TU-26B (Backfire) long-range bomber aircraft. Predictably, the Soviets did neither, and by the end of the year about seventy TU-26s were in service.

On 9 March 1978, the Soviet delegate to the twenty-nation U.N.

---

[7] The Belgium, Netherlands, and Luxembourg Economic Union.

conference on disarmament, in Geneva, presented a draft convention to ban the production, deployment, and use of neutron bombs. This was rejected by the American delegate, who remarked that it was "a curious proposition for the prohibition of a single type of nuclear weapon only," while conveniently ignoring several others already deployed in Europe. However, Carter announced on 7 April that he had decided to stop production of the neutron bomb. He said that the ultimate decision on the "incorporation of the enhanced radiation features into our modernized battlefield" would be made later, adding that he would be "influenced by the degree to which the Soviet Union shows restraints in its conventional and nuclear arms programs and force deployments affecting the security of the United States and Western Europe." The Russians were extremely pleased by this stroke of unexpected luck. However, on 26 October, Carter asked Congress to earmark funds for production of the neutron bomb.

In a major speech on 11 March 1977, retired Air Force Maj. Gen. George Keegan claimed that certain intelligence about the USSR had been either ignored or badly assessed by the U.S. administrations, which had been, and still were, acting on misleading views of Soviet capabilities and intentions. Throwing cold water on the notion of relying entirely on nuclear deterrence and the fondly held idea that, as nuclear war was too terrible to contemplate, neither the United States nor the USSR would ever embark upon it, Keegan asserted that the USSR was conditioning its people to the fact that a war between the two superpowers could be waged and won at any level, even a nuclear one, "and that it [the USSR] could emerge as a viable, controlled, surviving military entity." Keegan also said that the USSR was virtually on a permanent war footing and that "Soviet industrial, scientific and economic investment remains largely subordinated to the conflict purposes of the state." These and other comments by Keegan, together with information that the Soviet Union was making extensive civil defense preparations, caused many in America to pause and think.

The SALT II talks dragged on at intervals throughout 1978, but substantial differences between the two sides remained, and meetings between U.S. Secretary of State Vance and Soviet Foreign Minister Gromyko failed to settle them. Detente remained Carter's primary concern, and he closely linked it to the SALT II talks. Americans began asking why it was not working, why the Russians were not also trying to ease East-West tensions, and became increasingly uneasy as the talks dragged on fruitlessly. It was generally considered that the United States was making too many concessions that would endanger the security of the country. Eventually, though, it was decided to finalize the SALT II agreement and to settle for what had been agreed so far. SALT II was scheduled to be signed by Vance and Gromyko on 21 December 1978. However, on the 15th of that month a joint United States–China communique announced that full diplomatic relations would be established between the two countries as of 1 January 1979, and that ambassadors would be exchanged on 1 March. This considerably upset the Soviets, who, fearing this might be a first step in an alliance possibly hostile to the USSR, refused to sign the SALT II agreement. It is still debatable whether Carter's timing of this announcement was careless and tactless or deliberate.

Despite a U.S. intelligence report of 15 March 1979 that Soviet SS-18 missiles had been adapted to carry fourteen MIRV warheads instead of the provisionally agreed ten under the SALT II talks, and after over six years of frustration and Soviet intransigence, the SALT II agreement was signed with great pomp and ceremony on 18 June, in Vienna, by Presidents Carter and Brezhnev. It was to remain in operation until 31 December 1985, when it would be superseded by a hoped for SALT III agreement, talks for which were to begin as soon as possible.

The Americans had conceded much in the SALT negotiations in the belief and hope that the Soviets would be content to retain parity of military capability, and that it was best to consolidate upon those issues on which there was some agreement, leaving the unsolved ones for the SALT III negotiations. Immediately after the signing of SALT II, beginning on 24 June, the USSR began to pressure Turkey, which resulted in that country refusing to allow American aircraft to make verification flights through its air space. This meant that it would not be possible to monitor accurately whether the Soviets were in fact keeping to the agreement in all its aspects.

The main concession made by the American negotiators was not to insist on the inclusion of the Soviet TU-26 (Backfire) aircraft, which with midair refueling could make the round trip from the Soviet Union to the American mainland. Technically, as it could carry nuclear bombs, the TU-26 was clearly an "intercontinental offensive strategic weapon." The Soviets disagreed, falsely alleging that it did not have an intercontinental radius of action, and that in any case it was "not deployed so as to be a danger to the American mainland." The main American objection was the old one, that the Soviet ICBMs had greater "throw-weight" than those of the United States; and in a preemptive nuclear strike, with the improved Soviet CEP*, they might be able to destroy ninety percent of the some 950 Minuteman II and IIIs, the backbone of the "land leg" of the American nuclear deterrent triad.

The SALT II count was still based on the launchers, or means of delivery, owing to the difficulty in distinguishing and verifying single-headed missiles, multi-headed ones, and MIRVs, especially when they were deliberately intermixed (a deceit the Soviets exploited as much as possible). For example, the Soviet ICBM sites near the two Ukranian towns known to the Pentagon as "D and P" (Derazhnya and Perm-vomaisk) had a total of about 180 below-ground silos, or launchers, one-third of which contained SS-19s with multi-warheads, while the remainder housed the older and less formidable SS-11s, with only a single warhead. The United States was in much the same situation; for example, some of the ICBM Minutemen IIIs at Malmstrom, Montana, had MIRVs and others were multi-headed.

The signing of the SALT II agreement was one thing, but ratification by the U.S. Senate was another. While it hesitated and pondered during the remainder of the year, the Soviets blatantly carried out at least twenty-four underground nuclear test explosions. On 3 January, Carter announced that because of the intervention of Soviet armed forces in Afghanistan, Senate consideration of SALT II was to be deferred. Apart from this, Senate objections included the refusal of the USSR to link such talks with human rights issues in the Soviet Union, and Soviet involvement in the dispute between Somalia and Ethiopia in the Horn of Africa.

As a ploy to obtain American ratification of the SALT II agreement, at the MBFR talks in Vienna in October 1979, the Soviets offered to withdraw 20,000 men and 1,000 tanks from the guidelines area if Carter would abandon his plan to modernize NATO's nuclear theater weapons. Considering the Warsaw Pact had almost one million armed troops in or near the guidelines area, with some 27,000 tanks and 55,000 other armored vehicles, in practice this was really a puny gesture, even if it was meant sincerely.

This Soviet proposal was regarded with some skepticism by Western negotiators at the MBFR talks. No mention was made of formations, how many, or of what type, or what sort of tanks would be withdrawn. That numbers of men could be absent from duty for reasons of sickness,

---

*"Circular Error Probable," a jargon expression for an accuracy measuring formula, meaning that at least 50 percent of the warheads would fall within a circle of stated diameter.

leave, detachment, or training, and that many tanks could be off the road for inspection or mechanical reasons without being noticed. Also, the Soviets were continuing to introduce their new T-72 and T-64 tanks into forward formations to replace the older T-54s and T-55s, which would have to be withdrawn anyway. To give weight to their proposal, the Soviets produced some propaganda film and news photographs, captioned "Soviet troops and tanks being withdrawn," but the armored vehicles depicted were older models.

Apart from the SS-20 mobile missiles being deployed in western Russia, the European NATO allies were also very worried about other Soviet nuclear-tipped missiles ranged against them, which included some five hundred SS-4s with a range of about 1,200 miles, and some ninety SS-5s with a range of about 2,300 miles. Carter was somewhat pressured into producing a plan to placate them, which was referred to as being "to modernize NATO nuclear theater weapons." In practice this meant deploying in Western Europe 108 Pershing II missiles with a range of 1,200 miles (the Pershing I had a range of 400 miles) and 464 cruise-missiles on trucks that could target their warheads onto Soviet territory. The latter part of 1979 was spent in forging this U.S. package for NATO Europe, as some countries were reluctant to participate and have nuclear weapons on their soil.

The year ended disastrously for American relations with the USSR, as the Soviet invasion of Afghanistan destroyed American faith that the Soviets had ever been fully committed to detente, and obliterated all Senate thoughts of ratifying the SALT II agreement under terms so unfavorable to the United States. Confident Soviet leaders considered the USSR sufficiently superior over the United States in military capability to take this step in brinkmanship, in furtherance of the ultimate Soviet aim of global hegemony. A heavy Soviet imprint had fallen on the East-West negotiating tables during the seventies.

4  The Soviet Imprint on Europe

In 1985 we shall have attained most of our objectives in Western Europe, and the reversal of forces will then be so decisive that we shall be in a position to impose our will each time this is necessary.
— Leonid Brezhnev; to the Czechoslovakian Communist Party Congress; Prague, February 1977

SOVIET POLICY IN Europe in the seventies aimed to impose stricter control over the Warsaw Pact countries, increase Soviet influence in the neutral ones, drive a wedge between West European countries and the United States, and divide the NATO allies among themselves.

THE WARSAW PACT

In 1970 the Soviet imprint lay deeply on the Warsaw Pact states. The Soviet government had demonstrated its "iron fist" tactics on Czechoslovakia in August 1968, when Soviet forces invaded that country to ensure that a strong Moscow-oriented government would be installed in Prague, and that Alexander Dubcek, the liberal idealist, would be quickly deposed.

In November that year in Warsaw Brezhnev enunciated what became known as the "Brezhnev Doctrine," under which the Soviet government assumed the right to interfere, with military force if necessary, in the internal affairs of Warsaw Pact member states, if any one of them showed signs of breaking away from the Marxist-Leninist line to adopt pluralism or a liberal form of democracy. Brezhnev stated, "There is a limitation of sovereignty of Communist countries, which have only the right to self-determination so far as it does not jeopardize the interests of Communism in their own countries, or in any other state in the Communist Commonwealth."

The Balkan state of Bulgaria was regarded as Moscow's most faithful Pact member; indeed, the government led by Todor Zhivkov almost

slavishly followed Soviet wishes. This was partly because of traditional Bulgarian gratitude towards the Russians for helping them achieve independence from Muslim Turkish rule in 1878, both then being Christian countries; partly because of weak leadership; and partly because the Soviets had poured in aid to enable the Bulgarians to start an industrial base. Zhivkov, who became chairman of the Council of State in July 1971, when a new constitution was adopted, kept his country firmly in the Soviet orbit. Pressed against Greece and Turkey, both NATO members, Bulgaria was the southernmost bastion of the Warsaw Pact.

Czechoslovakia, from the Soviet point of view, was another vital strategic bulwark. The country was still involved in 1970 in the aftermath of the 1968 insurrection: accusations, counteraccusations, and trials culminated in 1972 with the sentencing of a number of dissidents to imprisonment. Gustav Husak had taken over the leadership of the

Czech Communist Party as first secretary in April 1969; in 1975 he took on the additional title of president. Rumbles of continuing discontent within the country and protests from writers, intellectuals, and others resulted in periodic minor amnesties and releases of dissidents from prison. Both the Czech Writers Union and the Slovak Writers Union were active critics of the Czech government. Reports of the lack of human rights within the country obtained wide publicity in the Western world, but had no more serious repercussions.

One country that caused the Kremlin some anxiety during the seventies was East Germany. Since their creation as separate states, the two Germanies held reunification as their ultimate aim. For the East German government, it would be when communism became victorious in Western Europe; and for the West German government, when there were free elections in East Germany. The main Soviet anxiety was in case an uncontrollable (by the Soviets) movement for the reunification of the two parts of Germany arose. The Kremlin leaders did not want this to take place unless it was on their own terms. The Soviets did not overlook the fact that if popular opinion became so overwhelmingly in favor of reunification on both sides of the Iron Curtain, and if East Germany was unable to continue as a Soviet satellite state, the situation might be used to manipulate West Germany, the keystone of NATO ground defense in Europe, into becoming a neutral buffer state within a re-unified Germany.

The West German Chancellor, Willi Brandt, worked hard and long for German reunification. His policy became known as Ostpolitik, but it was generally treated with caution by the Soviets, who did not dismiss it out of hand. They viewed the prospect of a reunified Germany with apprehension and distrust, even though it might become a communist state led by the veteran German communist Walter Ulbricht. The Soviets suspected Ulbricht of having delusions of grandeur and thought that if he controlled a reunified Germany he might become too powerful and too independent of the Kremlin. Talks on reunification had begun in December 1969, and the following month, Chancellor Brandt made a declaration on the normalizing of relations between the two countries. In May 1970, Brandt proposed a twenty-point treaty to improve mutual relations, which caused Ulbricht to hurry to Moscow for advice. In August, a Treaty on the Renunciation of the Use of Force, designed to be the basis for improved relations between the two Germanies, was signed in Moscow by Kosygin and Brandt. The Soviets kept a firm grip on these East-West negotiations, and the East Germans were not allowed either a free hand or a free voice.

As the Soviets became more interested in the tactic of detente and in obtaining universal recognition for the legality of East Germany's existence as a sovereign state, they came up against the stubborn Ulbricht, who was against detente and too much close contact with the West German government. In 1971, as he was old (seventy-eight years), ill, and inflexible, Ulbricht was pushed aside as first secretary of the German Republican Communist Party; but because of his great prestige, he was allowed to retain the title of chairman of the state committee, meaning that he remained as nominal head of state. He was replaced as first secretary by Erich Honecker, who assumed the additional office of chairman of the State Committee when Ulbricht died in 1973. The Soviets felt Honecker might be a more pliable tool in their hands.

Meanwhile, Brandt pushed hard with his Ostpolitik. In May 1972, a Traffic Treaty between the two Germanies was signed, easing tension over movement in and out of West Berlin. This was followed in November by a treaty to form the basis for better future relations between the two German states on the principle of equal rights. For example, East Germans were automatically accorded nationality and full citizen rights in West Germany, while West Germans were able to visit East Germany —which many did, mainly to see relatives. Far fewer East Germans were allowed to visit West Germany. The aim was to keep the spirit of a united German nation alive, but the West German expression "One Nation— Two States" was only included in the treaty in return for the recognition of East Germany as a sovereign state. East Germany was admitted to the United Nations in 1973, thus automatically gaining a degree of accepted and assumed legitimacy. In July a number of minor agreements were signed between the two states, including one to cope with natural disasters along their common frontier. By this time the Soviets were no longer interested in the idea of a reunified Germany—it was too dangerous to them.

In the second half of the seventies, frequent exchanges of visits between Soviet and East German leaders were still being made. To all intents and purposes, East Germany remained a satisfied and compliant Soviet satellite.

Nor did Hungary pose problems for the USSR. The mood of the people in Hungary had changed since the heady days of the 1956 rising, and although there were occasional dissident and political trials, and some political prisoners were in detention, there was comparatively little evidence of political instability or dissident activity in the country. In November 1972, Brezhnev visited Hungary, anxious about the effects its contacts with Western tourists were having, and to remind Janos

Kadar that his government's first loyalty was to Moscow. This warning may have sufficed as Hungary remained compliant and quiet during the seventies.

Poland, with an area of about 121,000 square miles and a population of 24.9 million (1976), was strategically significant. It lay across the potential route of any Soviet military advance westwards into Europe, was a Soviet corridor to East Germany, and was part of the probable land battlefield in any World War III. Speaking one language, the Polish people are a nation in the true sense of that word, and about 95 percent of them have remained Roman Catholics, despite Communist discouragement since 1945. After World War II, some 69,000 square miles of eastern Polish territory was annexed by the USSR; in exchange Poland received about 39,000 square miles of German territory.

For some years Polish trade unions had a remarkable degree of freedom of expression and action for a Communist country, but they remained strictly nonpolitical, obediently accepting Party domination. Commencing on 14 December 1970, disturbances and riots broke out, caused by large increases in the prices of food and fuel, in the Baltic ports of Gdansk, Gdynia, and Szczecin. These lasted for a week, until the troops were able to restore order. On the 20th, Vladyslaw Goumulka resigned as first secretary of the Polish Communist Party and was replaced by Edward Gierek. More unrest in some shipyards and certain textile factories erupted in January 1971, the ripples of which did not subside until September.

In February 1976, the constitution (of 1952) was modified and the title of the country changed to the Polish People's Republic. Private ownership of land and freedom of religion were recognized, as was the separation of state and church.

Mounting economic difficulties and mismanagement began to manifest themselves in a restlessness in the Polish United Workers Party. In June 1976 when the government again proposed increases in the prices of food and fuel, strikes and riots erupted. Troops again had to be brought in to restore order, but this time they did not use firearms against rioters, as they had done in 1970. The government cancelled the proposed increases. In September, a Workers' Defense Committee was formed, which eventually persuaded the government to grant a limited amnesty. For the rest of the decade the tension between trade unions and the government persisted, escalating in 1980–81 to alarming proportions.

The other Balkan member of the Warsaw Pact was Rumania, wedged between Bulgaria, the USSR, and communist Yugoslavia, with a population of 21.5 million (1976). The country was led by Nicolae

Ceausescu, who came to power in 1965 as first secretary of the Rumanian Communist Party; he additionally became president in 1974. Ceausescu had always tended to take an independent line as regards foreign policy, but this seemed to be tolerated by the USSR, perhaps because Ceausescu was a dedicated Communist, although he was also a dedicated national-ist. He and his Party kept a firm grip on the country, and there seemed to be little danger of pluralism creeping into Rumania. Ceausescu contin-ually practiced his brinkmanship with Moscow: in June 1970, for example, he paid a state visit to China, then openly antagonistic towards the USSR.

The following month, July, Brezhnev visited Rumania, ostensibly to renegotiate the existing Rumanian-USSR Friendship Treaty, but also to lecture Ceausescu. Resisting Soviet pressure, Ceausescu insisted on the inclusion of a clause on the right of Rumania to national sovereign independence, which cut right across the Brezhnev Doctrine and was a minor Soviet setback. No Soviet troops were stationed in Rumania, the last having left in 1964, nor were there any Soviet military missions or military advisers with the Rumanian armed forces.

One brief tremor in the Communist calm in Rumania came to light in February 1972. In what was known as the "Serb affair," Gen. Ion Serb, commander of the Bucharest military district, was arrested for passing on military secrets to the Soviet military attache. On the 16th of that month, an official at the Rumanian embassy in Vienna stated that Serb was no longer a general. Many precise details are still missing, but it seems that Serb had attempted a military coup against Ceausescu, as he opposed certain aspects of his policy, especially when it was at vari-ance with that of the USSR. It seemed that Serb could not muster enough pro-Soviet and anti-Ceausescu support. The full story is yet to be told.

During the seventies Ceausescu paid a number of visits abroad not only to Warsaw Pact countries, but to NATO and Third World countries as well, not all of which met with Soviet approval. He had visited Presi-dent Nixon in the United States in October 1970, and then again in December 1973. Another visit was made to President Ford in June 1975, which Ford returned in August that year. In April 1978, Ceausescu visited President Carter in Washington. In August Premiere Hua Guo-feng of China visited Rumania. Soviet leaders accused Ceausescu of being too friendly with capitalist countries, and also of sowing discord among communist ones. Ceausescu had visited Yugoslavia, and Marshal Tito had visited Rumania, which caused the Kremlin to fear that even-tually Rumania might opt out of the Warsaw Pact and join Tito in some form of independent, neutral Balkan pact.

In a major speech on 23 November 1978, Ceausescu declared there was "no imminent danger of war with the West." At a Warsaw Pact meeting a few days later, he refused a Soviet demand for "closer integration" of the Rumanian armed forces into the military framework of the Warsaw Pact, which would have meant placing them completely under Soviet command. Both in 1978 and 1979, Ceausescu refused to increase his defense spending, then about 3.2 percent of his national budget. He was pushing his brinkmanship to the utmost limits.

Soviet propaganda made good capital out of what became known as the "Sonnenfeld Doctrine," which emerged from a briefing to a group of ambassadors of both Western and communist countries, in Brussels, on 14 December 1975, by Helmut Sonnenfeld, a senior U.S. State Department adviser on communist affairs. The then accepted U.S. Administration policy was to support and give what help it could to aid "the independence, the national sovereignty and identity, and the autonomy of all the peoples and countries of Central and Eastern Europe." In seeming contradiction, Sonnenfeld said immediately after a NATO ministerial meeting, "It is in the long term interest of the United States to encourage East European countries to develop a more natural and *organic* relationship with the Soviet Union, and to respond to the clearly visible aspirations in Eastern Europe for a more autonomous existence within the context of a strong Soviet geopolitical influence."

Many saw this as a switch in American policy; in return for a free hand for the Soviets in Eastern Europe, the United States was free to take action against communism in Western Europe. This caused some Western alarm and confusion. Henry Kissinger, the U.S. secretary of state, had to step in and say, "There is no Sonnenfeld Doctrine," and to remark that Sonnenfeld's use of the word "organic" had been unfortunate. Called to testify in the U.S. House of Representatives in April 1976, Sonnenfeld denied he had advocated what amounted to allowing the "consolidation of Soviet domination over Eastern Europe." One wonders if the Sonnenfeld statement was too accurate for the comfort of the U.S. administration, or had been uttered prematurely.

The final assessment must be that in the seventies the Soviet imprint rested deeply on Warsaw Pact members, despite occasional rumbles of unease. Albania by this time was out of the Pact and under Chinese influence. All the Warsaw Pact governments were Marxist-Leninist, faithful to the Moscow line. Their armed forces were standardized, being woven into the military framework of the Pact with few signs of either military or political discontent, or of the military anywhere plotting a coup against Party leadership. The Serb affair in Rumania and

Ceausescu's brinkmanship seemed to be the exceptions to this rule. In the background was the persuasive shadow of the Brezhnev Doctrine.

THE EUROPEAN NEUTRALS

The policy of the USSR was to strive to gain influence with the neutral European states (Austria, Finland, Spain, Sweden, Switzerland, and Yugoslavia), to make treaties and trade agreements with them, and to encourage their Warsaw Pact satellites to do the same. For convenience, a brief comment on Malta is also included in this section.

Situated in the middle of Central Europe, tiny Austria has become the ideal image of a thriving neutral European country which has successfully remained independent of both NATO and Warsaw Pact military alliances. After World War II, Austria remained under Allied occupation until 1955, when the Austrian State Treaty formally reestablished that country as a sovereign independent state within its prewar frontiers. Mainly oriented towards the West, and having common borders with West Germany, Switzerland, and Italy, Austria received several million Western tourists annually during the seventies.

The Austrian national symbol is a spread eagle with outstretched talons, dangling from which is a gyve, from which hangs part of a broken chain. One fetter bears the symbol of the Soviet hammer, and the other the Soviet sickle. The symbolic significance of the broken chain cannot be lost on many repressed or dissident factions in Soviet satellite states, especially East Germany.

To gain influence, the USSR encouraged Warsaw Pact countries to enter into trade, economic, and other agreements with Austria. In September 1971, for example, such agreements were concluded with both Poland and Czechoslovakia. In December 1972, a diplomatic agreement was made with East Germany, and a full consular one followed in March 1975. Austrian relations with the USSR directly were cool but correct. For example, road and rail links across part of Czechoslovakia and between the two countries operated satisfactorily. In the seventies it could be said that Chancellor Bruno Kreisky successfully kept the Soviet imprint away from Austria and kept his frontiers open to the West.

It is often said that Finland, wedged between the USSR and Sweden, is not in the strict sense of that word a neutral like Austria, but was almost as much under the Soviet imprint as any Warsaw Pact satellite state. The Soviets certainly had a strong hold over the country, but as long as the Finns did not join NATO or any other non-Soviet defense pact, they were allowed almost unfettered domestic liberal democracy, great latitude in making foreign contacts, and wide scope to enter into economic, trade, and cultural agreements. This state of affairs has become known as "Finlandization." Current definitions of this expression include: a country that is subservient to its protector's foreign policy; a country within the sphere of influence of another; supine submission to Great Power domination; and creeping Sovietization. You can take your pick, or think up one more suitable to individual views and philosophies.

The reason for the Soviets allowing such freedom of liberal democracy and pluralism to Finland is usually ascribed to propaganda, an attempt to depict themselves as tolerant and liberal-minded in the hope of persuading Scandinavian countries to walk into the Soviet camp on similar terms. Undoubtedly, the Soviets have the necessary military strength to swiftly occupy Finland if they wished, and this possibility in the background must persuade Finnish governments to be very amenable to Soviet wishes.

Moscow certainly has interfered in the domestic affairs of Finland in the past. For years it insisted on the exclusion from ministerial office of the Social Democrats, the majority party. In the 1958 election, Communists won about a quarter of the seats in the Eduskunta, the single-chamber parliament; but when a coalition government was formed, the Communists were excluded. The Soviets stepped in to insist they be included. At that time the bulk of Finnish exports went to the USSR, so the Soviets halted all trade with Finland until this political condition was met.

With its wide-ranging universal contacts, Finland was the Soviet window on the free world which the Kremlin leadership found most useful. Helsinki, the Finnish capital, became the location for important international conferences, such as the one in 1975 that produced the Helsinki Accords.

In July 1970, President Urho Kekkonen went to Moscow to sign an extension of the 1948 USSR-Finnish Treaty of Friendship, Cooperation, and Mutual Assistance. In Soviet jargon "mutual assistance" means "military aid," and this treaty bound the Finns to go to the aid of the USSR if that state was threatened. In October, President Podgorny visited Finland to sign trade agreements. The Finns can hardly call themselves truly neutral, but they do.

With such trade, construction, and other agreements between Finland and the USSR, relations between the two states remained stable in the seventies. In 1973, Finland made trade and cooperation agreements with East Germany. Marshal Ustinov, the Soviet defense minister, suggested joint maneuvers in Finland in 1978, but the Finns refused.

In this instance the Soviets did not push the Finlandization fiction too far, in case it became counterproductive.

For some years Spain was considered by the U.S. administration to be a valuable potential member of NATO, but this was unacceptable to the European members because under Gen. Francisco Franco's regime, it was not a democratic country. It was isolated by them politically, although millions of West European tourists flocked to Spain's sunny beaches annually. Franco died in November 1975, after which Spain struggled to become a Western democracy under the approving gaze of West Europeans.

Relations between Franco's Spain and the USSR had always been bad. In World War II, for example, Franco sent his Blue Division to fight in Russia with the German Wehrmacht against the Russians. It was not until early 1975 that any formal contact between the two countries was made. Then, in January, some trade agreements were signed, and permission was given for Soviet civil aircraft to overfly Spanish territory; and in September, a fishing agreement was concluded. But on the whole, relations with the USSR remained frigid even after Franco's death, largely over the issue of gold repayment. During the Spanish Civil War (1936–39), the beleaguered Republican government sent the Spanish gold reserve (present estimated value being $2.5 billion) to the USSR for safekeeping. The Soviets were reluctant to return the gold to any other than a Spanish Communist government, which had not materialized as expected by them when Franco died. The Spanish government claimed the gold had been sold, and the money transferred by the Soviets to Spanish Republicans in exile. Eventually, on 9 February 1977, full diplomatic relations were established between Spain and the USSR, even though the gold issue had not been resolved.

When the Spanish Communist Party, led by Santiago Carrillo, was legalized, the exiled Spanish Communists trickled back to Spain. In the 1977 elections the Party gained 20 seats in the 350-seat Cortes. The Communists accepted the Spanish democratic constitution. In April 1978, the Spanish Communist Party openly rejected Leninism and threw off the Moscow Marxist-Leninist domination to become Eurocommunists.[1] In the election of 1979, the Party won 23 seats. The Soviet imprint that had rested briefly and lightly on Spain in 1977 was quickly removed.

[1] An expression coined by the media to differentiate it from rigid Marxist-Leninist doctrine. It embraces all the Communist parties in Europe that do not follow Soviet leadership and ideology but does not indicate a common doctrine. Most Eurocommunists believe in combining communism with a degree of political and personal freedom, but not all.

Another European neutral was Sweden, a NATO member. Sweden, which has not been involved in a war for about 150 years, has a comparatively small population of about 8.3 million people for its 173,500 square miles (1976). As Sweden is in an exposed and vulnerable strategic position should the Soviets ever decide to take a short cut to attack Norwegian ports, it maintains fairly large, efficient armed forces. Somewhat unusual as a neutral country, it has developed a flourishing armaments industry with profitable overseas markets for ships, aircraft, tanks, and other weapons.

Sweden had a small legal Communist Party which, in 1977, splintered into the Communist Left Party and the Swedish Workers Communist Party, but Communists generally had only a small following in the electorate. As a liberal democracy, Sweden is openly oriented to the West but maintains diplomatic relations with the USSR; in 1972, it added East Germany to its diplomatic list. The attitude of the Swedish government towards the USSR is rigidly correct and diplomatic; trade, economic, and other links are maintained. During the seventies the Soviets failed to cast any imprint on Sweden.

With only about 16,000 square miles and a population of only about 6.3 million (1976), securely perched in the Alps, the traditional West European crossroad point is Switzerland, long a neutral country and determined to remain so. During the war it became a center for espionage and third party negotiations; and although technically the Cold War is over, it retains this image. Switzerland has a world-wide commercial reputation, especially for banking, and its coded deposit accounts are notorious.

Once the home of the defunct League of Nations, Switzerland maintians diplomatic relations with most countries in the world, including the USSR. In 1972, it established them with East Germany as well. The Swiss city of Geneva still attracts important international conferences. Soviet Communist philosophy has little attraction for the Swiss as it is contrary to their way of life and business, and so the Swiss government has always fended off Soviet political overtures or advances. Traditionally a neutral country that has kept clear of all military alliances in modern times, its heart is with the West, and the Soviet imprint on Switzerland in the seventies was indiscernible, although the Soviet embassy staff at Berne, the capital, was one of the largest in the world.

The other European neutral country of considerable interest to the USSR was Communist Yugoslavia. Tito cooperated closely with Stalin immediately after World War II. In 1948, the two leaders quarreled and Tito broke all formal links with the USSR. His country since has remained solidly independent—but solidly Communist. Marshal Tito can perhaps be regarded as the first successful independent Eurocommunist national leader. Tito's state was able to survive economically in the Cold War period as Western markets were opened up to Yugoslavia.

In an effort to tempt the Yugoslavs back into the Soviet orbit, in 1955, Khrushchev visited Belgrade, where, with Tito, he signed a document on the principle of noninterference in internal affairs for whatever reason, whether of economic, political or ideological nature. This did not get the Soviets very far, but high-level contact between Yugoslavia and the Soviet union was maintained.

Brezhnev visited Belgrade in September 1971 but had to be content with a vague joint declaration that merely reiterated the right of individual countries to choose their own form of socialism. Tito wanted friendship, not domination; but Brezhnev wanted both. Feathers were ruffled, and in December, Tito declared he would use the Yugoslav army against his enemies, meaning the Soviets, whom he thought were preparing an armed invasion of Yugoslavia. Tempers subsided, and the following year Tito visited Moscow. In 1973, Brezhnev ordered the Bulgarians to try to persuade the Yugoslavs to enter some form of Balkan Pact with them, but this initiative failed miserably. Yugoslavs had deep differences with Bulgarians over territory claimed by both, an issue that was liable to erupt on the slightest provocation.

Tito tended to side with President Ceausescu of Rumania in his brinkmanship with Moscow, and in 1974 visited Rumania, where he signed a number of scientific, economic, and technical cooperation agreements. One of the latter bore fruit in a cosmetic sort of way in April 1975, when the first prototype of the Jurum fighter aircraft, a joint Yugoslav-Rumanian production, was put on show in Belgrade. This annoyed the Soviets, who liked to control arms development and production in their satellite countries. In September 1976, Tito rejected a Soviet request for port facilities on the Adriatic Sea coast.

In November, Brezhnev again went to Belgrade to a cold reception by Tito: neither leader would give an inch. After this the Soviets held off, waiting for Tito either to die or retire from office, at which point they anticipated Yugoslavia would disintegrate into chaos, upon which they hoped to be able to impose their imprint. To Soviet chagrin, Tito did not die in the seventies;[2] on the contrary, he was able to visit the United States in May 1979. Due to his stubbornness, no Soviet imprint at all was made on Yugoslavia during this decade.

[2] Tito died in May 1980 at age eighty-seven.

Malta, which strove unsuccessfully in the seventies to become and remain a neutral country, can be conveniently and briefly commented on in this section, although strictly speaking it is a Mediterranean state rather than a European one. During this decade Malta, a strategically valuable island, passed from British (and consequently NATO) influence to that of the Kremlin's agent, Col. Muammar Gaddafi of Libya. For many years until its independence in 1964, Malta had been a British military and naval base; and with its dockyards, naval repair, and refueling facilities, it was of immense value to the North Atlantic Alliance. In 1970, Malta was the base for NATO's Allied Forces, Southern Europe.

In June 1971, in a narrow election victory, Dominic Mintoff came to power as prime minister. He immediately demanded that the British pay immensely increased charges for the base facilities and provide other economic assistance, which Britain was in no way able to do. On 30 June, Mintoff terminated the defense and financial assistance agreements with Britain and banned U.S. warships from using Maltese naval facilities. In August, NATO Allied Forces had to move their southern Europe base to Naples, Italy.

In an attempt to play off East against West, Mintoff succeeded in obtaining diplomatic recognition from the Soviet Union in the latter part of 1971. He also made trade agreements with the USSR, Poland, and Rumania. These agreements were of small significance; the Kremlin had decided instead to use Colonel Gaddafi, who had come to power in Libya in 1969, as their agent. In July 1971, Libyan warships had visited Malta; in September, Gaddafi gave Mintoff some driblets of financial and other assistance; and in January 1972, Libyan technicians arrived to take over the running of Malta's Luqa airport.

Disappointed, Mintoff turned back to the British. On 26 March 1972, a seven-year Anglo-Maltese defense agreement was signed, containing a clause that the Maltese would not allow their airport, docks, or any military or naval facilities to be used by any Warsaw Pact armed forces, nor allow any of them to be stationed on the island. The fee for the use of the facilities was heavily increased again, but the United States and four other NATO European allies contributed to make up for what the British, then plagued by a falling pound, were unable to raise. Despite this moderate gesture to the NATO allies, Mintoff did not have much success getting economic assistance and trade pacts to help his barren economy. Nor were his contacts with Gaddafi very smooth or profitable, as the Libyan leader did not like Mintoff's deal with the British; also, arguments developed between the two leaders over the ownership of certain offshore oilfields.

In November 1977, Mintoff warned that if Western Europe would not provide the economic assistance he requested, he would have to "opt for military attachment with Arab countries," meaning Libya. Although his election majorities were small, Mintoff remained in power for the rest of the decade. He began to introduce repressive measures against his political opponents and to ban foreign journalists whose reports were not favorable to him. Meanwhile, Soviet leaders sat back quietly on the issue of Malta, leaving their agent Gaddafi to recruit it from the NATO camp.

The Anglo-Maltese military agreement terminated on 31 March 1979. Colonel Gaddafi himself was present at the ceremony of lowering the British flag in Malta for the last time. The last British troops and ships left the following day. Mintoff was left alone on his strategic Mediterranean island, as he put it, to be "entirely neutral and un-aligned" with his island country forming "a bridge of peace between Europe and Africa." The Kremlin leaders had played their cards well, and as the seventies closed the Soviet imprint had begun to hover over Malta.

THE HELSINKI ACCORDS

For a long time the Kremlin had been seeking to legalize and gain international recognition of the Soviet territorial acquisitions after World War II. Together with their Warsaw Pact allies, they had frequently suggested a conference of all European nations. This idea attracted some European nations; indeed, when in Moscow in October 1970, President Georges Pompidou of France had supported the suggestion for a European conference on security, although he emphasized that France's primary commitment was still to NATO. As West European nations recovered economically from the effects of World War II, memories of injustices began to fade and attention was given to the issue of accepting postwar national de facto boundaries.

This Soviet idea came to fruition on 3 July 1973, when the European Security Conference opened at ministerial level in Helsinki, Finland. It became known as the "Conference on Security and Cooperation in Europe" (CSCE). In September, the conference proper began its sessions at Geneva, and representatives attended from every country in Europe, from both sides of the Iron Curtain (except Albania), and also from the United States and Canada. The West regarded the CSCE as a liaison between all European countries that might make a significant contribution to detente. The Soviets wanted it to ratify the territorial divisions of Europe that had taken place since the end of World War II and to recognize the sovereignty of East Germany.

The main subject on the agenda was security in Europe. There came to be four topics in all, the others being cooperation in economics and other technical fields; cooperation in humanitarian and similar fields; and a follow-up on the conference. These four subjects became known as "baskets," as the national representatives wrote their original suggestions for the agenda on slips of paper which were then placed in separate baskets according to the basic subject.

Western states were deeply concerned at the lack of individual freedom inside the USSR and Soviet restrictions on movement from the Soviet bloc to the West. The USSR was urged to relax these restrictions, but the Kremlin put up considerable resistance to suggestions for the free flow of information and people between East and West. On 10 March 1974, Brezhnev accused Western nations of deliberately blocking progress in the conference by concentrating so much on the human rights issue. The year 1974 brought considerable doubts to Americans as to the Soviet sincerity in regard to detente.

Eventually, on 28 July 1975 at Helsinki, the heads of thirty-five national delegations signed a 30,000-word document called the "Final Act," which outlined the guiding principles in high moral tones and sometimes obscure language. To the Soviets it was, of course, a considerable triumph as existing European national boundaries were recognized by all signatory states. The sovereignty of East Germany was implied and accepted. On 7 October 1975, the USSR signed the new Friendship Treaty with East Germany, which deliberately omitted all reference to eventual German reunification.

Not all guidelines were so welcome. One of the conditions in Basket one was that states should notify the others of all major military exercises involving 20,000 men or more, in advance, and invite foreign military observers to see them. On 11 December 1975, Joseph Luns, the NATO secretary general, complained that on at least two occasions the Soviet Union had failed to give advance notice of, and invitations to, large military exercises. It was not until February 1978 that the Soviets invited military observers from the United States, Britain, and the Benelux countries to attend a five-day military exercise in western Russia; they were shown very little.

Nor was the human rights campaign everything it could have been. In September 1973, trials began of two prominent Soviet dissidents,

Pyotr Yakir and Viktor Krasin, for "anti-Soviet agitation and propaganda." Another Soviet dissident widely known outside the USSR was the novelist Alexander Solzhenitsyn, who in an interview with the Western press declared that the "violence of the Soviet regime is greater than that in Greece, Spain, or Turkey." On 13 February 1974, Solzhenitsyn was expelled from Russia, being the first Soviet national to lose his citizenship and be deported since Leon Trotsky in 1929. When Solzhenitsyn later came to the United States, President Ford refused to meet him, as he did not want to spoil the atmosphere of detente by offending the Soviet government. Ford overlooked the fact that on several occasions Brezhnev had publicly met and praised anti-Western personalities who visited or took refuge in the USSR.

The Soviet human rights accord was an extremely bad one and the Soviet government was vulnerable in this respect, but the American administration did not seem to make much use of this lever in negotiations, especially in relation to the SALT II talks. There was a growing suspicion that for some reason the American administration was deliberately shying away from the issue.

From the day President Jimmy Carter took office in January 1977, he worked assiduously on human rights in the USSR, which hit the Soviets where it hurt. By this time several prominent Soviet dissidents were surfacing embarrassingly and being given publicity by the world media. On 10 February 1977, Carter sent a personal letter of encouragement to Andrei Sakharov, the Russian dissident scientist, which not only offended against normal accepted diplomatic protocol, but infuriated the Soviet government which was proving to be extremely susceptible to this form of criticism. This unwitting Carter barb struck deep. The USSR mustered all its diplomatic means and propaganda to persuade individual NATO countries to pressure Carter to ease off. NATO allied support for the Carter human rights campaign in the USSR noticeably declined.

Indeed, on 10 July 1977, when Helmut Schmidt, the West German chancellor, was on a visit to Canada, both he and Premiere Pierre Trudeau openly agreed that Carter's human rights policies were harming detente. The Carter campaign against Soviet internal political repression lost its intensity, and so the one effective weapon available was not used, as the spirit of detente was considered to be more important. Although persuaded to ease off, Carter still clung to his human rights philosophy and was upset by the spate of trials of Soviet dissidents in the Soviet Union, which began in April 1978 and dragged on through the summer.

NATO EUROPE

As regards NATO Europe, the Soviet peace strategy was to maintain, and extend if possible, full diplomatic contacts with all its nations; to negotiate economic, trade, and technical cooperation agreements with them; and also for individual Warsaw Pact states to forge similar agreements with individual NATO European nations, hoping that such a cross-pattern of linkage would orient NATO Europe towards the Soviet bloc and weaken its NATO resolve and alliance with the United States. A large number of such treaties and agreements had already been concluded; some were operating well, especially from the Soviet point of view, and some were not.

Soviet leaders worked hard, but unsuccessfully, to persuade the French to sign a friendship treaty. The French had gone as far as they were prepared to go: they were not prepared to abandon NATO and walk into the Soviet camp.

The next major NATO European country the Soviets tried to subvert was West Germany, whose problems with reunification have already been mentioned. During the seventies numerous minor trade and other agreements between the USSR and West Germany were concluded, but Soviet and German suspicions of each other remained.

Kremlin leaders made no progress with Britain, the other major NATO European country, despite a Labor government being in power for most of the decade. The British remained inherently suspicious of the USSR and its approaches. The seventies got off to a bad start as far as the Soviets were concerned, and Foreign Minister Gromyko's visit to London in October 1970 was not a success. In June 1971, the British government summarily expelled ninety Soviet diplomats and other personnel for alleged involvement in espionage, which cooled relations between the two countries for some time. A number of trade and technical agreements were concluded during the seventies, but that was all.

Guarding NATO's open vulnerable northern flank was Norway, a priority Kremlin target. Norwegians remained wary of Soviet intentions and were reluctant to upset or change the delicate status quo around the North Cape area. It was not until 7 March 1974 that a joint USSR-Norwegian agreement was concluded for the construction of a year-round airport on a small island near Spitsbergen, in the Arctic Ocean. Days afterwards, this was followed by a state visit to Moscow by the Norwegian prime minister. In July 1979, the USSR-Norwegian fishing agreement in the "gray area" of the Barents Sea was extended, but generally the Norwegians were not looking for any closer links with the Soviets. An incident of NATO interest occurred on 28 August 1979, when a Soviet TU-22 (Badger) aircraft crashed on Hopen Island, southeast of Spitsbergen. Its wreckage and its "black box" were not handed over by the Norwegians to the Soviets until 15 November, after having been minutely examined by NATO experts, much to Soviet chagrin. One up for the Norwegians.

At the beginning of the decade, before Italian Eurocommunism became so pronounced, the Soviets set their sights on Italy. In November 1970, Foreign Minister Gromyko visited Rome. In October 1972, the Italian prime minister, Guilio Andreotti, visited Moscow to sign trade and other minor agreements. An Italian consulate was opened in Leningrad, and a Soviet one in Milan. After that, few fresh Italian-Soviet high-level contacts were made.

Turkey, NATO's southeastern bastion, has a common frontier with the USSR. In April 1972, President Podgorny visited that country. but all that resulted was a joint declaration on "The Principles of Good-Neighborly Relations between the USSR and the Republic of Turkey," which did not mean very much. Turkey was then a loyal NATO ally and deeply suspicious of Soviet intentions. In 1974, Turkish armed forces invaded Cyprus and remained in occupation of part of that island; this caused a rupture with Greece, which supported the Greek Cypriot cause. U.S.-NATO military aid to Turkey ceased, and the Turks closed down all but one of the U.S.-NATO missile monitoring stations on its territory, which was a magnificent gift to the Soviets. Left with an ailing economy, Turkey was practically ostracized by its NATO allies.

The Soviets sought to take advantage of this situation. In July 1975, they made certain credit facilities available to the Turks, and then promised more, but with strings attached. In December, Kosygin visited Ankara, the capital, but his attempt at political blackmail was unsuccessful. The customary joint declaration was not issued on the termination of this visit, owing to Turkish objections to the USSR's wording. The Turks considered the Soviet draft too close to a nonaggression declaration.

In April 1978, Carter asked Congress to lift the American arms embargo on Turkey, but Western aid was slow to arrive. In June, Turkish Prime Minister Bulent Ecevit visited Moscow. The Soviets agreed to supply Turkey with three million tons of oil a year in exchange for Turkish grain. Turkey was then in a state of economic crisis. This time a joint declaration was produced, entitled "A Political Document on the

Principles of Good-Neighborly and Friendly Cooperation''; it was a pale copy of the 1972 declaration. Despite shabby treatment by its allies, Turkey remained loyal to NATO.

Under Soviet encouragement a large number of treaties, agreements, protocols, and pacts were made between individual NATO and Warsaw Pact countries on a wide variety of subjects, from fishing to double taxation, and from extracting natural gas to cultural exchanges. It seemed that the Soviet plan was to spin a web of cross-agreements on almost any mutually acceptable subject, no matter how trivial. NATO countries made these agreements largely in the interest of furthering detente. This pattern largely complimented the Kissinger policy of linkage between the United States and the USSR.

The Soviets ruthlessly manipulated these agreements as political blackmail when it suited their purpose. For example, in October 1973, when the Yom Kippur war was at its height and arms and equipment for the Israelis were being shipped from West German ports and airfields, the Soviet Energy Corporation cut off the natural gas that was piped in quantity into Germany. The supply of natural gas was not resumed until the West German government had embargoed the transport of all military material for Israel from its soil. Concurrently, the USSR insisted on using its overflying rights from Turkey for its aerial arms lift to Egypt and Syria, and persuaded the Turkish government to refuse such rights to the U.S. To the Kremlin's satisfaction, Greece and Italy, both NATO allies, refused the United States transit facilities for equipment and personnel to Israel.

In January 1972, the European Economic Community (EEC), was enlarged by the addition of Britain, Denmark, and the Republic of Ireland, making it a nine-nation economic pact. In a speech in March, Brezhnev for the first time recognized the EEC as a reality and ceased to criticize it. The Soviets had their Council for Mutual Economic Assistance, more usually referred to as COMECON, consisting of all seven Warsaw Pact members plus Mongolia and Cuba. The Soviets regarded it as a power lever over resources and trade. The USSR exported oil and raw materials to COMECON countries at subsidized prices; and trade with them, and between members, was on favorable terms so that Communist states would not be tempted to look for cheaper and better markets in the West. It also meant that if COMECON countries did not toe the Moscow line, their favorable trading advantages would abruptly cease until they came round again to the Soviet way of thinking. COMECON was used as a Soviet form of economic blackmail.

DIVIDING THE NATO ALLIES

Throughout the seventies, Brezhnev worked to divorce the United States from its NATO European allies and did his best to exploit differences and suspicions that surfaced from time to time. On 18 February 1970, President Richard Nixon, who had been in office for only just over a year, produced his Report to Congress, called "U.S. Foreign Policy for the 1970s: New Strategy for Peace," in which he expanded on his doctrine of "stimulated self-help for foreign countries" in need of support, which he had first enunciated in June 1969, to be based on a "peace through partnership" theme.

Nixon also renounced the isolationist policy and said that the U.S. would continue to play a full part in world affairs. He assured Europe, Asia, and Latin America that they were still of primary importance to the United States. To give confidence to the West Europeans, Nixon wrote: "Europe is as indispensable as Alaska to the United States." During 1970, he reaffirmed the American commitment to NATO Europe several times; and during his tour of that region in the fall, he emphasized the American determination to resist Soviet aggression, especially in the Mediterranean area.

The adoption by the United States of the flexible response strategy to any Soviet attack had not been welcomed by all the NATO European allies, who had begun to doubt whether the U.S. president would ever use the nuclear weapons in defense of NATO European soil, and to suspect that the will to do so was no longer there. For a long time the NATO European allies had sheltered comfortably under the American nuclear umbrella, doing as little as possible about their own defense capabilities. They had been shaken out of this sense of security by the flexible response strategy, which required them to have large defense forces to enable the "other conventional options" to be credible. During 1971, both Nixon and his defense secretary, Robert McNamara, had on several occasions to restate their defense commitment to the NATO European allies, and also to declare they would not make any bilateral agreements with the USSR involving the reduction of American combat troops in that theater. On 21 December, Nixon assured Brandt that "the American commitment to Europe will remain unchanged."

When Nixon visited Moscow in May 1972, one of the several agreements he signed with Brezhnev, was a twelve-point statement on "Basic Principles of Relations between the United States and the USSR." It mainly called for reciprocity and mutual restraint in international affairs and respective spheres of influence. However, the USSR ignored this agreement and continued to act without restraint in areas well outside its own traditional sphere of influence. The Soviets also insisted that this agreement did not cover national liberation movements.

The Yom Kippur War, which began on 6 October 1973 when Egypt and Syria attacked Israel, brought the United States and the USSR into dangerous confrontation with each other. The shadow of World War III momentarily hovered over the Middle East. The course and analysis of this war has been described elsewhere,[3] and here it is only necessary to say that the Arabs fought with Soviet arms and the Israelis largely with American ones; the rate of weapon destruction caused both the Americans and the Soviets to mount massive air and sea lifts of replacements, spares, and ammunition, as neither wanted their own arms to be badly outclassed. Loss of prestige and revealed flaws and weaknesses might seriously alter the strategic balance of arms between the two superpowers, either one way or the other.

By 24 October, the Egyptian Third Army in the southern part of the Suez Canal region was besieged by Israeli troops. That day, President Anwar Sadat of Egypt asked Brezhnev to send Soviet troops to help him. Through intermediaries, Brezhnev suggested to Nixon that a joint American-Soviet armed force be sent as a "unilateral institution of suitable measure." Nixon refused as he did not want Soviet combat troops flooding into the Middle East. Brezhnev's response was the so-called "tough-note," in which he said that if the United States would not cooperate in enforcing a cease-fire, the Soviets might be obliged to consider acting alone.

Nixon's response was to declare a Defense Condition Three, or in the jargon a "DEFCON 3," which went into effect in the early hours of the 25th, putting U.S. armed forces worldwide on "Red Alert." This was action the Soviets understood. There is still debate and controversy over whether the alert was a deliberate act to divert attention from Nixon's Watergate problems, but there is no doubt that it was effective, as the Soviets were ready to move, having mobilized airborne and other divisions. The critical confrontation between the two superpowers was gradually defused.

Apart from bringing the "oil weapon" to the notice of the world, the Yom Kippur War brought about a change in NATO European attitudes, especially towards the United States, whose DEFCON 3 had been declared without any prior consultation with its allies. This made them apprehensive that they might become involved in a World War III without their consent. NATO European allies were also concerned that

[3] See Edgar O'Ballance, *No Victor, No Vanquished* (Novato, CA: Presidio Press, 1979).

quantities of military items from NATO stockpiles in Europe had been flown to Israel (which was not even a NATO member) without the host nation even being informed. NATO European nations imposed restrictions against the American air and sea lift to Israel. The NATO base at Lajes in the Azores, in Portuguese territory, had initially been used by the Americans for this purpose without Portuguese permission. Belated permission was only given in return for U.S. support in the United Nations on an unpopular colonial issue, Portugal then still being a colonial power. On 26 October, West Germany refused to allow any more shipments of military supplies from its ports to Israel. This was the first sign of any real difference between West Germany and the United States.

The Yom Kippur War demonstrated that the NATO European nations had a distinctly regional concept of defense, and that their strengthening economy was making them more politically independent of the United States. This brought objections to lack of consultation and misuse of NATO stockpiles in Europe. France, which had always cautioned against placing too much reliance on detente, now called for a common West European defense policy. The Americans were also disappointed as they felt their NATO European allies had deserted them in a period of international tension.

In November 1974, when visiting West Germany, the U.S. Defense secretary again had to promise there would be no reduction in the U.S. military contribution in that country, but he added that there might have to be a shift in ratio of support to combat troops. Later, on 24 September 1978, Hans Apel, the West German defense minister, openly questioned the value of the NATO annual reinforcement of European military exercises, stating that they were unnecessarily provocative; he urged that a NATO political review of them be instigated. The differences that surfaced and were aired between the United States and its NATO European allies as a result of the Yom Kippur War were to the distinct satisfaction of the Kremlin. The Soviet peace strategy was working well.

In May 1977, Carter persuaded his reluctant NATO European allies to increase their annual defense spending by 3 percent in real terms. On 3 August, he confirmed the American commitment to use nuclear weapons in defense of NATO European territory. To assuage his allies' uneasiness, Carter promised on 5 January 1978 to send another 8,000 U.S. combat troops to boost the strength of the American contingent in Europe.

At a meeting held on 18 April 1978 in Denmark, the NATO Nuclear Planning Group agreed to the American plan to modernize nuclear weapons in Europe. This included introducing the neutron bomb into Western Europe. West Germany immediately agreed to have the bombs on its soil, which brought violent protests from the Soviet Union. The Soviets were delighted by the reluctance of certain NATO European countries to have nuclear weapons on their soil, their demonstrations and protests against such weapons, and the failure of some to meet their promised 3 percent increase in military budgets. The Soviets read into this attitude a disinclination to fight or become involved in war at all.

At a NATO Summit meeting on 30 May in Washington, Carter stated, "The Warsaw Pact countries, especially the USSR, have steadily expanded and modernized their conventional forces beyond any legitimate requirements for defense. They are now able to attack with large armored forces." The one bright spot in Europe for the Americans was on 9 October 1978, when Turkey agreed to reopen four of the former U.S.-NATO monitoring bases. On the whole, in the seventies the Soviets made considerable gains in Europe, while the United States suffered a series of setbacks.

5 The Soviet Imprint on the Middle East

Among Arab countries, the Soviet Union has strengthened its relations with Syria, Iraq, Algeria, South Yemen and Libya, and also the Palestine Liberation Organization. Certain forces have recently been making persistent attempts to undermine Soviet-Egyptian relations.
—Leonid Brezhnev; Twenty-Fifth Congress, 24 February 1976

SOVIET POLICY TOWARDS the Middle East was the simple but devastating one of destabilizing the region and breaking the power of the Arab League. Soviet objectives were to regionalize the area into more malleable sectors, eliminate all American and Western influence, and establish the influence of the USSR more firmly. The USSR wanted to dominate the Suez Canal and the Red Sea passage from the Mediterranean Sea to the Indian Ocean, so as to control the flow of oil from the Middle East and Persian Gulf territories to Europe and Western countries.

With Third World countries generally the Soviets used bribery, bullying, and blackmail, first of all to obtain influence, and then to gain a foothold for Soviet personnel. The process usually began with a calculated supply of arms, either free or at a very low price, and economic aid in small amounts, so that the target country came to rely on this assistance and ask for more. More arms and aid were offered, usually if possible under "friendship" agreements that prevented the recipient from obtaining arms from or dealing with Western or other sources, thus making the USSR the sole prop in the country's defense and economic fields.

Since World War II, the Middle East had been a dangerous flash point, largely because of conflict and wars between Arabs and Israelis, and other issues, such as the still homeless Palestinian refugees. The Arab-Israeli War of 1973—the Yom Kippur War to the Israelis, and the War of Ramadan to the Arabs—ended in a standoff, but it revealed to the Arabs the power of their oil weapon and how effectively it could be

61

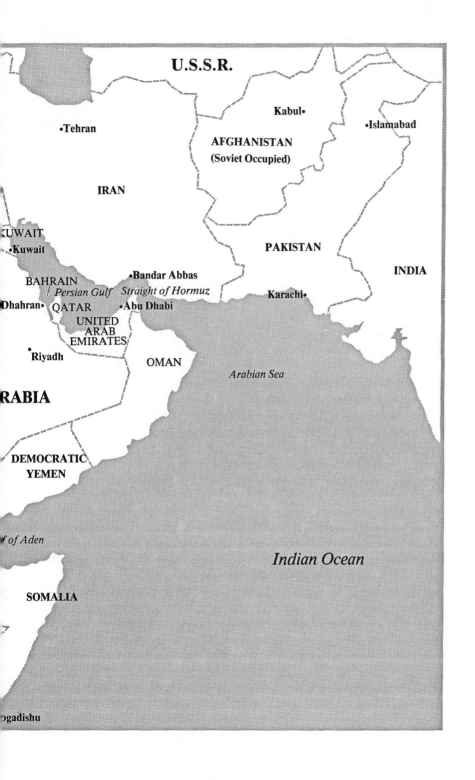

used against the West. Western Europe was desperate for oil, and at times cared little how it was obtained, often to the embarrassment of the United States. The Soviets did their best to exploit these differences.

Other conflicts in the Middle East in the seventies included the Egyptian-Israeli war of attrition that did not end until August 1970; the civil war in Jordan against the Palestinian Fedayeen in 1970–71; the Lebanese civil war of 1975–76, which never really stopped; the Iraqi civil war against the Kurds that continued until 1975, with later eruptions; the three-day border war in July 1977 between Egypt and Libya; and the twenty-three day war early in 1979 between North Yemen and South Yemen. The Middle East also spawned the growth of terrorism, both Palestinian and international, aided secretly and selectively by the Soviet KGB.

The Soviet imprint in 1970 lay patchily across the Middle East, resting heavily on Egypt, Syria, Iraq, Algeria, and South Yemen. Soon to fall on Libya, it was felt more lightly in North Yemen, Sudan, Lebanon, and the Palestine Liberation Organization; and not at all on Bahrain, Kuwait, Jordan, Oman, Qatar, Saudi Arabia, or the United Arab Emirates. The solidly pro-American bastion in the Middle East was Israel, extremely hostile to the USSR mainly because it would not allow free emigration of Russian Jews. Hostility was reciprocated by the Soviet Union, as it considered Israel an American satellite state that blocked Soviet ambitions in that region and a symbol of Western imperialism. During the seventies Egypt and Sudan managed to brush off the Soviet imprint, and by the end of the decade Egypt was offering facilities for the American Rapid Deployment Force project. On other target Arab states, such as Iraq and Syria, Soviet influence deepened.

EGYPT

In 1970, the most important country in the Arab Middle East was Egypt, known as the United Arab Republic until September 1971, when it reverted to its older and better known designation. Having an area of about 385,000 square miles, Egypt is strategically sited, bordering the Mediterranean Sea and the Red Sea, and including the vital Suez Canal, close to shipping since the 1967 war. To the east of the canal, the Sinai Peninsula, legally Egyptian territory, was occupied by the Israelis. The population of Egypt in 1970 was about 33 million, increasing at the rate of a million a year. The country had reached a higher stage of economic development and industrial advancement than most other Arab states.

In the 1950s, President Gamel Abdel Nasser of Egypt, after being refused by the West, had turned to the Soviet Union for economic aid and arms. Soviet aircraft, missiles, tanks, guns, and other military equipment were provided in quantity, and with them came numerous Soviet military advisers and technicians. By 1970, the Soviets considered Egypt their client state and felt their imprint rested firmly on it. They were coming to regard Egypt as one of their main stepping stones in the Middle East, and one that might lead into the African continent. On the other hand, Nasser regarded his country as an unaligned Third World neutral, and himself as leader of the Arab States.

The USSR had provided Egypt with more sophisticated weapons, such as surface-to-air missiles (SAMs), to counter Israel's combat aircraft, many American-built, which had gained the freedom of the skies over Egypt during the 1967 war. The Americans had given the Israelis electronic countermeasure pods (ECMs) to affix to their aircraft to counter the Soviet-manned radar search and tracking devices possessed by the Egyptians. This caused a proxy war between the U.S. and the USSR that became known as the Electronic War, the first major one of its type in military history.[1] Referred to as the War of Attrition by the Egyptians, it really began on 21 October 1967, when an Egyptian-manned Soviet-made KOMAR class missile naval craft sank the Israeli destroyer *Eilat* with a Soviet Styx surface-to-surface missile. It was the first action of its kind in naval history and caused navies to tend to shear away from reliance on gunnery at sea and to favor missiles instead.

The Soviet SAMs were placed in groups, or belts, and then in "box formations" that crept eastwards across the desert between Cairo and the Suez Canal, progressively restricting Israeli air activity over Egypt. The Suez Canal physically separated the opposing armed forces on the ground. On 7 January 1970, the Israelis made the first of many deep penetration aerial bombing raids into the interior of Egypt. On the 22nd of that month, Nasser rushed to Moscow to demand weapons capable of countering these Israeli attacks.[2] He was successful: more sophisticated SAMs and improved radar detection and tracking devices soon arrived in Egypt, as did Soviet-piloted MiG-21J aircraft, and later a few MiG-23s as well.

By the end of March, "boxes" of SAM-3s were being slowly leap-frogged eastwards. Despite Israeli air attacks that frequently destroyed

[1] See Edgar O'Ballance, *The Electronic War in the Middle East: 1968–70* (Hamden, CT: Shoe String Press, 1974).
[2] Nasser asked for SAM-3s. Egypt already had SAM-2s, which had not been fired in the 1967 war, the later excuse being that they had "too many limitations." The Egyptians had begun receiving Soviet SAM-7s in 1969.

these weapons, more seemed to appear overnight in their places. Soviet-piloted aircraft assumed the defense of Egypt proper, and Israeli aircraft were edged out from Egyptian air space, as they could not risk clashing with Soviet pilots. Within three months, six Soviet squadrons, some 200 Soviet pilots, and 150 Soviet MiG aircraft were patrolling the Egyptian skies. The Egyptians received still more updated Soviet SAMs and radar, and the Israelis more improved American ECM pods. It was Nasser's "electronic summer," which he accurately predicted would be one of "electronics by day, and infrared by night."

Soviet weapons in Egypt included over 1,000 tanks, 1,000 other armored vehicles, 1,000 guns, and about 150 FROG short-range missiles. It was estimated that up to 15,000 Soviet personnel were involved in controlling, manning, and supervising the SAMs, radar, and antiaircraft guns (ZSU 23mm x 4). Another 3,000 or so Soviets formed an entirely separate command, staff, and logistics organization that was completely independent of the Egyptian military command structure. But the Soviets had their price, which in this case was the use of Egyptian ports and air bases; this enabled them to give supporting facilities and air cover to their Mediterranean fleet. The Soviets had priority on naval facilities at Alexandria, Port Said, and smaller Egyptian Red Sea ports, such as Ras Benas; they also openly controlled about six of the main Egyptian air bases. On 7 August 1970, a cease-fire between the Egyptians and the Israelis across the Suez Canal, largely brought about by the efforts of U.S. Secretary of State William Rogers, terminated the Electronic War but not the Arab-Israeli confrontation.

On 28 September 1970, Nasser died in Cairo of a heart attack. He had previously spent some weeks in June and July in the Soviet Union undergoing medical treatment. A charismatic leader, he had greatly inspired the Arab States by standing up to Western "imperialism" in 1956, even though many of them regarded his actions as controversial. Nasser's last political act, on the day before his death, had been to persuade King Hussein of Jordan and Yasir Arafat, chairman of the Palestine Liberation Organization, to observe a cease-fire in their civil war in Jordan. Nasser was succeeded by Anwar Sadat, the vice president, who was a different personality, a deep thinker who tended to be a unifier rather than a divide-and-influence leader, as Nasser had perforce to be.

Sadat soon began developing his plan to attack Israel. One of his first moves was to withdraw Soviet military personnel manning the SAMs, radar, ZSUs from the forward areas "for their own safety";

this was completed by the end of March 1971. A number of Soviet military personnel had been killed and wounded in the Electronic War, but details were never made public. Sadat's objective was to give his Egyptian officers full control of these weapons so they could learn the techniques and tactics and gain experience.

Sadat continued Nasser's policy of close liaison with the Soviet Union, so from the Soviet point of view the decade was starting well. On 15 January 1971, President Podgorny of the USSR was present with Sadat at the formal inauguration ceremony of the Aswan Dam. The sudden withdrawal of promised U.S. and World Bank credits to construct the dam in 1956 had thrown the Egyptians into the arms of the Soviets. The new Aswan Dam provided electric power and enabled large tracts of land to be brought under cultivation. Instead of wasting out into the Mediterranean, the surplus waters of the River Nile formed a huge reservoir, known as Lake Nasser, around which a fishing industry developed. The Soviets, who had made considerable contributions to completing the Aswan Dam, made more agreements with the Egyptians, promising credits, expertise, and equipment for hydroelectric power stations and an electrification scheme.

When Podgorny again paid a four-day visit to Cairo, commencing on 25 May, he persuaded Sadat to sign a fifteen-year "Treaty of Friendship and Cooperation between the Soviet Union and the United Arab Republic." Soviet friendship pacts usually contained clauses extremely advantageous to the USSR, such as allowing them to establish bases, use existing military facilities, and have the exclusive right to supply arms. This 1971 friendship treaty with Egypt was the first of this type made by the Soviet Union with a Third World country.

Sadat visited Moscow on 11 October 1971 for discussions with Brezhnev. Their joint communiques stated that agreement had been reached on measures aimed at increasing Egypt's military strength. Soviet arms in quantity poured into Egypt. In 1972, Sadat made two more visits to Moscow, one in February, and the other in April; Soviet Defense Minister Grechko and a military team visited Egypt in both February and May to assess Egyptian military requirements; and on 13 July, Aziz Sidky, the Egyptian prime minister, also visited the USSR for talks.

Communiques issued after each of these visits all expressed joint satisfaction at the military cooperation between the two countries, and so it was some surprise to the world at large, and certainly to Soviet leaders, when on 18 July, only two days after Sidky's trip to Moscow, Sadat ordered all Soviet military personnel to leave Egypt. They were estimated to number about 21,000.[3] With their families, they left quietly within a few days. A small number, about a hundred, remained to work on the new SAM-3s. Sadat confiscated all Soviet military material on Egyptian soil for the state. Without the aid of Soviet technicians though, it was thought the Egyptians would not be capable of operating the complicated Soviet weaponry.

Sadat was now well advanced with his plans for war against Israel, and he knew that the Soviet military personnel in Egypt, with their own separate lines of communication in Moscow, could frustrate and even abort his plan. The Kremlin did not want a Middle East war, mainly because it thought the Israelis would again win, discrediting Soviet arms in Egyptian and other Arab hands. The Soviets thought they had been using Sadat as their puppet, but all along Sadat had been using them. Sadat outsmarted Brezhnev.

Although abashed and angry, the Soviets did not give up easily. Prime Minister Sidky was invited to Moscow to talk the matter over, which he did in October 1972, as Sadat wanted more Soviet arms and military equipment, but without Soviet personnel. The Soviets hesitated. In February 1973, Sadat's security adviser, Hafez Ismail, was sent to the USSR to ask for more arms; but he managed to extract only a Soviet promise to send military aid to Egypt if it was attacked by Israel. The Soviets first refused to send any more sophisticated arms, such as MiG-23s, SAMs, radars, or ZSUs, but then indicated they might relent and send limited quantities of arms and spares.

The Yom Kippur War began suddenly on 6 October 1973, when the armed forces of Egypt and Syria simultaneously attacked Israel. Much has been written about this war, but here it is sufficient to say that the last cease-fire between the combatants came into force on the 28th. On 21 December 1973, a Middle East Peace Conference assembled at Geneva, attended by representatives of the United States, the USSR, the United Nations, and the combatant nations, with the exception of Syria and Iraq. It was a brief one-day meeting that adjourned, never to be reconvened in the seventies, despite frequent Soviet calls for this to be done. The Soviets wanted to ensure they were not excluded from any Middle East peace settlement.

As soon as the Yom Kippur War cease-fire came into effect, the massive flow of Soviet arms, spares, and other military material ceased abruptly. The Soviets refused to replace the heavy Egyptian battle losses

[3] According to Mohammed Heikal in *The Road to Ramadan* (London: Collins, 1975).

of weaponry. When Gromyko visited Cairo in March 1974, Sadat asked for weapons to replace those he had lost in war. The Gromyko visit communique stated that the USSR would not send any new weaponry to Egypt unless it was coupled with a Middle East peace settlement. However, the Soviet Union agreed to send Egypt small amounts of military spares in return for the continued use of naval facilities at Alexandria. On 18 April 1974, exposing the Soviet blackmail, Sadat said, "Egypt can no longer count on the USSR as the sole supplier of arms, because the USSR has refused all requests for the last six months."

Sadat then turned away from the Soviet Union and looked towards the West for assistance. Diplomatic relations between Egypt and the United States, severed in 1956, were resumed. Nixon visited Cairo on 12 June, when a declaration of "United States–Egyptian Friendship and Cooperation" was made, as were agreements for the U.S. to provide Egypt with nuclear technology for peaceful purposes and economic and other aid. Later in the year, both Britain and France provided financial and other aid to Egypt; both promised to supply arms as well.

Sadat continued to complain that the Soviets would not send him arms, but this may have been for American consumption, as a number of Soviet MiG-23s arrived in Egypt in September 1974, together with a number of Soviet personnel. In fact, the number of Soviet technicians in Egypt steadily increased between 1974 and 1976. Egypt decided in September 1974 to buy eight Soviet-built TU-154 jet airliners; but on delivery these were found to have many defects. One crashed on a training flight, killing two Egyptians and six Russians, and the other seven were returned to the Soviet Union in March 1975, when the order was cancelled.

Realizing they were losing out to the West in Egypt, the Soviets tried again, in October 1974, to resume economic aid in return for an air base for maritime aircraft and more naval facilities. The Egyptians resented this offer, and personality clashes between national leaders further marred relations. For example, Brezhnev's invitation to visit Cairo in January 1975 was suddenly cancelled without explanation on 30 December 1974. Sadat continued his complaints that the USSR had consistently failed to meet Egyptian arms requirements since the war of 1973, and hinted that the Kremlin was pressuring him to stop looking for arms from the West. Certainly, the Soviets openly criticized Sadat for allowing Western investments in Egypt.

On 25 April 1975, the Soviets again called for the reconvening of the Geneva Middle East Peace Conference, and for a seat to be given to the Palestine Liberation Organization. The Soviets had just recognized the PLO as one of their official "Movements of Liberation," and so it became deserving of support. On the previous day, Gromyko stated that the USSR would guarantee the survival of the State of Israel if it withdrew from territories it had occupied since the 1976 war. The Israelis refused to withdraw and flatly declined to sit at the same negotiating table with a representative of the PLO, which they regarded as a terrorist organization.

During 1975, U.S. Secretary of State Kissinger practiced his "shuttle diplomacy," flitting from capital to capital to negotiate with heads of state and prime ministers. In his search for a Middle East peace settlement that would exclude the Soviet Union, he managed to persuade Israel to withdraw eastwards back across the Suez Canal. After being closed since 1967, the canal was again opened to shipping on 5 June 1975.

That month the Egyptians concluded a $900 million arms deal with the British, which probably forced the pragmatic USSR to send a few more arms to Egypt. These amounted to about forty MiG-23 aircraft, more missiles, and spares for the Soviet sophisticated weaponry. However, Sadat still insisted he had received no new arms and that the Soviets were only completing prior commitments. The Second Sinai Agreement was signed on 2 September, catering for further Israeli withdrawals, pledges to resolve the conflict peacefully, and promises of massive American aid and arms to both Egypt and Israel.

Soviet-Egyptian relations deteriorated further, and on 15 March 1975, Sadat abrogated the 1971 USSR-Egyptian Friendship Treaty, complaining that the Soviets wanted to impose heavy military and economic restrictions on his country. In a major speech on 26 March, Sadat said, "The Soviet Union wishes to exert military and economic pressure on us in order to force us to go on to our knees," adding, "In a year or eighteen months all the arms I have will turn into scrap iron because . . . the Russians are withholding spare parts and the means to overhaul aircraft engines. The Soviet Union has even refused India permission to supply spare parts for Egypt's MiG-21 jets."

Sadat also said that the Soviet Union was demanding the immediate payment of interest on the Egyptian debts incurred by purchasing Soviet armaments. Moreover, some of this payment was to be in hard currency, not trade. Sadat said that the Soviets "refused all compromise solutions." Naval facilities at Alexandria were withdrawn from the Soviets as of 1 April, and in a speech made in Paris, Sadat said, "I can confirm that Egypt has closed the refitting and maintenance facilities accorded to Soviet fleets in Egyptian ports." The Soviet reply was that during the past year they had supplied Egypt with seventy-five aircraft and all the spare parts contracted for; they claimed they had fulfilled all their undertakings, and also admitted there were Soviet military technicians working in Egypt. These were estimated to number almost 3,000.

The Egyptian debt to the USSR was now huge, and Egypt was not able to meet the interest repayments, or at least was reluctant to do so, as the Soviets would not stretch out the repayments or modify the interest rates. As the Soviet Union was Egypt's biggest trading partner, any suspension of debt and interest repayments would harm the Egyptians more than the Soviets. However, a Soviet trade delegation visited Egypt in April 1976 and signed a new trade agreement that gave the Egyptians a balance-of-trade surplus of $140 million, to be used to pay off Soviet debts. But this did not placate Sadat, who was looking for alternative markets, particularly in the West. Despite poor relations, Gen. Mohamed Gamasy, the Egyptian defense minister, flew to Moscow on 29 April to attend the funeral of Marshal Grechko.

The Egyptian government made allegations of Communist responsibility in instigating the Cairo "food and fuel" riots of January 1977, which caused Soviet-Egyptian relations to deteriorate further. On 19 February, an editorial in the Soviet periodical *Pravda* personally attacked Sadat following the publication of his memoirs. Sadat's reply, made in a speech on American television in April while on a visit to Washington, was that he had "waited for at least two years for the delivery of fifty refurbished MiG-21 jet fighters, but only now have been informed that the aircraft were arriving."

Egypt came into dispute with its next door neighbor, Libya. The Soviets took the Libyan side in the issue, and in April 1977 sent a diplomatic note to all the Arab embassies in Moscow, except that of Egypt, in which they alleged that Egypt was attempting to provoke an armed clash with Libya by reinforcing its armed forces near the Libyan border; and that Egypt wanted to seize Libyan oil for itself. However, on 8 June, Egyptian Foreign Minister Ismail Fahmi again traveled to Moscow, where Brezhnev told him of his desire to improve relations with Egypt. On 6 October, Sadat imposed a ten-year moratorium on the repayment of Egyptian debts to the Soviet Union; the Egyptians were finding other markets.

The Middle East peace stalemate was broken on 21 November 1977, when Sadat made his dramatic journey to Jerusalem. The following day he addressed the Israeli Knesset. This paved the way to the Camp David Accords and the eventual signing of the Egyptian-Israeli peace treaty. This bold initiative was disliked by the other Arab states, most of which ganged up and isolated Sadat, claiming he had betrayed the Palestinians by making peace with Israel.

The Soviet reaction was given by Gromyko, who alleged that Sadat had "aimed at exploding the Geneva Peace Conference before it is even convened again." The Egyptian ambassador was recalled from Moscow on 4 December; and on the 6th, in an interview with the *New York Times,* Sadat complained that the Soviet government "never played a constructive role in the Middle East and did not want a peace settlement to be reached." On the 7th, the Egyptian government closed down some, but not all, of the several Soviet and Soviet-bloc consular offices and cultural centers in Egypt.

On 30 December 1979, the day before the end of the seventies, Sadat announced he would provide military facilities in Egypt for American troops to enable them to defend the Arab Gulf countries from Soviet aggression or subversion. The Soviet imprint had faded from Egypt.

SUDAN

One other Arab state upon which the Soviet imprint lay in 1970 was Sudan, where in May 1969 Col. Gafaar Mohammed al-Numeiry had led a successful coup. Situated south of Egypt, with a Red Sea littoral, Sudan is a huge country, mainly scrub and sand, of some 986,000 square miles, with only a small population of just under 16 million (1970). In the southern province of Equatoria, its negroid minority of about four million was in rebellion against the central government until February 1972. Two main rivers, the White and Blue Niles, meet at Khartoum, the capital. Sudan largely relied on its inaccessibility, long distances between towns, and lack of good land communications as its natural defenses. Formerly a British-Egyptian condominium, Sudan had gained independence in 1956. The British left behind a small Sudanese army, with a few British weapons.

When he launched his coup, Numeiry had to make a tactical alliance with the Sudanese Communist Party, which had a membership of probably 100,000 and claimed to influence about one million people. Seeking economic aid, Numeiry visited Moscow and, in the usual Soviet manner, was given a trade agreement and promises of Soviet arms. Within a few weeks, Soviet aircraft, tanks, other arms, and vehicles began arriving in Sudan, accompanied by the inevitable Soviet military advisers and technicians. Soon about 1,800 Soviet military personnel were at work in Sudan. The Sudanese armed forces, raised on a voluntary recruitment system, increased from about 27,000 men to well over 50,000, and then still higher. At least forty Soviet aircraft arrived before 1970, and Soviet warships visited Port Sudan, on the Red Sea. On 1 January 1970, the

Kremlin was congratulating itself for successfully imposing the Soviet imprint on Sudan, a country that gave the USSR strategical advantages in its long-term aims. In Sudan's annual Independence Day Parade on 25 May 1971, Soviet SAM-2 missiles and other Soviet weaponry were displayed for the first time.

In addition to the influx of Soviet military advisers and technicians came a number of KGB personnel. Their object was to gain control of the large Communist Party, and then to manipulate it to turn Sudan into a Communist state. All political parties other than the Communist Party had been declared illegal and were suppressed by Numeiry, who became chairman of the Revolutionary Council and then president of the state. The Communist Party established at least four large front organizations and gained control of the trade unions.

Realizing what was happening, Numeiry quickly dropped his tactical alliance and on 12 February 1971 declared he would destroy the Sudanese Communist Party. But he hastened to add that this would not affect his close relations with the USSR, which was supplying him with economic, trade, and military aid. On 11 May, he ordered the dissolution of the Communist Party and its front organizations and imprisoned many communists. He had in fact unwittingly forestalled a Communist plot to seize power in Khartoum.

Well organized, patient, and supported by the KGB, the Communists tried again. On 19 July, a Sudanese army officer, Maj. Hashem al-Atta, successfully led a group of left-wing officers in a coup that unseated Numeiry. The Soviet ambassador in Khartoum hurried to congratulate Atta. However, when news of this coup reached Cairo, Sadat immediately dispatched the Sudanese military contingent on duty in the Suez Canal zone back to Khartoum. With this detachment and other loyal soldiers, Numeiry, who had escaped in the initial coup, made a successful countercoup and regained power on the 22nd.

Numeiry extracted deadly revenge, executing a score of Communist plotters and imprisoning hundreds more. When the Kremlin learned that Numeiry was back in power and that many Communist leaders had been detained, a frantic telephone call was put through to ask him to spare their lives. He is reputed to have replied, "They were hanged this morning." Numeiry executed fourteen leaders of the Communist Party, expelled a majority of the Soviet military personnel, including all the KGB men who could be identified, and declared a senior member of the Soviet embassy staff to be persona non grata. Numeiry stated that the plot against him had been carefully organized and operated by the KGB; while in Beirut, Lebanon, on 4 July, the Organization for Communist

Action, a KGB front, stated that Major Atta's regime would not have collapsed but for the aid given to Numeiry by the governments of Egypt and Libya.

On 1 August 1971, after Soviet protests at his purges of Communists, Numeiry recalled the Sudanese ambassador from Moscow. On the 5th, he triumphantly stated, "There is no place in Sudan for Communism, and we will not accept the Soviets as colonizers." The Soviet imprint seemed to lift from Sudan, but traces remained; diplomatic relations, although strained at times, were maintained for the remainder of the seventies. Also, for the time being a small number of Soviet military technicians stayed to work on the Soviet material possessed by the Sudanese. The Soviets took about 60 percent of the Sudanese cotton crop, the main export. On 24 August 1971, Numeiry made an economic cooperation agreement with the Chinese, followed by a military cooperation one in January 1972. A complete rift between Sudan and the USSR was only prevented by the mediation of both Egypt and Libya, then both in the Soviet camp.

Another incident of notorious interest in Sudan occurred on 1 March 1973, when eight Black September Organization terrorists[4] seized the Saudi Arabian embassy in Khartoum, taking everyone inside hostage, including a few visiting diplomats. On the 2nd, the terrorists killed three of them: George Moore, the retiring American ambassador; his successor, Cleo Noel; and Guy Eid, the Belgian charge d'affairs. Sudanese security forces launched an assault on the embassy building, in which all eight terrorists were captured and the remaining hostages freed.

Although evidence pointed to the fact that this was a Palestinian terrorist exploit (the object had been to obtain the release of PLO terrorists held in detention in several countries), Numeiry openly blamed the KGB, alleging the Soviets had given considerable assistance, hoping the incident would bring about his downfall and a Communist regime could be installed in Khartoum. Now solidly in power, and definitely anti-Communist, Numeiry imprisoned many Communists, expelled many non-Sudanese Arabs, and banned all Palestinian activities in his country. Nonetheless, Numeiry still retained links with the USSR.

During 1977, Sudanese-Soviet relations deteriorated. Numeiry, who was in sympathy with Moslem Somalia, accused the Soviets of sending arms to Ethiopia. In May, the remaining Soviet military personnel, about ninety technicians, were expelled from the Sudan. The Sudan-

---

4 See Edgar O'Ballance, *The Language of Violence* (Novato, CA: Presidio Press, 1979).

ese minister of information stated this step had been taken because the Soviet military equipment in use with the Sudanese armed forces had become obsolete, and the Soviets had not sent any spare parts to keep it operative.

On 6 June 1977, the Sudanese foreign minister denied that Sudanese armed forces were about to attack Ethiopia; on the 15th, five Sudanese diplomats were expelled from Moscow; and on the 19th, the Soviet cultural center in Khartoum was closed down; but the tenuous diplomatic links between the two countries still held. The Soviet ambassador was recalled from Sudan in July but returned in May the following year. By the end of the seventies the deep Soviet imprint on Sudan had faded, and only pale traces remained.

SYRIA

One of the more confused Arab states in the Middle East was Syria, which had an area of about 70,000 square miles and a population of about 6 million (1970). In 1970, the Soviet imprint rested heavily on Syria. After an internal struggle within the ruling Baathist party, Gen. Hafez Assad, the defense minister, came to power as prime minister on 13 November 1970. After a referendum, he then became president on 14 March 1971. Assad was the fourteenth president to take office since Syria became independent in 1943, in which period there had been twenty changes of government, some violent. Assad was also the first member of the minority (10 percent) Alawite section of the Shiite sect to become President; the others had all been members of the majority (70 percent) Sunni sect of Islam. Agricultural methods in Syria were backward; having no oil in quantity for sale, the economy was very poor in relation to that of some of the Arab oil states; but the country did have a strategically valuable stretch of Mediterranean coastline, with several ports and harbors.

The previous regime, that of President Nureddin Attassi, had isolated itself from its Arab neighbors, partly because of its opposition to the 1970 cease-fire in the Electronic War, and partly because of its brief military intervention in Jordan on the side of the Palestine Liberation Organization, during the Jordanian civil war, in September 1970. Also, its relations with the Soviet Union had become abrasive, owing to harsh treatment meted out to the Syrian Communists. Assad, whose policy was to cooperate with the left-wing parties, set out to improve relations with the Soviet Union; in February 1971, with a large delegation, he went to Moscow to meet Brezhnev. The Soviets welcomed him as a change from Attassi, and the joint Assad-Brezhnev communique spoke of the "major importance of contacts between the Soviets and the Baathist Party." In February 1972, a Soviet delegation visited Damascus and concluded the usual Soviet-type technical and economic agreements. China was also wooing Syria at about this time, promising credits and agreements.

In March 1972, Assad brought four left-wing parties, including the Syrian Communist Party, into a coalition with his ruling Baathist Party, known as the Progressive Front of National Union; and there generally were at least two Communist ministers in his government. Assad allowed his Baathist Party to operate only within the armed forces or among students.

Just previously, in May 1971, a crisis had blown up in the Syrian Communist Party. One faction wanted to free the Party from the Moscow rein and to be able to make decisions independently. This rift was healed to some extent by Soviet intervention, and all seemed to be going the Soviet way for a while, but eventually the break came in December 1973. Those members who wanted to cast off Moscow domination formed their own party at a congress held in January 1974. Thus, two conflicting Communist parties operated in Syria in the seventies. The Soviets condemned the breakaway Communists, who advocated war with Israel, the establishment of a Palestinian state, and the rejection of United Nations resolutions, recognizing Israel. The Kremlin, not wanting a Middle East war, which it thought might escalate into a superpower confrontation, declared their policy "not realistic and a recipe for a Third World War."

Over the years Syria had been deliberately drawn into the Soviet orbit, as the Soviet leaders saw it as a valuable, strategically-sited Middle East puppet state. The Soviets wanted to use Latakia and other Syrian ports and harbors, and also Syrian air bases, for their maritime cover of the Soviet Mediterranean Fleet. The Soviets had been supplying Syria with increasing quantities of arms since the mid-1950s; and when the Syrians were badly beaten by the Israelis in the Six Day War of 1967, losing most of their aircraft, tanks, and guns, the Soviets quickly re-supplied them with replacements.

By 1970, the Syrian armed forces, which were about 110,000 strong, possessed about 800 tanks of various sorts, 800 guns, and over 500 other armored vehicles, as well as eight SAM-2 batteries. The air force had about 210 combat aircraft, and the navy about twenty-two small coastal craft, including six KOMAR class missile boats with the Styx missile. Practically all this material was Soviet-made and supplied.

With the Syrian armed forces were at least 2,000 Soviet military personnel.

Assad wanted more weapons, and in May 1972, Marshal Grechko, the Soviet defense minister, together with the chiefs of staff of the Soviet air force and navy, and a team of experts, arrived in Damascus to see what was needed. A Soviet agreement to strengthen the Syrian armed forces was concluded. Soon more modern Soviet arms in quantity were arriving in Syria—MiG-21 aircraft, SAM-2s, SAM-3s, ZSU antiaircraft guns, radar detection and tracking devices, modern tanks, and guns. By the end of the year over 2,300 Soviet military personnel were with the Syrian armed forces. Each unit had an adviser, and Soviet personnel manned some of the SAMs, ZSUs, and radar devices.

In conjunction with the Egyptians, Syrian armed forces attacked Israel on 6 October 1973 and fought well initially on the Golan Plateau. Then the Israelis rallied and inflicted heavy losses on the Syrians, who fought back. For the first four days of the war, the Syrians would not allow the commander and senior staff of the Soviet Military Mission into their Headquarters Operations Center; but as the battle went against the Syrians, the Soviets insisted on the pain of withholding ammunition, spares, and replacement weapons. The USSR had instant and accurate information from its satellite imprints of the battlefield. When the Soviet Military Mission saw the Syrian war plan, which was a very bad one, it insisted that the Syrian forces engaged in battle immediately abandon their tanks and guns and withdraw to a strong defensive line to prevent annihilation by the Israelis.

On 27 February 1974, Gromyko went to Damascus to talk about replacing arms lost by the Syrians in battle, but his price was a friendship and cooperation treaty, to which Assad refused to commit himself. Gromyko was equally unsuccessful when he again visited Syria the following month. The Soviets realized that a militarily weak Syria was vulnerable to an Israeli attack, and so decided to send a limited number of weapon replacements. When Assad visited Moscow in April, the resulting communique mentioned the "importance of consolidating Syrian defensive power." By the end of 1974, the Soviet-constructed Tabka Dam on the River Euphrates, which had been inaugurated in July the previous year, came into full operation to provide much-needed hydroelectric power and irrigate more land. Similar projects were dangled before Syrian eyes to tempt Assad to accommodate Soviet requests. Gromyko again visited Damascus in February 1975, asking Syria to call for a resumption of the Geneva Middle East Peace Conference, which the Soviets were keen to reactivate to counter the dazzling Kissinger "shuttle diplomacy."

In May 1976, Prime Minister Kosygin went to Damascus to try to reconcile Syria and Iraq, which once again were in dispute with each other, this time over the Lebanon issue, and to join together in a "Rejection Front" in protest against the Second Egyptian-Israeli Disengagement Agreement (of September 1975). Kosygin arrived in Damascus on the 29th and was still there on 1 June when, just as it seemed the Lebanese Christians might be defeated by the Muslims, Assad sent a military expeditionary force into Lebanon to their aid. Kosygin, who remained in Syria until 4 June, had not been given any prior warning of this, which displeased the Kremlin leaders. Also, Assad had unwittingly jumped the Soviet gun and thwarted a KGB plan to install a left-wing PLO-dominated government in Beirut. The Syrian puppet was not responding as the Soviet puppet-master expected. Although the Assad-Kosygin communique spoke of the two countries working together "to end the bloodshed in Lebanon," a period of stilted cooperation followed, lasting many months, during which the Soviet military personnel with the Syrian armed forces were reduced to less than 1,800 in number. The supply of Soviet arms in quantity ceased, although a trickle continued to reach Syria, and Assad withdrew all Soviet facilities at Syrian ports.

Eventually, to break the ice and to the satisfaction of the Soviet leaders, Assad went to Moscow on 24 February 1978 to try to improve relations and to persuade the Soviets to rearm his forces with modern material, as his Soviet weaponry was becoming worn and out-of-date. Assad had not paid for the last Soviet rearmament program (of 1974–75) and probably owed the USSR some $2 billion, which he could not pay. Although they had bailed him out on previous occasions, this time the Arab oil states showed little inclination to pay his debts.

The Soviet plan was to form a southern tier of Arab satellite states in the Middle East, including Lebanon, Syria, and Iraq. The Soviets persuaded Assad to heal his breach with Iraq as a first step. The Camp David Accords had excluded Soviet partition. A huge rearmament program for the Syrian armed forces was put into effect, providing modern aircraft, tanks, missiles, and guns. It started well but soon began to run down because Assad would not come to the Soviet heel: the Soviets could not persuade him to sign a friendship and cooperation treaty.

The Soviets wanted Syria and Iraq to confederate, but Assad was reluctant to do this. In October 1978, Assad met Brezhnev in Moscow, but they failed to agree on the amount of Soviet military aid to be sent to Syria. Brezhnev was only prepared to "fulfill existing commitments" and said he wanted to wait to coordinate joint Syrian and Iraqi supplies, so they would not be duplicated. In November, Syria recalled its ambassador from Moscow; and in December, Assad suddenly canceled a visit to Moscow. A period of huff and hurt feelings followed.

However, Syria was of strategic value to the USSR and was not to be lost over trivia. In January 1979, the Syrian defense minister was sent to Moscow to meet Marshal Ustinov, the Soviet defense minister. Arrangements were made to increase military supplies, including the new Soviet T-72 tanks, which were then superior to anything possessed by the Israelis. This time Assad responded by signing the National Charter of Joint Action with Iraq, providing for "political and economic cooperation and complete military unity." On 30 January, Syria and Iraq concluded a mutual defense pact and agreed on a plan to create a unified state, under the Soviet imprint. Syria was then hoping that Iraq would pay its arms debts to the Soviet Union; but old enmities between Syria and Iraq surfaced, and this plan fell through. The Soviet ploy had failed and Syria was left alone, more deeply still in Soviet debt.

In March 1979, Gromyko visited Damascus to talk to Assad, but neither could persuade the other to see things their way. The communique after this meeting was really a Soviet call to all Arab states to look to the USSR in their opposition to the Egyptian peace treaty with Israel. It said, "The Soviet Union is prepared to go on acting as hitherto, and to cooperate with not only Arab states with which the Soviet Union has friendly relations, but also other Arab states which maintain a realistic and worthy position."

Meanwhile in Syria considerable unrest had developed. Interfactional fighting and assassinations broke out between the Sunni Muslim Brotherhood, a hard-line Islamic religious secret society, an offshoot of the Egyptian one, and the ruling Alawite minority. In February 1979, over two-hundred members of the Syrian Muslim Brotherhood were awaiting trial; and between June and October, over one hundred Alawites were assassinated. Sectarian strife flared up in certain cities, and troops had to be brought in to try to restore order. On 6 June, sixty-three army cadets, all believed to be Alawites, were killed in a Muslim Brotherhood attack on the artillery school in Aleppo.

The internal situation in Syria became so violent and chaotic that the KGB began plotting to get rid of Assad. The Soviets thought he was fast losing all authority and that the opposition would soon smother him. The Soviets did not want to back a loser. Assad had imprisoned a number of Communists and was placing a heavy hand on the two existing Syrian Communist parties, although both in theory were legal and each had a representative in his government.

The KGB was also active within the Syrian armed forces. It was both training and using certain selected officers with Soviet sympathies in counterterrorist warfare against the Syrian Muslim Brotherhood, which was strongly anti-Soviet. A number of Soviet officers became involved in this underground warfare and a few were killed; death by a "street vehicle accident" became a common method of assassination in Syria for a period. The KGB was also working to penetrate the Syrian officer corps at all levels to cultivate officers who could be persuaded to accept, and work for, Soviet ideals and aims, and who would remain loyal to Kremlin policy in the event of a coup against Assad or a general upheaval in the country.

However, Assad visited Moscow on 20 October 1979 and persuaded Brezhnev to continue to back him and send him more military aid. The Soviets asked for the resumption of naval facilities at Latakia and other Syrian ports, but this was refused. Also, Assad still refused to entertain the idea of a friendship and cooperation treaty: he was playing hard to get. At this moment, having again fallen out with Iraq, he was hoping that Colonel Gaddafi of Libya would pay his arms debts to the USSR for him.

The decade ended with the Soviet imprint resting more heavily on this country than at the beginning. Months later (October 1980) after Gaddafi had reneged on his promise to help Syria financially, Assad at last signed a Soviet friendship and cooperation treaty. The joint communique on this occasion said that the Soviet Union and Syria had adopted measures "with a view to reinforcing the defense potential of Syria." Syrian leaders in reply expressed "extreme satisfaction" on the Soviet promise to provide substantial amounts of arms, including MiG-25 aircraft.

IRAQ

The Soviet imprint had been evidenced in Iraq since it had begun to receive arms from the USSR after the 1958 revolution. Having an area of about 172,000 square miles, wedged between Arab Syria and Persian Iran, Iraq is a rich oil-producing country, exporting about 3.5 million barrels a day (1970) from the Shatt al-Arab, the demarcating waterway with Iran, out through the Persian Gulf. With a population of just over 11 million people (1970), it is a country of dissimilar regions, with about 2.3 million Kurds in the northern mountainous region, about six million Shiites in the eastern provinces adjacent to Iran, and about three million Sunnis, who provided the ruling regime. Iraq was on the edge of the Arab world, a traditional frontier country against the Persians.

President Ahmed Hassan al-Bakr, chairman of the Revolutionary Command Council, had been in power since a coup of 1968, although his vice president and foreign minister, Saddam Hussein (Taraki), was rapidly becoming the power in the land even in 1970. The ruling regime was Baathist, representing a socialist and secular philosophy; and the expression "Baathist Regional Command" meant the Iraqi brand of Baathism, as opposed to its severed Syrian part. The Kremlin wanted to fit Iraq into a Soviet-controlled southern tier of satellite states and to deepen its influence on the government. In August 1970, an Iraqi delegation led by Saddam Hussein was invited to Moscow for discussions. The Iraqi armed forces then numbered about 94,000 men and possessed about 600 tanks, other armored vehicles, and guns; some SAM-2 missiles and most of its 230 combat aircraft were Soviet, but not all. As Iraq had money from oil exports and could buy hardware anywhere, the Soviets had to move cautiously.

The Iraqi Baathist government had two main internal problems politically: the Kurdish revolt that had been in progress since 1961, and an active Communist Party. Fighting for autonomy, the Kurds had been supported spasmodically by the shah of Iran, who sent arms and supplies to them across his frontier. Although ostensibly trying to become more friendly with the Baghdad government, the Soviets viewed the Kurds and their cause sympathetically, but always insisted they gave them no military aid. Even if this was true, which is doubtful, the USSR certainly gave sanctuary to Kurdish insurgents; their leader, Mullah Mustafa Barzani, had spent years in exile in the USSR. In March 1970, the Baghdad government made an autonomy agreement with the Kurds, fighting ceased for the time being, and five Kurds were taken into the Iraqi cabinet.

The long-running, almost traditional dispute with Iran over navigation rights on the Shatt caused the Iraqi government, between October and December 1971, to expel about 35,000 Iranians living in Iraq. Further expulsions were prevented only by Soviet intervention.

In February 1972, Saddam Hussein led another Iraqi delegation to Moscow, for talks with the Brezhnev Trio, who expressed concern at the pressure put on the Iraqi Communist Party, which dutifully followed the Moscow line. Hussein was able to say he had already had successful discussions with Communist leaders to see if they would cooperate with the Baathist government, and many had been released from detention.

This was followed on 6 April 1972 with a visit by Kosygin to Baghdad, where a Soviet-Iraqi Friendship and Cooperation Treaty was concluded. While in Iraq, Kosygin attended the inauguration ceremony of the Northern Rumaila oil field, which had been appropriated by the government from the Western-owned Iraq Petroleum Company in 1961 and since developed with considerable Soviet assistance. Relations between the two countries seemed to improve.

On 14 May, two Communists were brought into the government,

and the Communist Party agreed to subscribe to the proposed National charter, which was to be the basis for a new constitution. On 17 July, the National Action Pact made between the Baathists and the Communist Party officially recognized the Communist Party as a legal organization for the first time since its formation in 1934. The two parties formed the Progressive National Front the following year. The Baathists needed Communist support against the restless Kurds.

When the Kurds stopped fighting in 1970, one condition was that a Kurdish vice president would be appointed; another was that there would be Kurdish representation on the Revolutionary Command Council. These and other promises were not fulfilled, though, and the Kurds were further provoked when the government nationalized the Kirkuk Oil Field, which they regarded as being on "Kurdish" territory. In March 1974, the Kurdish insurgency flared up again, and the shah recommenced supplying them with arms. On the 23rd of that month, Marshal Grechko visited Baghdad to cool the situation but cut short his stay when he was unable to do so.

On 19 September 1974, Hussein went to Moscow to ask the Soviets to mediate in the Kurdish insurrection, but they refused to become involved as they obviously had interests in both camps. Eventually an agreement was made between the shah of Iran and Hussein at an OPEC Summit meeting in Algiers on 6 March 1975. The shah promised to cease sending arms to dissident Kurds in Iraq; in return the Iraqis were to relinquish their long-time claim over the whole of the Shatt al-Arab waterway, regard its center as the national boundary; and make other concessions. On the 7th, the shah closed his frontier to the Iraqi Kurds, and their revolt soon fizzled out.

President al-Bakr had visited Moscow in September 1972 and met Brezhnev, being the first Iraqi head of state to do so, and had been successful in obtaining more Soviet arms. The visit communique stated that the two countries had agreed on measures "to enhance the combat readiness of Iraqi armed forces." The Iraqis briefly intervened in the Yom Kippur War of 1973, on the Golan Plateau, with some small armored formations. After that war, the USSR sent Iraq over one thousand tank transporters, the lack of which had been a big handicap to the Iraqis in moving their tanks quickly over long distances to the battlefield.

A period followed in which Soviet-Iraqi relations deteriorated, the Iraqis complaining the Soviets were not fulfilling certain conditions of the 1972 friendship treaty, especially in regard to trade and cooperation. Iraq developed trade links with the United States, West Germany, and

France, which prompted the USSR to make another trade agreement with Iraq. In 1976, the French agreed to install a nuclear center and plant near Baghdad, which considerably displeased the Kremlin.

The Iraqi government became critical of some of the USSR's policies overseas, especially its presence in Ethiopia. During the Ethiopia-Somalia confrontation in the Horn of Africa, the Iraqis gave arms, supplies, and support to Somalia. Iraqi leaders also thought the Soviets were too conciliatory towards Israel and began to talk of affording diplomatic recognition to the United States.

With the Kurdish problem static, if not completely solved, the Iraqi government felt it no longer needed the Communist support and so turned against the Communist Party. Many Communists were imprisoned, and a campaign of persecution against them began. This purge caused many Communists to move north into Kurdish territory where there were still spasms of active dissidence. Later (in January 1979), nine Arab Communist parties protested to the Baghdad government about its treatment of Communists. Sometime in the spring of 1978, the Baghdad government executed twenty-one Communists, some of whom had been under sentence of death for almost three years, for "attempting to subvert the armed forces." Precise dates of the executions were not made public, but confirmation was officially given on 7 June. In mid-March 1979, the Iraqi Communist Party left the coalition with the Baathists, and soon afterwards the two Communist members of the cabinet were dismissed.

Although relations with Iraq had become strained, Soviet responses were restrained. The Kremlin did not want to lose its imprint on the country. The Soviet protest was even mild when, in March 1978, without giving any valid reason, Iraq ordered the USSR to move its embassy from its site near Baghdad's presidential palace out to a suburb; electricity and water were cut off to enforce Soviet evacuation of the building. In April, the Iraqi government loudly protested against the Soviet-instigated coup in Afghanistan.

Despite Iraq's harsh treatment of Communists and its trade with Western and other nations, which involved arms deals, or perhaps because of all this, the Soviets made a serious attempt to improve the relationship. They almost turned the other cheek. In December 1978, Hussein was invited to Moscow and offered practically all the arms he wanted, in return for which the Soviets asked for a military presence at certain Iraqi ports and air bases and for an increased Soviet presence in Iraq. This was agreed on.

On 16 July 1979, in a quiet palace coup, President al-Bakr was pushed aside and Saddam Hussein took his place. This meant little change in policy; Hussein had been making all the major decisions for some time. The young, vigorous, and ambitious new president was determined to take on the mantle of the shah of Iran as "Policeman to the Gulf," the shah having left Iran for the last time in January 1979.

Marshal Ogorkov, the Soviet chief of staff, hastened to Baghdad in August to congratulate Hussein. The president asked for more arms, the cancellation of some debts, and extended loans and credits, all of which were conceded. In return the Soviets wanted an "open presence" at Iraqi ports and air bases, but Hussein refused. Hussein also asked for extra Soviet military personnel to train his armed forces more quickly in the use of new arms being received from the USSR. Instead, suddenly about 2,500 Russians were flown from Iraq to Afghanistan, leaving probably about 16,000 Soviet and Warsaw Pact allied personnel in the country.

Hussein now began to move the paramount political power from the armed forces that had traditionally held it, and which had indeed projected him into power, to his expanding National Baathist Guard, which he was turning into a part-time political militia. Indoctrinated to be loyal only to the Baathist Party, meaning himself, this militia was to become a safeguard and counterbalance against the armed forces. When Hussein asked for Soviet help to form this political militia, some 600 Cubans were flown in from Aden. Brezhnev could not spare any more Russians for such tasks. At the end of the seventies, the Soviet imprint still lay fairly heavily on Iraq, as Hussein could not manage without Soviet arms and personnel. Only his oil wealth gave him an illusion of independence and neutrality, as it enabled him to shop in Western and Third World arms bazaars.

LIBYA

Libya was another Arab country on which the USSR schemed to implant its imprint in the seventies, having most success in the latter part of the decade. An African state with about one thousand miles of Mediterranean seaboard, Libya became independent in 1951, being the first "emergent" colonial country to be created by the United Nations. It comprised the three desert provinces of Tripolitania, Cirenaica, and Fezzan. Having an area of about 810,000 square miles, of which about 93 percent is barren desert, it is one of the largest countries in Africa, with only a tiny population of less than two million people (1970 estimate), of whom the large majority live in the coastal region.

On 1 September 1969, a military junta led by Col. Muammar al-Gaddafi seized power from the aging King Idris and proclaimed a Socialist Republic. Gaddafi adopted a violently anti-Zionist policy, and on 7 November offered training and financial support to Palestinian terrorist groups. At the time of the coup, the U.S. had a large military base in Libya at Wheelus Airfield (since renamed Okba ben Nafi). The British had a base near Benghazi; they also had a friendship treaty with Libya. In October, Gaddafi demanded the withdrawal of the American and British bases, which were evacuated the following year.

The small Libyan armed forces of about 22,000 men had mainly British weapons, together with some American and French aircraft. More Western weaponry was on order at the time of the coup, but delivery was held up when Gaddafi's attitude became apparent. A Libyan mission to London failed to persuade the British government to go ahead with the order for 188 new Chieftain tanks, and the British-Libyan treaty was terminated in 1972.

The Soviets made tentative approaches to the new Libyan regime and even sent a few free tanks and guns (older models, of course). All were unsuccessful: Gaddafi came out strongly against communism and criticized the USSR for its policy of detente with the West, calling it a "betrayal of the antiimperialist cause." Gaddafi came down hard on the illegal Libyan Communist Party. Many of its members were detained, others fled the country, and communist books and literature were publicly burned. Libyan oil was in full flow by 1970, which gave Gaddafi considerable wealth and the options that went with it.

Gaddafi became immensely popular in his own country, carrying out certain much-needed material reforms, such as in housing and water supply, which together with his personality made him into a national hero. This fact was overlooked by Westerners and Arabs who made fun of his initial naivete and lack of experience in international affairs. A number of attempts were made to assassinate him in the seventies, which had the marks of the KGB on them; little is known in detail, though, owing to strict Libyan censorship. Some assassination attempts were foiled by the loyalty of his staff and followers. One attempted coup against him, in August 1975, resulted in an opposition government-in-exile establishing itself in Cairo, with Egyptian approval.

The first four years of the decade are notable for Gaddafi's quarrels with his fellow Arab heads of state, caused by his frank criticism and general lack of tact; also notable were his successive but unsuccessful efforts to merge Libya with one or another of the Arab states. He saw himself as taking on Nasser's mantle as leader of a united Arab nation and could not understand why Arabs generally did not welcome him in this role. He was at the stage when he thought money should be able to buy anything.

On 15 April 1973, Gaddafi proclaimed his Cultural Revolution, based on a strict Islamic way of life from which all foreign influences were to be purged. "People's committees," some 1,800 in all, were set up throughout the country to put the Cultural Revolution into effect. The following year, also in April, Gaddafi relinquished his post as chairman of the Revolutionary Command Council to devote himself to "ideological and mass organizational work." He thoughtfully retained control of oil production, finance, and his position as commander in chief of the armed forces. In September 1975, he issued the first part of his *Green Book,* containing some of his political theories. He called his "Third International Theory" the alternative to capitalist materialism and communist atheism. Later, in September 1978, Gaddafi stated he was relinquishing all administrative duties in order "to devote himself to revolutionary action"; but he continued to retain all the real power in his own hands.

Finding it difficult to obtain arms in the quantity he wanted for prestige purposes from Western sources without restricting conditions, Gaddafi at last responded to Soviet invitations in 1974. France had been supplying Libya with Mirage aircraft, but only on condition they would be used solely for the defense of the country. When Gaddafi lent some of them to Egypt in the war of October 1973, French cooperation in this respect momentarily slackened. On 14 May 1974, a delegation led by Abdul Salaam Jelloud, the Libyan prime minister, went to Moscow, where a number of the usual Soviet-type agreements were concluded for economic, agricultural, and scientific aid and trade. Taking advantage of the extremely poor relations between Libya and Egypt and influenced by their increasing difficulties with Sadat, the Soviets took the opportunity to send a few token modern arms to Libya.

The Soviets followed this up: in May 1975, Kosygin went to Libya—the first time a Soviet leader had ever visited that country—and more agreements for cooperation in various fields were signed. One important agreement increased the flow of Soviet arms, with attendant Soviet military personnel, to Libya. The Soviets asked for facilities at Libyan ports and airfields, but Gaddafi would not agree. When Omar Abdullah Meheisi, the Libyan planning minister (later the leader of the Libyan government-in-exile in Cairo) visited Moscow that same month, the Soviets agreed to "cooperate in the use of atomic energy for peaceful purposes" and to help train Libyan scientists to develop Libyan nuclear potential. The Soviets promised to establish in Libya an atomic center that was to include "a nuclear reactor with a capacity of two megawatts, increasable to ten." Although a start was made on this project, the Soviets soon had second thoughts, or perhaps never meant it seriously, so no further progress was made. Since coming to power Gaddafi had a fixation about acquiring a military nuclear capability; in his early period in power, in 1971, according to one authority, Mohammed Heikal, he tried to buy a "small atomic bomb" from China, only to find such items were not for sale, even in arms black markets.

When the Soviets began their usual blackmail tactic of demanding more concessions, with the threat of slowing down arms supplies if they were not forthcoming, Gaddafi once again turned to France, a country to which he was supplying large quantities of oil (in 1975 Libya supplied France with about 30 percent of its domestic requirement). France resumed delivery of Mirage aircraft and other military material. More-over, on 22 March 1976, the French government agreed to build a nuclear power plant in Libya. This upset the Soviets who had no option but to continue and even increase their arms supplies to Libya, as they did not want to lose what influence they thought they had gained; perhaps they also wanted to upstage the French. Relations between the USSR and Libya ostensibly improved. In December 1976, when Gaddafi paid his first visit to the Soviet Union, the Soviets tried to persuade him to sign their usual friendship and cooperation treaty, but Gaddafi fought shy of this.

The first public display of Soviet weaponry in Libya was on the National Anniversary Parade, on 1 September 1976, and included T-62 tanks, artillery, light armored vehicles, SAM-2s, SAM-3s, and some SCUD missiles. President Sadat of Egypt assessed the value of Soviet arms delivered to Libya by the end of the year as exceeding $1 billion. Libya then had over 700 Soviet tanks and 220 other armored vehicles; by the end of the following year, it had at least 1,200 tanks, sixty SAMs, twenty-five ZSUs, thirty MiG-23 aircraft, and twelve TU-22 bombers. Selected conscription was introduced in 1977, and the armed forces rose in strength to 37,000 by the end of 1978, and then to over 50,000 by the end of 1979. Conscription tended to make Gaddafi less popular with his own people, especially as women were included, which upset male Muslims. Gaddafi also nationalized all housing in the country, which made him unpopular with many who owned more than one house, in-cluding his own military officers, who by corrupt means were building houses—of which there was an acute shortage—and leasing them out for their own private profit.

In August 1978, Gaddafi established diplomatic relations with China. This prompted the Soviets to send even more arms to Libya, until 130 out of the estimated 280 combat aircraft were Soviet-made. The Libyan army soon had over 2,000 tanks, many of which were kept in crates or storage (along with military material received) for sheer lack of trained personnel to maintain, let alone operate, them. Soviet military personnel were concentrated at a few inland camps and bases; although Gaddafi had received some Soviet missile naval craft, he would not allow the USSR to use any of his ports or naval facilities.

In the early 1970s, Gaddafi became notorious as the so-called Terrorists' Paymaster General. He financed several terrorist groups, both internatonal and Palestinian, for devious reasons and certainly gave sanctuary, arms, and training facilities to many terrorists from many countries. When these terrorists would not carry out the specific exploits he demanded of them, he recruited mercenaries and formed his own terrorist organization, the National Arab Youth, who carried out a number of terrorist acts. In the latter three years of the decade, Gaddafi organized "hit squads" that roamed Europe, and perhaps farther afield, searching for and killing Libyans who had fled abroad and refused to return home on Gaddafi's orders.

The Soviet KGB was active in Libya and may have been responsible for the motivation and expertise—faulty though it proved to be—of the several assassination attempts on Gaddafi. The Soviets would have liked to install another Arab leader in his place, one who might be less erratic and unpredictable and more consistently amenable to Kremlin policy. The KGB was behind the anti-Western, and in particular anti-American, feeling in Libya that persisted throughout the seventies. This manifested itself on 2 December 1979, when anti-American riots were whipped up in Tripoli and the U.S. embassy burned down.

After a cold start in the seventies, the Soviets had succeeded in placing an imprint on Libya, and while it could not be said that the country had become a compliant Soviet satellite state, it had certainly become a client one. Gaddafi had plenty of money to diversify his arms sources, but the Soviets tried to persuade him not to look elsewhere by sending him weapons in saturation quantities. Gaddafi has accumulated a massive amount of armaments, far more than his expanding conscript army could absorb in years; so either he is a "magpie," cannot resist a good military bargain, or is being deliberately used by the Soviets to stockpile arms in great quantities for future use by their proxy troops in Africa. Perhaps the truth is a mixture of all three surmises.

Kremlin leaders regarded Libya as their modest success story, even though Soviet ships were not allowed into Libyan ports, nor were Soviet aircraft allowed to use Libyan airports or airfields. The decade closed with reports that Gaddafi was stepping in (after the French pulled out) to finance the "Islamic nuclear bomb" project being worked on in Pakistan.

SOUTH YEMEN

South Yemen was the only Arab country with a Marxist government, but it was one of the most strategically valuable. The former British protectorate of Aden had emerged in November 1967 as the Independent People's Socialist Republic of Yemen. The title was changed on 30 November 1970 to the People's Democratic Republic of Yemen, a status upgrading by Communist values. Situated on the southwestern corner of the Arabian Peninsula, with extensive naval and military facilities at the port of Aden (its capital) and elsewhere, which had been left behind by the British, it largely controlled the southern entrance to the Red Sea, being almost opposite the French colonial port of Djibouti. Allowed the use of naval facilities in Aden's harbor during the 1973 war, Egyptian warships were able to seal off that sea from the south. Having an area of about 112,000 square miles—180,000 square miles if the several off-shore islands are included, the ownership of some of which are in dispute—South Yemen has a valuable 700-mile coastline. Its population is tiny, being barely 1.6 million (1970 estimate), its people uneducated, and its economy barren and undeveloped. To its north is North Yemen, an uneasy and unfriendly neighbor; both countries want to take over and absorb each other, which causes occasional border fighting.

Early contact had been made by South Yemen with the Soviet Union and China, both of which gave some economic aid. The president of South Yemen visited Moscow in February 1969, where he signed a number of the usual Soviet agreements, including one for a supply of Soviet arms in return for a Soviet presence in the country and the use of military and naval facilities in Aden and elsewhere. Deliveries of Soviet arms began in 1970, and soon the South Yemen armed forces, numbering about 18,000 men, which had inherited a certain amount of leftover British military equipment, acquired 200 Soviet tanks, six small coastal craft, and about a dozen combat aircraft, including MiG-17s and MiG-21s.

South Yemen became a haven and training ground for a wide variety of terrorist groups of many nationalities and aims, the abandoned British-built barracks and camps being ideal for these purposes and the airport at Aden very convenient to transient terrorists. The KGB was extremely active in South Yemen, as were fairly large numbers of Soviet, East German, and other Warsaw Pact countries' military advisers and technicians. In the early terrorist boom years of the decade, terrorists freely operated from this safe sanctuary with the help and approval of the government. For example, the Marxist South Yemen government gave sanctuary and support to the Popular Front for the Liberation of the Occupied Arab Gulf, a guerrilla liberation movement that operated into the adjacent Dhofar province of neighboring Olman, whose Sultan Qaboos, who came to power in July 1970, was distinctly pro-Western. In March 1977, Fidel Castro visited Aden, and in his wake came small numbers of Cuban advisers and organizers to add their subversive expertise to that of other communist states.

In a military coup on 26 July 1978 by the pro-Moscow South Yemen National Liberation Front, President Salem Rubayyi Ali was executed, and his place taken by Ali Nasser Mohammed. On his way home from a visit to Ethiopia, on 16 September 1979, Kosygin stopped in Aden to meet the new president. Under Soviet sponsorship, South Yemen had joined COMECON as a member with observer status.

In October 1979, Mohammed visited Moscow in return. On the 25th, a USSR–South Yemen Friendship and Cooperation Treaty containing the usual Soviet conditions and obligations was signed, as were other agreements on economic and technical cooperation. The combined number of Soviet, Warsaw Pact, and Cuban personnel in South Yemen were to be raised from 9,000 to 15,000. More arms arrived from the Soviet Union, and by the end of the decade South Yemen had over 400 tanks, SAMs, ZSUs, about thirty Soviet aircraft, and a total of twenty small Soviet coastal craft, including four OSA class craft armed with the Styx missile.

Relations between South Yemen and North Yemen varied from poor to bad during the seventies. Active border fighting broke out on two occasions, in 1972 and in 1979. South Yemen's relations with Saudi Arabia were continually bad, their regimes being ideologically opposed. The attack by dissident armed forces on the Grand Mosque in Mecca, Saudi Arabia, on 20 November 1979, was launched from South Yemen, where further backup groups of armed men waited for the signal to cross the border into Saudi Arabia.

When the seventies ended, the government of South Yemen was firmly allied with that of the USSR, and reports indicated that the Soviets were enlarging the naval bases and constructing submarine pens at Aden and two or three other places along the South Yemen coastline, as well as at the island of Socotra. Throughout the seventies the Soviet imprint rested firmly on South Yemen.

NORTH YEMEN

The Arab Republic of Yemen is smaller than its southern neighbor, being about 75,000 square miles, but has a larger population of about 6.5 million people (1970 estimate). It is more usually known simply as "North Yemen" to differentiate it from the People's Democratic Republic of Yemen. Only slightly more developed than South Yemen, North Yemen was viable at a low agricultural subsistence level. A large part of the national income during the seventies was derived from the large expatriate labor force, estimated to be some two million workers, who sent remittances home. North Yemen has a short Red Sea coastline, but its strategic value is reduced because its only port of any note, Hodeida, is usually silted up, and lighters have to be used to offload ships.

The civil war that had been in progress in North Yemen since 1962[5] between the "Royalists," backed by Saudi Arabia, and the "republicans," backed by the Egyptians and the Soviets, was won by the republicans. A Royalist-Republican peace agreement was signed in May 1970. In February that year, a government had been formed by Muhsin al-Aini, previously the Yemeni ambassador to the USSR, who was in sympathy with the Moscow brand of communism and had developed favorable contacts with the Soviets. During the civil war Soviet arms and vehicles had been doled out in small quantities to the Republicans, and some arms had been left behind when the Egyptians finally pulled out in 1969.

The North Yemen government wanted union with South Yemen, expecting to dominate any such merger, and a number of seats were reserved for South Yemen members in the National Convention, but the South Yemen government was not receptive to the idea at all. In fact, a small frontier war erupted between the two Yemens early in 1972 and continued until October; under Arab League persuasion, the two states ended hostilities and eventually agreed to form a union. However, hostile feelings remained between them, and the union did not take place. In 1974, the Saudis pressured the North Yemen government into renewing

[5] See Edgar O'Ballance, *War in the Yemen* (Camden, CT: Shoe String Press, 1971).

the Taif Treaty (of 1934) by seizing the two Yemeni provinces Jizan and Najran, which they continued to occupy.

In 1975, the armed forces of North Yemen numbered about 32,000 and possessed about thirty Soviet T-54 tanks, one-hundred BTRs, and twenty aircraft, including Il-28s and MiG-17s. Promises of more modern Soviet arms had been slow to materialize, and the Soviets had been demanding concessions, including naval facilities at Hodeida. The Saudis persuaded the North Yemen government to sever its links with the Soviets. During 1975, North Yemen rejected belated offers of MiG-21s, refused to take delivery of a batch of Soviet tanks and other weapons that arrived by sea off Hodeida, and expelled all Soviet military advisers and technicians. By June 1976, the military break with the USSR was complete, but certain economic and development agreements continued. The Saudis had arranged to have North Yemen receive American arms in place of Soviet ones; the total price of $130 million would be paid by Saudi Arabia. This arrangement took some time, and the American arms did not reach North Yemen until 1978.

On 15 October 1978, a military coup against Ali Abdullah Saleh, who had become president in June,[6] was instigated by the National Democratic Front, a group of North Yemeni dissidents and tribesmen operating from the sanctuary of South Yemen. A number of executions and detentions followed this attempt, which worsened relations between the two Yemens. The story of North Yemen in the seventies was the uneasy one of political killings, attempted coups, and internal struggles for central power. On 10 October 1978, about one-hundred North Yemeni students in Moscow briefly took over their own embassy to protest the executions and detentions. The Kremlin wanted to change the North Yemen government and was manipulating Yemeni students to this end.

On 24 February 1979, war again broke out between the two Yemens. South Yemen troops and guerrillas of the North Yemen National Democratic Front invaded North Yemen. On the 28th, under Saudi persuasion, the United States reluctantly agreed to rush North Yemen sixty-four tanks and twelve F-5E aircraft. The following day, through the Saudis, the North Yemen government engaged seventy Taiwanese pilots and technicians to fly and service the expected Phantoms, in return for which the Saudis agreed to supply Taiwan with oil at favorable prices for five years.

Mediation by the Arab League military commission brought the

---

[6] His predecessor, Ibrahim al-Hamdi, had been assassinated in October 1977.

fighting to an end on 18 March. The Arabs had feared that the Americans would intervene militarily to save North Yemen. Reconciliation talks followed, and again the unification of the two Yemens was vaguely agreed on. Once this agreement had been made, the United States immediately cooled off. American arms supplies ceased, as the U.S. administration feared the weapons would fall into the hands of a Marxist South Yemen government if a union materialized.

As soon as American arms deliveries ceased, North Yemen turned again to the USSR, and the Soviets agreed to send at once at least ten MiG-23 aircraft, one-hundred T-55 tanks, other weapons; and about one-hundred Soviet personnel. The Soviets were back in business in North Yemen: these arms were their Trojan Horse to obtain entry into that country. Saudi Arabia retaliated by cutting off all economic and financial aid to North Yemen, which had been averaging about $300 million annually. During the seventies, the Soviet imprint at first rested lightly on North Yemen; then it began to fade, only to suddenly deepen in the last year of the decade.

JORDAN

The Kingdom of Jordan was so much regarded as being in the Western camp that it tended to be forgotten, overlooked, and neglected. It was certainly not under the Soviet imprint, although it was a Soviet target country. With an area of about 37,000 square miles and a population of about 2.6 million people (1974), the country is divided in two by the River Jordan; the eastern part (formerly Trans-Jordan) is mainly inhabited by tribal Arabs, and the western part (formerly part of British-mandated Palestine), consisting of the Biblical provinces of Judea and Samaria, was known as the West Bank. The West Bank, inhabited mainly by Arabs, had been invaded and occupied by the Israelis in the 1967 war. About 700,000 Palestinian refugees were in camps on the East Bank of Jordan in 1966. After the 1967 war, various Palestinian Fedayeen ("Men of Sacrifice") guerrilla groups under the umbrella of the Palestine Liberation Organization settled on these refugee camps, using them as sanctuaries, recruiting centers, and training bases. Friction between the PLO groups and the Jordanian government developed into civil war in 1970 and 1971, during which King Hussein's troops drove the Fedayeen from the country.

Not an economically viable state, Jordan survived on Western subsidies and economic aid. Its small armed forces of about 60,000 men (1970) were equipped with Western, mainly American, arms and equipment. After the 1973 Yom Kippur War, Hussein sought more arms, especially SAMs, in case of aerial attack from Israel. When Nixon visited in June 1974, he promised continued American economic and military aid. In November, negotiations began for Jordan to obtain eighteen batteries of U.S. HAWKs SAMs, but these dragged on fruitlessly. the U.S. Congress insisted the HAWKs be in fixed positions to keep them from being used against Israel.

King Hussein had been solidly anticommunist, anti-Soviet, and pro-Western in his views, contacts, and actions, but he was so frustrated at delays in obtaining the Hawk missiles, that he was provoked in July 1976 to visit Moscow, where he met Brezhnev. Brezhnev promised him arms in quantity, including modern SAM-3s, but the condition was that the USSR must be Jordan's sole arms supplier. This caused Hussein to hesitate before falling into the Soviet trap. Fortunately, the U.S. administration saw the red light in time, and the Hawk deal was concluded by September (under the condition that the missiles be "on fixed defensive lines only"). The lesson was that certain pro-Western Third World countries could be overneglected. His brief fit of pique and Soviet flirtation over, Hussein held off the Soviet imprint from his kingdom for the remainder of the decade.

LEBANON

Tiny Lebanon, with an area of only about 4,300 miles and a population of less than three million (1970), had been saved from a left-wing take-over in 1958 when U.S. Marines landed on its East Mediterranean beaches. Lebanon was a "confessional state," meaning that it contained several religions and sects and that high political offices and appointments were allocated on the basis of religious denominational strengths. It was then assumed that the Christians had a 6:5 ratio against the Muslims, so the president was always a Christian, the prime minister always a Muslim, and so on. Despite its Christian majority, Lebanon was considered an Arab state and was a member of the Arab League.

The long-standing internal stresses and rivalries in this multireligious country were aggravated by the influx in 1948–49 of Palestinian refugees. In 1970, they numbered about 160,000. Seven thousand or so PLO Fedayeen guerrillas driven out of Jordan in 1970–71 also settled in Lebanon, mostly in refugee camps; but owing to relatively small armed forces, the government was unable to assert its full authority over them. Supplied with Soviet arms, the ubiquitous AK-47s being in prominent evidence, the PLO groups became confident and arrogant, and like the cuckoo in the nest, sought to dominate and then take over the country, as they had failed to do in Jordan. Mounting friction between the Christians, who also had their armed militias, broke out into full-scale civil war in April 1975. Despite often misleading political labels for the various armed groups involved, the civil war polarized into a battle between the Christians and the Muslims as the Lebanese army disintegrated on factional lines and the central government lost all control. In June 1976, Syrian armed forces intervened to save the Christians from defeat and then remained in the guise of the Arab Deterrent Force, a so-called peace-keeping body sponsored by the Arab League.

Israel allied itself, secretly at first and then openly, with the Christians, which threw the various Muslim guerrilla groups into the arms of the KGB. The civil war nominally ceased in November, but spasmodic outbursts of violence continued. It was to the advantage of the Soviets to keep the area unstable. Ostensibly, there was no Soviet imprint on Lebanon, but the Soviets were working away behind the scenes; indeed, in June 1976 they had been on the point of helping a left-wing Muslim coalition government into power, only to be thwarted by Syrian invasion. The KGB shadow fell on the many guerrilla PLO groups, which sometimes fought each other as much as the Christians. A brief Israeli occupation of part of southern Lebanon in March 1978, prompted by a Palestinian terrorist raid into Israel, was replaced by the United Nations Interim Force in Lebanon, a peace-keeping force that vainly tried to prevent Palestinian guerrillas from infiltrating Israel to commit terrorist exploits. In Lebanon in the seventies, the Muslims generally looked hopefully towards the USSR, while the Christians looked to Israel and the West.

SAUDI ARABIA

There was no Soviet imprint on Saudi Arabia in the seventies, but that country must be briefly mentioned because of its economic and monetary importance, and because it was the world's largest exporter of oil to the West. A huge desert kingdom of about 927,000 square miles, it claims a population of about eight million. A census was taken in 1975, but its results were never made public, the suggested reason being that the Saudi population was much smaller than they dared admit in a country that employed a foreign labor force of over two million. Saudi Arabia was solidly anti-Soviet and anticommunist; it looked to the West to sell its oil, and indirectly to the United States, in its role as a superpower ranged against the USSR, for protection. A solitary Soviet trade consul was the only Saudi acknowledgment of the existence of the Soviet Union.

On the surface all seemed well internally in Saudi Arabia during the seventies, despite prognostications by some experts that discontent and revolution were simmering just below the smooth facade. Saudi Arabia was run on somewhat patriarchal lines by King Khalid and the large "family of some 3,000 Royal Princes," who were extremely sensitive to comments abroad on Saudi customs, which were mostly alien to those of the West.

Suddenly, on 20 November 1979, a group of just over three hundred armed men seized the Grand Mosque in Mecca and were besieged there by Saudi security forces for about a fortnight, before they were all captured or killed. French antiterrorist personnel were secretly flown in to bring the siege to a successful end. The Saudis officially announced that the motive of these attackers was religious, and that a mahdi—a sort of messiah or prophet who appears from time to time in history and is proclaimed a religious leader—had surfaced and been brought by his followers to be proclaimed at the Grand Mosque in Mecca.

The real reason was more significant: the motive was political. With the help of the KGB and armed with AK-47s and other Soviet weapons, this group intended to take King Khalid hostage (he was due to pray at the Grand Mosque) and declare the Hejaz province, which contained the holy cities of Mecca and Medina, to be independent of Saudi Arabia. Other groups of supporting insurgents of mixed nationalities were waiting in South Yemen near the Saudi border; after the initial success signal, they would move into Hejaz province and consolidate a successful secession. Egyptian intelligence got wind of the plot, though, and warned King Khalid to stay away from the Grand Mosque in time.

ARAB GULF STATES

In the seventies there was no Soviet imprint on the Arab Gulf States, that is those of Bahrain, Kuwait, Oman, Qatar, and the United Arab Emirates (Saudi Arabia is also technically an Arab Gulf State). The United Arab Emirates was hastily put together by the British in 1971, before they pulled out, and consisted of seven coastal emirates: Abu Dhabi, Ajman Dubai, Fujairah, Sharjah, Umm al-Qaiwain, and Ras al-Khaimah. They comprised an area of about 32,000 square miles and had a population of about 655,000 (1975). These emirates had formerly been known as the Trucial States because they had all made nineteenth-century truces with the British in return for protection against the formidable gulf pirates. They were all relatively backward, underdeveloped, individualistic, and suspicious of each other; some of them were oil-producers and some were not. The nearby sheikdom of Qatar and the offshore island of Bahrain, both oil producers, refused to join this UAE confederation and remained independent states. These states, including Bahrain and Qatar, were vulnerable, both externally and internally, to Soviet subversive activity; but during the decade, although they were priority targets, the Soviets had little success.

Kuwait, one of the world's biggest oil exporters, is also small, being only about 7,500 square miles and having an indigenous population of about 1.1 million (1971 estimate). Although underdeveloped, it became a paradise welfare state for its citizens through its oil wealth; the government was able to hire foreign labor to do practically all the work that had to be done. This huge foreign labor force was an acute security hazard and probably outnumbered the indigenous people. Kuwait looked to the West to sell its oil, for its development needs, and also for its arms. The Kuwaiti government had been given a Soviet "salesman's sample" of a few FROG-7s in the sixties, but could not be persuaded to buy any Soviet arms at all: the Kuwaitis feared and distrusted the USSR.

The other main gulf state was the Sultanate of Oman. In a vitally important strategic position, with a seaboard of about 1,000 miles, it guards the southern part of the Straits of Hormuz, the entrance to the Persian Gulf. With an area of about 120,000 square miles and a population of about 750,000 (1973), it is underdeveloped. Oil production began in Oman in 1965, but its output was comparatively small during the seventies. Oman was still under British influence; and with British help, Qaboos bin Said, a Sandhurst-trained cadet, ousted his father in July 1970 and assumed the Sultanate. The British gave both military and economic help, and Sultan Qaboos made efforts to develop his country.

An insurrection in the southeastern province of Dhofar, adjacent to South Yemen, had bubbled fitfully since 1965. Instigated by the KGB and helped by the South Yemen government, the insurgents called themselves the Popular Front for the Liberation of Oman and the Arab Gulf; this title changed in August 1974 to the Popular Front for the Liberation of Oman. Using South Yemen as a sanctuary, supply corridor, and training ground, the insurgents became more active in the early seventies, putting about 1,000 armed guerrillas into the Dhofar province to carry out insurgent warfare in its coastal and desert areas.

Help to fight this communist-aided insurrection was given by the British, the shah of Iran, and King Hussein of Jordan, and it was gradually contained. In May 1973, from the shelter of Aden, its spokesman boasted that the movement's intention was to "liberate all the Emirates of the Gulf." In March 1975, 300 British officers, 2,000 Iranian and 6,000 Baluchi troops, some British Special Service detachments, Jordanian military engineers, and Pakistani pilots were fighting about 1,500 guerrillas in Dhofar. In December that year, the sultan announced that he had driven the main body of the insurgents back across the South Yemen border; and in March 1976, he announced an amnesty to all Popular Front fighters who surrendered. The following month, Qaboos declared the insurrection had been crushed: he had successfully fought off the Soviet imprint. This should give heart and comfort to pessimists who believe that Communist-inspired and supported insurrections in underdeveloped countries of the Third World must inevitably be successful.

THE ARAB LEAGUE

One of the USSR's objectives was to break the power of the Arab League, an organization that loosely bound together the diverse and quarrelsome Arab states. In 1970 it had sixteen member-states with headquarters in Cairo. Its organizational framework was dominated by Egyptians. The Arab League did its best to mediate between Arab states in their wars and differences with each other. By reason largely of religion, the Arabs were generally anticommunist and anti-Soviet; the Arab League reflected this attitude, and so it became a target of Soviet subversion. The Soviets wanted the Arab states to remain divided rather than to unite, since individually they would become more vulnerable. In September 1971, Bahrain, Qatar, and Oman were admitted as members; in December, so were the United Arab Emirates; and as the membership scope widened, Mauritius was admitted in October 1973, Somalia in February 1974, and the Palestine Liberation Organization and Djibouti in September 1977.

The Camp David Accords and the Egyptian-Israeli Peace Treaty were unpopular with Arabs generally and rejected out of hand by many. At the Baghdad Summit meeting in November 1978, which Egypt did not attend, Egypt's membership in the Arab League was "frozen," and the headquarters and secretariat of the Arab League moved from Cairo to Tunis. Without Egyptian support, the league was less successful than formerly. Although it was not of their making, the Soviets considered this diminution of the effectiveness of the Arab League, which was generally hostile to them, to be a peace strategy success.

THE PLO

The Palestine Liberation Organization came into being in July 1964, being Egyptian-sponsored.[7] It developed into an umbrella organization for a number of Palestinian terrorist groups with varying political views, but all with the overall objective of destroying the State of Israel and returning the Palestinian refugees to their "rightful" home. The largest terrorist group was that of Fatah, led by Yasir Arafat, who eventually became the chairman of the PLO; another was the Popular Front for the Liberation of Palestine, led by George Habash, a Christian Arab; the others (there were about a dozen in all) were smaller, but some of them had a powerful terrorist potential. Secret KGB money, arms, and other assistance were selectively given to some of these terrorist groups, most of which used South Yemen as a sanctuary and training ground under KGB guidance.

Although he would not have any of its Fedayeen fighters or terrorists on Egyptian soil, President Nasser sought to use the PLO in his plans to dominate Arab countries. In August 1970, he had in fact brought about a cease-fire in Jordan between the PLO and King Hussein's army because he did not want the PLO to be eliminated from the Middle East equation. In January 1970, when visiting Moscow, Nasser had taken Arafat with him; on Nasser's recommendation, the Soviets gave Arafat $1 million. The PLO was then short of funds, and Arafat was having difficulty persuading the rich Arab oil states to produce the money they promised him. Gradually the Arab states paid up — partly for propaganda reasons, to prove their support for the Palestinian cause; and partly as protection money, as they and their oil installations were so vulnerable to terrorist activity. By the mid-seventies, using in addition terrorists methods of ransom and enforced contributions, the PLO had accumulated considerable funds.[8]

In November 1973, Arafat took a PLO delegation to the USSR, but it was not until August of the following year that he was allowed to

---

[7]See Edgar O'Ballance, *Arab Guerrilla Power* (Camden, CT: Shoe String Press, 1973).
[8]According to *Time* Magazine of 12 July 1977, "The PLO is probably the richest, best financed revolutionary terrorist organization in history [and has] at least $60 million invested in U.S. business concerns."

open a PLO office in Moscow by Brezhnev, who had at last consented to see him. Brezhnev now pledged support for a seat for the PLO at the stalled Geneva Middle East Peace Conference. At the Arab Summit at Rabat, Morocco, in October 1974, Arafat gained agreement from Arab heads of state that the PLO would be regarded as the sole representative of the Palestinians. Arafat had succeeded in outflanking his old enemy, King Hussein, who had also implied that he spoke for the Palestinians.

On 13 November 1974, Arafat was invited to address the United Nations General Assembly, when he made his famous "olive branch or gun" speech.[9] Recognition by the USSR of the PLO as an approved "movement of liberation" followed.

The PLO spent the remainder of the decade spreading its influence, working on building a reputation for "respectability and responsibility," and opening offices and establishing missions in capital cities; meanwhile, Arafat traveled extensively to lobby governments. He made progress, especially in Western Europe, but the much sought after American recognition of the PLO eluded him. Throughout, the Soviets supported Arafat, insisting that the PLO be a party to any Middle East settlement that involved Palestinians. The Soviets saw the PLO as a valuable weapon in its peace strategy, and they did their best to put their imprint on it.

THE MAGREB

The Arab countries of Algeria, Morocco, and Tunisia are usually known collectively as the Magreb. All three are members of the Arab League. Algeria and Morocco were traditionally hostile to each other, their tensions at times erupting into minor border skirmishes, and they seemed to take opposite views on controversial Arab issues. Algeria, for example, was a "rejectionist" state, calling for the destruction of Israel by force, while Morocco was a "moderate" one.

The Kingdom of Morocco, with a population of about 16 million (1970) and an area of about 180,000 square miles, is strategically sited, with territory controlling the southern part of the narrow Straits of Gibraltar, the entrance from the Atlantic into the Mediterranean Sea. Generally, King Hassan looked to the West for his main contacts and trade, although from a religious and cultural aspect he had to look to the Middle East. In the sixties, he had flirted briefly with the USSR

9"I have come bearing an olive branch and a freedom fighter's gun. Do not let the olive branch fall from my hand."

and had been sent the usual "salesman's samples" of weapons, including 120 T-54 tanks, ninety "Czech" BTRs, twenty-five self-propelled SU-100s, and twelve MiG-17 aircraft (which were still in crates in 1970).

Hassan had not fallen for this ploy, and his relations with the USSR remained aloof and distant, if correct. His armed forces were equipped with Western arms, mainly American and French. In October 1971, Kosygin visited Morocco, but only succeeded in obtaining two small agreements, one on fishing, and the other to construct a power station. Kosygin was shown the door by Hassan.

In 1975, when the Spanish evacuated their colonial territory in northwest Africa, part of their Rio de Oro colony—a coastal desert strip—was claimed by Morocco, which had made a deal with the Spanish government to divide that former colonial area with Mauritania. This Moroccan claim (and indeed the Mauritanian one, too) was resisted by a freedom fighter group known as POLISARIO,[10] which was supported and supplied by Algeria. A drawn-out desert guerrilla war continued in an indecisive fashion until the end of the decade.

While no Soviet imprint of any note rested on Morocco, it did on Algeria, one of the largest countries in Africa, having an area of about 885,000 square miles and a population of about 14 million people (1970). Its armed forces were entirely equipped with Soviet arms and material. Algeria exported oil and natural gas to Europe and the United States, but for its political ideology it looked towards Moscow. In October 1971, Kosygin visited Algeria; this was reciprocated in October 1973, when head of state Houari Boumedienne went to the USSR. On both occasions, and on others, too, the usual economic, scientific, technical, and other agreements were signed.

Smaller Tunisia, with only about 63,400 square miles of territory and a population of about 5.7 million (1970), is a Mediterranean country wedged between Algeria and Libya, both "rejection" states. Tunisia was a "moderate," being considered one of the more advanced Arab countries that tended to look towards Europe and the West for economic interests, especially to France, having only minimal contact with the USSR. It was the first Arab country to talk about modifying Ramadan, the period of one month a year when all Muslims must abstain from food during daylight hours, which had a severe retarding effect on the life of a country.

---

[10]Meaning "Popular Front for the Liberation of Saguira el-Hamra and Rio de Oro."

ISRAEL

As regards Israel in the context of this book, it is sufficient to say that relations between the USSR and Israel were bad, there was no Soviet imprint on that country at all, and the tiny Israeli Communist party was inconsequential.

6 The Soviet Imprint on Africa

We say to the Soviet Union and its allies . . . get your hands off Africa. The Continent needs tractors, not guns."
— President Numeiry of Sudan, 1 May 1977

DURING THE SIXTIES the Soviets, in competition with the Chinese, had schemed and intrigued for influence in Black Africa, that is, the sub-Saharan part of Africa and the Horn of Africa. They had successes and failures. Soviet intervention in Guinea and Senegal had been successful; but in the Congo (Zaire), it had not. In fact, despite considerable aid given to certain individuals and liberation movements, especially in former British colonies, the leaders in Zaire showed ingratitude and rejected the Moscow form of communism.

Nevertheless, the Soviets still regarded Africa as a fruitful ground for subversion and worked to convert potential national leaders to their Marxist-Leninist creed. The Kremlin considered, in its arrogance, that they would be unlikely ever to achieve national independence without Soviet backing. In the seventies the Soviets decided to be more selective in Africa, and to concentrate their efforts mainly, but not exclusively, on the Portuguese colonies, the Horn of Africa region, Rhodesia, and Namibia.

Big changes took place in Africa in the seventies. On 15 January 1970, the civil war in Nigeria against the breakaway Biafra was ended by an infusion of Soviet arms to the federal government. In March, the white minority Rhodesian government declared the country to be a republic, illegally breaking away from nominal British sovereignty. In their three main African colonies, Angola, Mozambique, and Portuguese Guinea, the Portuguese faced large-scale insurrections, largely fueled by the Soviets, which they were generally able to contain, retaining control of the main cities and towns, but losing wide areas of the countryside to the freedom fighters. The revolution in Portugal in April 1974 ultimately brought independence to the Portuguese African colonies. Soviet interference in Angola caused a civil war to erupt there, into which the USSR poured arms and Cuban proxy troops.

In September 1974, Emperor Haile Selassie, who had dictatorially ruled Ethiopia (Abyssinia) for forty-four years, was pushed from his throne, thus releasing tensions that brought war to the Horn of Africa region. The Soviets abandoned their satellite state of Somalia and sent arms and Cuban proxy troops into Ethiopia to fight the Somalis. The seventies were an era of Soviet proxy warfare. A CIA report stated that by the end of 1978 there were in Africa about 6,500 Soviet and Warsaw Pact, and 37,000 Cuban, troops. Another CIA report stated that between 1955 and 1978, 13,420 Africans had been given military training in the USSR.

The USSR spread its influence in Africa through various means. For example, in 1977, the Soviet Union was beaming out 1,699 hours of broadcasting to Black Africa. The following year over 20,000 overseas students in the USSR were from Black Africa; and over 7,000 Soviet and Warsaw Pact personnel were working on economic and construction projects on the African continent. A 1979 report of the Soviet Committee of External Economic Relations stated that during the decade thirty-eight trade and fifteen fishing agreements had been made with Black African countries; that air transport links were established with twenty Black African states; and that 25 percent of Aeroflot's overseas flying was over Black Africa.

I once asked a Nigerian why he had chosen to go to Moscow for his university education, rather than to an American or West European university. He said that the Soviets made it so easy for the Africans, providing them with everything they needed, including pocket money, transportation, and accommodation, without any obligations at all. To get to a Western university, the African student had to either pay his own fees and expenses, seek special sponsorship, or hope for a partial subsidy. Also, the minimal university entry standards were very much higher in the West than in the USSR.

PORTUGUESE TERRITORIES

Portuguese Guinea

Portuguese Guinea is a small enclave on the west coast of Africa, wedged between Senegal and Guinea, both former French colonies. It has an area of about 14,000 square miles and a population of just over half a million people, about one-third of whom are Muslim. In 1970, the Portuguese had about 26,000 troops in the colony engaged on

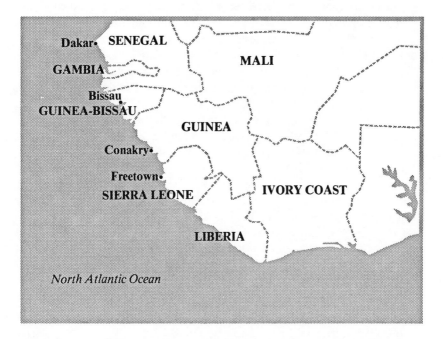

counter-insurgency operations. A guerrilla independence movement known as PAIGC (Partido Africano da Independencia da Guine e Cabo Verde), led by Amilcar Cabral, was fighting inside Portuguese Guinea. The PAIGC had both Soviet and Chinese arms, but Chinese supplies tapered off towards the end of the sixties, and from 1970 onwards only Soviet material was received.

Cabral claimed that about three-quarters of the country, including the Cape Verde Islands some 300 miles offshore, was under his control. Delegates from the PAIGC and other African liberation movements attended the Solidarity conference held in Rome in June 1970. The governments of both Senegal and Guinea were openly sympathetic and helpful to the PAIGC movement. They both allowed Soviet arms for the insurgents to cross their territories and allowed the PAIGC to establish training camps in them.

The PAIGC headquarters was at Conakry, the capital of Guinea, on the seashore. About 6,000 PAIGC freedom fighters were training in Senegal, about 1,500 in Guinea, and on an average of about 2,500 were operating inside Portuguese Guinea. The Portuguese authorities claimed that during 1970, for example, they captured forty-nine tons of rifles and small arms, and half a million grenades. President Sekou Toure of

Guinea was one of the African emergent national leaders who had remained loyal to the Soviets, and he had continued to collaborate with them. In 1970, the Soviets established a naval presence at Conakry; during 1973, a Soviet air force presence was added.

During 1972, more Soviet arms began to reach the PAIGC, including 122 mm rocket launchers, automatic weapons, land mines, and a few SAM-7s. That year the Portuguese claimed they killed 909 rebels. On 9 April 1973, a Portuguese aircraft was brought down by a SAM-7 missile, and in the following months four other aircraft were hit and at least three helicopters shot down by the same means.

In January 1973, Amilcar Cabral was assassinated by members of the Cape Verde faction of his PAIGC. He was replaced as leader by Aristides Pereira. The PAIGC was on the point of fragmenting, but was held together by mediation efforts by both Algerian and Cuban representatives. On 27 September, a PAIGC spokesman announced from "liberated territory" the formation of the independent Republic of Guinea-Bissau and a provisional government. Bissau was the country's main city and port. The new state was immediately recognized by the USSR, and then by some seventy other countries. A United Nations resolution of 2 November welcomed the new republic and on the 19th, it became a member of the Organization of African Unity (OAU).

Following the revolution in Portugal, President Antonio Spinola, a former governor of Portuguese Guinea, promised independence for all Portugal's African colonies. Guinea-Bissau officially became independent the following year, on 10 September 1974. Francisco Mendes became its first president. The Cape Verde Islands would not agree to become part of Guinea-Bissau; they became a separate republic in July 1975. The Republic of Cape Verde became a magnet to the Soviet navy; East German and Cuban personnel quickly arrived to expand the harbor and airport facilities. In 1976, Soviet technicians took over the control of the airport.

Mendes visited Moscow in February 1975, where he met Kosygin. Soviet aid was promised, and the usual type of Soviet agreements on military, economic, technical, scientific, and cultural aid and cooperation were signed. A Soviet trade mission was established in Guinea-Bissau. The Soviet imprint settled heavily on Guinea-Bissau and the Republic of Cape Verde, both extremely valuable strategic territories on the West African coast.

Mozambique

The Portuguese colony of Mozambique, on the African east coast, has an area of about 297,600 square miles. A census was taken in 1960,

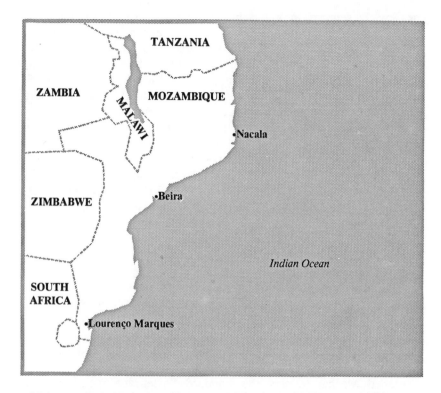

which put the population figure at 6.6 million, but it was estimated to have increased to about ten million by 1970. Mozambique is in an important strategical position, having about 1,500 miles of Indian Ocean coastline and good facilities at the ports of Beira, Lorenco Marques, and Nacala, controlling the busy channel between Mozambique and the island republic of Madagascar, about 240 miles away.

The main guerrilla insurgent organization was known as FRELIMO (Frente da Libertacao de Mocambique; the Front for the Liberation of Mozambique), which had been formed in 1962. Led by Samora Machel, whose headquarters was at Dar es-Salaam, in Tanzania, it was receiving military aid and weapons mainly from China, Eastern Europe, and Sweden. About 90 percent of FRELIMO's arms were of Chinese origin.

In 1970, there were about 7,000 active freedom fighters, some in Mozambique and the rest either in neighboring Zambia or Tanzania, both of which gave training and other facilities to FRELIMO and accepted its refugees and exiles. The Portuguese had about 70,000 troops in Mozambique, but Machal claimed he controlled about a quarter of the country. During 1972, when the Chinese military aid all but dried up, the Soviets stepped in and sent weapons to FRELIMO, including SAM-7s, antiaircraft guns, rocket launchers, and automatic weapons.

On 14 April 1972, FRELIMO guerrillas shot down their first two Portuguese aircraft over northern Mozambique, and in the following months two more aircraft were hit by SAM-7 missiles. On July 1973, the freedom fighters, using Soviet 122 mm rockets, attacked the Cabora Bassa Dam, a prestige target under construction in the north of the country. In March 1974, another 10,000 Portuguese troops arrived in Mozambique.

After the revolution in Portugal and Spinola's statement that the African colonies would be given their freedom, a truce was eventually arranged between the government forces and FRELIMO. In September, a brief "White Revolt" flared up, instigated by the Portuguese settlers. FRELIMO formed a provisional government with Samora Machal at the head. Mozambique became an independent republic on 25 June 1975. Machal became the first president, and Lorenco Marques, renamed Maputo, became the capital.

The Soviets stepped in quickly and helped the new republic form a small army: one tank, nine infantry, and three artillery units, equipped with Soviet T-34, T-54 and T-55 tanks, guns, mortars, and antitank missiles. A tiny air force was also formed and given eight prestige MiG-23 aircraft. With this Soviet material came Soviet military and technical personnel. On 29 March 1977, Podgorny visited Mozambique, where he persuaded Machal to sign the standard Soviet-type friendship and cooperation treaty and other agreements on the usual Soviet pattern. By 1978, there were over 300 Soviet advisers and technicians with the Mozambique armed forces. About 200,000 Portuguese settlers had left the country, depriving it of many essential skills, but the key men were quickly replaced by East Europeans. The USSR also provided a number of experts, including doctors, scientists, and agricultural experts, to work on development projects. The Soviet imprint lay heavily on Mozambique.

Angola

The large Portuguese colony of Angola, on the western side of southern Africa with a small population of only 5.7 million (1972 estimate), is potentially rich in mineral and agricultural wealth. Its South Atlantic seaboard is almost 1,000 miles long. Luanda, the capital, is a thriving and fairly well equipped port, and there are other smaller ports along the coastline. The railroad from Zambia and Zaire, along which 45 percent of Zambia's copper production is exported, terminates at the Angolan port of Benguela.

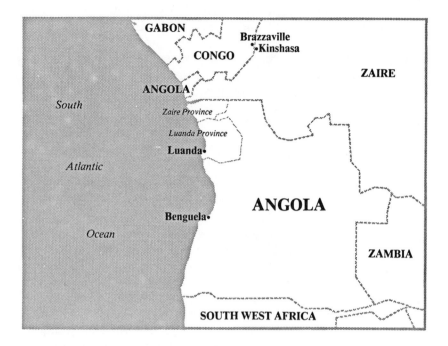

Insurgency against the Portuguese authorities had been in progress since 1961, and at one time there were as many as eleven different political guerrilla groups. By 1970, only three major ones remained active. Generally, the Portuguese troops managed to contain the insurgency fairly easily; their task was made easier by the bitter rivalry between the insurgent groups, the defections from one to another, and the splintering of them.

One of the main groups was the FNLA (Frente de Libertacao de Angola), founded in 1957, and led by Holden Roberto from his exile in neighboring Zaire. In 1962, the FNLA set up a revolutionary Angolan government-in-exile, also established in Zaire. The FNLA had not been invited to send representatives to the Rome Solidarity Conference in 1970. The Chinese, who had been supplying arms and other aid, stopped in 1974; the FNLA came to be largely dependent not only on Zaire, but also on the Democratic Republic of Congo. The FNLA was allowed to use Congo broadcasting facilities at Brazzaville, the capital.

Another insurgent group was called the MPLA (Movimento Popular para a Libertacao de Angola). A Marxist movement led by Agostinho Neto, it had been supported by the Soviets since its formation in 1961. The MPLA had its origins in the Angolan Communist Party, itself an offshoot of the Portuguese Communist Party, and it gained support from both intellectuals and workers in Luanda. Unlike the others, the MPLA did not confine itself to one ethnic group or region. In 1972, it boasted 10,000 members, but its leaders were scattered in exile or adjacent African countries. Zambia gave some cautious help, but was careful not to go too far, in case the Portuguese closed the Benguela railroad.

The third active insurgent group, a splinter faction from the FNLA, was UNITA (Uniao Nacional para a Independencia Total de Angola), formed in 1966. It was led by Jonas Savimbi, the only guerrilla leader actually remaining inside Angola, and drew its support from the southern part of the country. The MPLA again split in early 1973 when its "eastern command" severed itself from the main body; moreover, right up until the Portuguese revolution of April 1974, Neto was plagued with quarreling factions within his movement and had difficulty holding it together. At one point Soviet aid was withheld to try to enforce unity on this Soviet-supported MPLA. A feature of the insurgency in 1973 was the appearance of more effective Soviet weapons, such as the 122 mm rocket launcher and RPG-7s. One source, the Institute for the Study of Conflict (London), stated that between 1960 and 1974, the MPLA received over $55 million worth of Soviet arms.

Liberation from Portuguese rule caught the Angolan insurgent groups unprepared, as all three were extremely hostile towards each other, so the Portuguese authorities had to continue to govern until power could be transferred to one authority. Several months were spent persuading the three movements to work together. Eventually they came together at Mombassa, Kenya, and agreed to form a three-party coalition government to govern the country until elections could be held. Independence Day was set for 10 November 1975. The coalition government was formed in January 1975 but soon broke down, and a serious struggle for national power exploded into civil war. Within months some 400,000 Portuguese settlers left Angola.

The flow of Soviet arms to the MPLA increased as that group tried first to make itself master of Luanda. Soon Soviet and East European ships and aircraft were bringing in guns, automatic weapons, grenades, and SAM-7s in quantity. The airports at Brazzaville and Point-Noire, an Atlantic port in Congo, were staging posts for the Soviet arms lift. A CIA report estimated that between March and December 1975, the Soviets provided the MPLA with over $200 million in military aid.

Fighting began in Luanda between the MPLA and the FNLA in April 1975. Neto had been able to pull his group together again and fielded some 4,000 guerrilla fighters. Soon Soviet tanks and guns began to arrive, and by July the MPLA had driven the FNLA out of the capital completely. Based in the south, UNITA tried to negotiate a settlement with the MPLA, but failed; in August 1975, it declared war on the MPLA. In October, the Cuban troops began to arrive in Angola, first by air, and then by sea, as did more Soviet weaponry. In November, Soviet military advisers arrived in Luanda; and by the end of that month, all the Chinese who had been advising the FNLA had departed, leaving the field clear for the Soviets. The Cuban buildup was rapid, from 2,500 troops in the country in November to 11,400 by the end of December. The MPLA army had also risen in strength to 13,500. On 29 January 1976, the U.S. Defense Department stated there were 2,848 Soviet military advisers in the whole of Africa, of whom 300 were in Angola.

When the Cuban proxy troops arrived, the MPLA held only Luanda, a stretch of coastline on either side, and a narrow wedge-shaped section of territory extending eastwards into the center of the country, which was compressed from the north by the FNLA and from the south by UNITA. There was also some intervention by Zaire troops in the north, and by South African ones in the south, but it was fairly ineffective. The Cubans began expanding the wedge-shaped area, turning first on the FNLA forces to press them backwards, and then turning on the UNITA. By February 1976, the MPLA, spearheaded by Cuban troops, had successfully occupied a broad central sector of the country; and in March, UNITA announced that it had to revert to guerrilla warfare.

Some U.S. military assistance was given to the UNITA—FNLA guerrilla forces. In the spring of 1975, President Ford had authorized $300,000 for UNITA, given through Zaire; but later, when the Cuban proxy troops swung the war in favor of the MPLA, Congress voted on 19th December to cease all military assistance to the UNITA-FNLA coalition forces, thus handing victory on a plate to the MPLA. Had American arms and other military assistance been promptly sent, Angola probably would have become Cuba's Vietnam. For example, UNITA leaders claimed to have 2,000 trained guerrilla fighters and enough arms to endure a two-year guerrilla struggle, but the FNLA was desperately short of weapons and supplies. Had the Americans assisted the FNLA, its war against the MPLA would not necessarily have resulted in a Communist victory.

The Angolan civil war subsided. The UNITA and FLNA guerrilla groups withdrew into the bush to lick their wounds, but remained in being as guerrilla armies. The MPLA tentatively claimed its control over two-thirds of the country.

Meanwhile, the last Portuguese troops had departed by Independence Day, 10 November 1975, and Neto, the MPLA leader, immediately proclaimed from Luanda the establishment of a People's Republic of Angola, which was instantly recognized by the USSR. The following day, the FNLA and UNITA entered into a coalition with each other against the MPLA and announced from Huambo (Nova Lisboa), a port on the coast, the establishment of a rival Angolan government, which had two prime ministers, one from each group.

The Soviets helped the MPLA government form a small conventional army—initially one armored, nine infantry, one commando, and one air defense regiment, all equipped with Soviet weapons, including eighty-five tanks. A small air force was formed and given thirty-three Soviet aircraft, mainly MiG-17s and MiG-21s. Cuban troops in Angola during this period probably numbered about 20,000, but within a few months they were reduced to 12,000 or less, as most of them were needed by their Soviet masters elsewhere in Africa.

In October 1976, a Soviet friendship and cooperation treaty was signed by Neto, allowing the Soviets the usual facilities at Angolan ports and airfields. In December 1977, the MPLA held its First Congress in Luanda, where it formally declared itself to be a "Vanguard Leninist Party" that would be guided by the Kremlin principles of scientific socialism. In April 1978, Neto visited Moscow: he had been firmly hooked by the Soviets. On 8 December 1979, a thirty-five man Soviet military mission arrived in Angola.

THE HORN OF AFRICA

The region traditionally known as the Horn of Africa (its coastal outline is thought to be like a rhinoceros's horn jutting out into the Indian Ocean), consisting of Somalia, Ethiopia, and the French colony of Djibouti, has an area of some 750,000 square miles and a population of about 32 million people (1970). Its strategic position is one of extreme importance, its Indian Ocean and Red Sea coastline extending for almost 2,000 miles. It is an area of ethnic rivalry and tension, and during the seventies, the Soviets interfered massively in its internal affairs.

Somalia, the fusion of former British and Italian colonial territories, was in dispute with Ethiopia over the possession of the desert province of Ogaden. Ethiopia, that ancient landlocked Christian kingdom, had survived for centuries against surrounding hostile Muslim states and armies. It was ruled dictatorially by the aging Emperor Haile Selassie, who some time after World War II annexed the former Italian colonial territory of Eritrea bordering the Red Sea. The Ethiopian government

HORN OF AFRICA

was involved in a long-running insurgency problem against Eritrean freedom fighters struggling for independence. Between Somalia and Eritrea on the Red Sea coast was Djibouti, which provided the only rail link from that port to Addis Ababa, the Ethiopian capital, far inland.

Somalia

After a brief period as a U.N. trust territory, Somalia gained independence in 1960. In October 1969, its president was assassinated, and an army faction led by Gen. Mohammed Sayed Barreh seized control of the country. This coup was instigated and helped by the Soviets, who had taken a deep interest in Somalia and its strategic port of Berbera. The Soviet Union had initially given $5 million in military and other aid to this economically barren state. The Soviet-backed coup put Somalia on the Kremlin's road to "scientific socialism." A Revolutionary Council was formed, which produced both a Central Committee and a ruling Politburo. Barreh became president and kept a tight grip on his country. In the sixties, Somalia had accepted aid from the USSR, China, and the West. In June 1970, Barreh stated that American aid, which had amounted to $3.4 million in 1969, had been suspended because Somalia was developing trade relations with North Vietnam.

Having an area of about 246,000 square miles and a population of just under three million, of whom the majority were nomadic herdsmen, Somalia had a bare-subsistence pastoral economy. Apart from the port of Berbera and the capital, Mogadishu, there were few towns of any size or importance. Despite his country's poverty, Barreh had dreams of a "Greater Somalia" consisting of the Somali-speaking ethnic block that included portions of Ethiopia, Kenya, and Djibouti.

The Somali armed forces were small in 1970, being about 14,000 strong. The army—four armored and nine mechanized units—had some British light armored vehicles and other weapons but had already received Soviet material, including 150 T-34 tanks, 200 BTRs, and 100 guns. The small Somali air force possessed about twenty MiG-15s and MiG-17s; and its tiny navy had a few small Soviet coastal craft.

Relations with adjacent Ethiopia were bad, and during the sixties there had been a number of skirmishes between opposing frontier forces over alleged cattle-raiding activities. There were about two million Muslim Somali-speaking tribesmen in the Ogaden province (part of Ethiopia), and the Western Somali Liberation Front (WSLF) had emerged as a guerrilla liberation movement which had been openly and consistently backed by the Mogadishu government. Barreh, when he appeared on the scene, continued to support the WSLF. Later, although not an "Arab" nation, Muslim Somalia became a member of the Arab League in 1974.

In November 1971, Barreh visited Moscow and signed a number of the usual Soviet-type agreements, which virtually gave the Soviets a free hand in Berbera and other places in Somalia. Marshal Grechko, the Soviet defense minister, visited Somalia in February 1972, after which Soviet military constructional activity increased; and a start was made at building a small naval base with submarine pens at Birihao, which was only forty miles from the Kenya border. After Soviet military personnel were ejected from Egypt in July 1972, the Soviets began to take a deeper interest in Somalia.

In June 1974, Barreh denied that the Soviets had any bases in his country; but the following month, after a visit by Podgorny to Somalia, a Soviet-Somali Friendship and Cooperation Treaty was concluded, under which the Soviets were granted considerable military concessions. The United States was then supporting and aiding Ethiopia. The Soviets sent Somalia a few MiG-21 aircraft and 150 Soviet technicians. More Soviet arms followed. Within two years, the Somali armed forces increased in strength to over 20,000 men. They possessed about 250 Soviet tanks, including T-54s and T-55s; 350 BTRs; and twenty-five aircraft, including a few MiG-23s. In January 1976, the Soviets began delivering the first of fourteen OSA missile naval craft armed with the Styx missile.

The Soviets were constructing a large base at Berbera, including an airfield with a 15,000-foot surfaced runway able to accommodate the large, long-range Soviet naval reconnaissance aircraft; extensive naval facilities; a tactical nuclear missile handling and storage area; and barrack accommodation. Another airfield was being constructed near Mogadishu. U.S. intelligence agencies were apparently unaware of this massive Soviet construction program until 6 June 1975, when a U.S. satellite imprint of Berbera revealed it. Both the Soviet and Somali governments again denied the facilities were of a military nature. The Somalis invited a U.S. congressional delegation to inspect the new installation at Berbera; they found that beyond all doubt it had a military purpose, and that the port was becoming the main logistical base for the Soviet Indian Ocean fleet. Without finding a convincing answer, one may wonder why the Somalis invited the Americans.

During the first part of 1977, the Soviets toyed with both Somalia and Ethiopia and became increasingly impatient at Somalia contacts with Saudi Arabia. The Soviet plan was to gain paramount influence in both countries and they hoped both could be persuaded to cooperate with each other harmoniously under Soviet guidance, to eliminate all Western influence from the Horn of Africa.

In April 1977, Podgorny visited Somalia to preach patience to the Somalis over the Ogaden problem, but he was unsuccessful. The following month, Barreh launched an attack against Ethiopian forces, in support of WSLF activities, to try to regain control of the Ogaden province. At first the Somali armed forces were successful. Expecting Soviet support and more aid under the terms of the friendship and cooperation treaty, Barreh announced he would allow extended naval facilities for Soviet warships. However, the Soviets did not want a war to break out between Somalia and Ethiopia. In July, the Soviets began phasing out their military advisers and technicians from Somalia; and then they withdrew their ships eastwards from Berbera across the mouth of the Red Sea to the port of Aden, in South Yemen.

On 9 August 1977, the Ethiopians admitted that a successful Somali offensive had been launched across their last defenses in Ogaden, and that the Somalis had gained possession of the whole province after six weeks' fighting. The Soviets then suddenly employed their blackmail tactic and refused to send any more ammunition, fuel, spares, or weaponry to Somalia. This eventually caused Barreh, on 13 November, to renounce the friendship and cooperation treaty; to eject the almost six-thousand Soviet personnel remaining, and also the forty-four Cubans; and to withdraw permission for the Soviets to use his naval and other facilities. The Berbera naval base was soon deserted and empty.

By the end of the year, the Somali armed forces were stalled by lack of fuel, ammunition, and supplies. Just previously, on 2 September, the Soviets had made an agreement to supply massive amounts of arms to Ethiopia. They blatantly deserted their ally, Somalia, and changed sides in the middle of a local war, regarding Ethiopia as the better prize.

Now fully involved in war with Ethiopia, Barreh sought other allies and sources of arms, but with little success. On 30 August 1977, France had agreed to send arms to the value of $5 million to Somalia. That month, the Americans said they would be prepared to supply defensive weapons; but on 1 September, they withdrew the offer when they realized the scale of the Ogaden fighting. In return for collaboration in the hijacking incident at Mogadishu, on 17 October 1977, which was successfully resolved mainly by West Germany counterterrorist personnel, the West German government provided $18 million, which was mostly spent by the Somalis on Soviet arms and spares from Egypt. Barreh again applied to the United States for aid to replace that of the USSR, but on 23 November, he said this had been refused.

During 1977, two opposing strategic moves were made involving the Horn of Africa, one by Fidel Castro of Cuba, and the other by President Numeiry of Sudan. In May, Castro proposed forming a "progressive front," in which he wanted to involve North and South Yemen, Ethiopia, and Somalia; but Somalia demanded that the Ogaden problem first be solved. Numeiry's proposal, the same month, was for a "zone of security," in which he wanted Sudan, Somalia, Saudi Arabia, and the two Yemens to cooperate to restrict involvement in the region by the Soviet Union, and the United States and Israel. Numeiry said, "We say to the Soviet Union and its allies . . . get your hands off Africa. The Continent needs tractors, not guns." Neither leader was able to get his proposal carried.

On 9 March 1978, the undeclared war in the Ogaden province came to an end when Barreh stated that all Somali troops had been withdrawn from that province. He had not been able to obtain Western arms to replace Soviet ones, and so had to give up the fight. A few French anti-tank weapons had reached him on the battlefield, but that was all. The Western Somali Liberation Front guerrilla army vowed to fight on. Somali material losses had been heavy; it was calculated they had lost 225 out of the 350 Soviet tanks, and more than half the 56 Soviet combat aircraft. The Somali armed forces had been increased to over 50,000, and the People's Militia to 20,000.

On 9 April 1978, a group of air force officers and others mounted an unsuccessful coup against Barreh, because they felt he had broken with the USSR too prematurely, and had accordingly lost the war. Throughout the year, despite strenuous efforts, Somalia was unable to obtain Western military aid. In October, the situation was so critical that Barreh had to make cringing overtures to the Soviet Union, begging for help. He released many pro-Soviet detainees from his prisons as a peace-offering. During 1979, the Soviets began quietly trickling back into Somalia to reactivate the Berbera base. The Soviet imprint that had disappeared from Somalia was reappearing. The Carter administration had missed a great opportunity in the Horn of Africa.

Ethiopia

Ruled autocratically for nearly half a century by Emperor Haile Selassie, Ethiopia in 1970 was considered by the United States to be a "base rights" country, which was given considerable American military assistance in return for the use of a large communication base at Kagnew, near Asmara, in Eritrea. This was a huge "listening station" run by the U.S. army, part of the worldwide network, code-named USM-4, covering Egypt, the Arabian peninsula, the Persian Gulf area, and parts of North Africa. Over $100 million annually was channeled into the Selassie regime in military and other special aid.

Addis Ababa, the capital, was also the headquarters of the Organization of African Unity, which had been largely formed by Selassie, who hoped to influence African affairs through it. The Ethiopian armed forces, recruited on a voluntary basis, amounted to about 43,000 men. Selassie operated a "divide and rule" policy within the armed forces so they could not gang up against him. He also operated a patronage system, and arbitrary dismissal was common. The military equipment was mainly American, with a few British and French weapons. There were also a couple of Soviet helicopters, Soviet "salesmen's samples." The air force had about fifty U.S. combat aircraft and some French helicopters. The U.S. Military Assistance and Advisory Group (MAAG) consisted of over a hundred officers, mainly employed in training roles.

The Israelis were also active in Ethiopia in 1970, training the police and being involved in constructional and other projects as part of their policy of building up a belt of friendly Black African states south of the hostile Muslim ones. After the Yom Kippur War of 1973, the Israelis lost out in this strategy and pulled out from Ethiopia. Selassie had begun to try to play America, the Soviet Union, and China off against each other. In 1971, he visited China and signed trade and other agreements, but he also obtained Soviet arms as well as those he was receiving from the United States. It was estimated that from the end of World War II until 1974, Ethiopia obtained over $400 million in U.S. military aid and millions of dollars more in economic assistance. Over 25,000 Ethiopian military personnel were trained in the United States, and at one stage the MAAG rose to over 300 American officers.

Early in 1974, increasing unrest in the Ethiopian armed forces and general internal dissent, beginning with the demand by troops for more pay, led to strikes, mutinies, the arresting of officials by the armed forces, and the formation of a Supreme Military Council to bargain with the civilian government. Related concessions by Selassie and the release of political prisoners led to the assumption of power by a provisional military government headed by Gen. Aman Andom, the chief of staff, which deposed the emperor on 12 September 1974. Selassie was kept in detention until he died on 27 August 1975 at the age of eighty-three.

The governing Provisional Military Administrative Council, which later came to be known as the Dergue, meaning "committee," held radical views. The Soviets stepped in and offered to take over the role held by the United States, and to supply military and other assistance, but only on condition that the MAAG and all other American personnel be expelled. Initially, the Dergue held back, suspicious of Soviet intentions and also because some members favored making contact with China instead, which was still operating in some African states and had a good record of not interfering in internal matters of the countries it helped.

Hoping a moderate, pro-Western element would eventually come to power in Ethiopia, the Americans retained their relationship with the Dergue for the time being and continued to send arms at previously agreed levels, amounting to about $12.4 million annually. During 1975 and 1976, American weaponry sent to Ethiopia included some M-60 tanks, F-5E aircraft, and a few F-5A aircraft transferred from Iran. At first the Dergue seemed anxious to have a continued, and indeed increased, supply of American arms to bring its military material inventory to a level higher than that of Somalia. The U.S. administation hoped that by continuing to send limited quantities of arms, it would not only keep the local military balance in the Horn of Africa, but also show other African states that even though revolutions might occur, the Americans would not desert their allies.

When the Dergue realized that only limited quantities of arms were forthcoming from the United States, an Ethiopian delegation visited Moscow in December 1976 and obtained an agreement with the Soviets to provide arms to the value of about $385 million. These Soviet arms were slow to arrive. The Soviets wanted the U.S. MAAG out of Ethiopia first. When Carter assumed office in January 1977 and began to expound his human rights policies, the Dergue made up its mind to opt for the Soviets. On 23 April, the MAAG, down to forty-six officers, was expelled. The Americans had lost out in Ethiopia, and the Soviets rushed in to take their place.

Meanwhile, during 1975 and 1976, the Dergue was faced with large-scale rebellion in its annexed province of Eritrea. Other provinces were also demanding autonomy from the central government, many such demands being tribally motivated. The Dergue eventually had to admit that ten out of its fourteen provinces were in active revolt. In February and again in July 1977, there were purges within the Dergue; eventually, Lt. Col. Mengistu Haile Mariam, who had seized power in February 1976, emerged the victor. He at once cracked down heavily on his opposition.

During 1976, the Dergue increasingly adopted Marxist doctrines, purged moderate elements, and brutally repressed the antisocialist (meaning anticommunist) counterrevolutionaries. In February 1977, Mengistu became president of the Dergue and head of state; in May, he visited Moscow, his first trip ever out of his own country. He had talks with both Brezhnev and Ustinov. The Soviets eagerly and quickly moved into Ethiopia, partly because they thought the Dergue was in imminent danger of falling; partly because they saw the country becoming fragmented, and a possible Marxist government about to be lost to the Socialist world; and partly because they regarded Ethiopia as the key to the Horn of Africa. They were therefore willing to swap a foothold in Somalia for one in Addis Ababa.

In February 1977, Ethiopian and Somali troops clashed in the

Ogaden province; the following day, Fidel Castro visited Addis Ababa; and on 17 April, the first fifty Cuban soldiers arrived in the country. Castro promised to send another 250 Cubans, all alleged to be "medical personnel." On 25 July, the Dergue admitted the war against Somalia was going badly for them; in September, they began to organize a huge peasant militia for defense. The promised Soviet arms were still slow to arrive, causing Mengistu to complain the Soviets were more concerned with Somalia than Ethiopia, even though they had ceased giving aid to that country in July. Mengistu then again turned to the Americans, but Carter insisted on human rights reforms and the exclusion of all Soviet military personnel before resuming military and economic aid.

Rejected by the United States, Mengistu visited both Moscow and Havana. Military munitions were urgently needed by his cut-off, half-mutinous army in Ogaden. This time he was more successful. The Soviet ambassador in Addis Ababa confirmed that Moscow had "officially and formally" halted all military aid to Somalia and was now supplying Ethiopia with "defensive arms." These included 200 T-54 and T-55 tanks, BTRs, antitank missiles, 48 MiG-21s, and a few MIG-23s. Some of the aircraft were flown in by Cuban pilots. Soviet military transport aircraft flew arms to Ethiopia, filing false flight plans and overflying Yugoslavia, Turkey, Pakistan, Egypt, and Sudan without permission. By the end of October 1977, over 400 Cuban and 200 Soviet military personnel were in Ethiopia.

On 24 November 1977, the Soviets began their gigantic airlift of Cubans and weaponry across Africa from Angola into Ethiopia. They concurrently mounted a sealift as well, which turned the tide of war decisively against Somalia. The previous day, the Somali armed forces had mounted an armored and artillery attack on the surviving Ethiopian stronghold of Harrar, on the edge of the Ogaden province. It was a desperate gamble to win a military victory before the Cubans and more Soviet arms flooded into Ethiopia. On the 27th, Cuban-led units launched a counterattack; and on the 30th, the Somali army fell back.

On 1 January 1978, the Dergue was in a strong position and all doubts had vanished as to whether it would survive. A Supreme Military Committee was established to recover the whole Ogaden province, suppress the rebels in Eritrea, and bring to heel the dissident provinces; it consisted of seven Ethiopian senior officers, three Cubans, and eight Soviets, all under the command of a Russian general who was technically an adviser. By this time well over 2,000 Cuban and 1,000 Soviet military personnel were in the country, leading and training Ethiopian units, manning sophisticated weaponry, and flying combat aircraft.

During the first two months of 1978, more Cuban personnel and Soviet arms flooded into Ethiopia and were pushed forward to the Ogaden battlefield, all organized and coordinated by Soviet generals and their staffs. Soon there were 20,000 Cuban, Soviet, and East Germans in the country, as well as a South Yemen contingent, nearly 2,000 strong, with some armor and twenty-four MiG aircraft. By March, the Somalis were in full retreat.

The Ethiopian army was increased to about 90,000 men, reorganized and equipped with modern Soviet weaponry, including 500 tanks, 500 BTRs, and 300 guns of various sorts. The air force soon possessed over fifty MiG-21s and twenty MiG-23s; and the navy, which had bases at Massawa and Assab on the Red Sea, took delivery of three OSA missile naval craft. East Germans began improving the capacity of the Assab harbor. The ground forces were backed by a People's Militia of about 120,000 men, formed into ten divisions, which was given some political training.

In November 1978, Mengistu again visited Moscow, where he signed a Soviet friendship and cooperation treaty and other agreements of the now common type. In the seventies the United States had been skillfully eased out from Ethiopia, and the Soviet imprint appeared in its place.

Eritrea

In 1952, the former Italian colony of Eritrea was placed by the United Nations under Ethiopian administration on a federal basis. In 1962, it was annexed by the Addis Ababa government as Ethiopia's fourteenth province. This annexation meant that landlocked Ethiopia had access to the Red Sea. Eritrea has an area of about 45,700 square miles, a 600-mile stretch of Red Sea coastline, and a population of about three million people, the majority of whom are Muslims (although it is thought that about 43 percent are Christians). This annexation was unpopular, and gave rise to a number of Eritrean resistance groups who demanded either autonomy or independence, and who were encouraged and supported in varying degrees by the Soviet Union, China, and several Arab states. In 1970, a state of emergency existed in many parts of Eritrea, with some 40,000 Ethiopian troops in uneasy occupation.

One of the principal resistance groups was the Eritrean Liberation Front (ELF), formed in 1958, which demanded autonomy. Having a predominantly Marxist leadership, the ELF had its headquarters in Damascus, Syria. In 1970, it claimed to control large sections of the province by using tactics of sabotage and avoidance. In its early years the ELF had received some weapons and training from the Egyptians, but by 1970, Libya was its main source of funds. The ELF claimed to have about two thousand guerrilla fighters in the field, a Christian element still among them. In the first half of the seventies, the ELF received aid from the Soviet Union, Somalia, Libya, Iraq, and South Yemen. Its Christian element declined.

A split in the ELF leadership in 1970 brought into existence the Eritrean People's Liberation Front (EPLF), a Marxist organization led by Ramadan Mohammed Nur. The Soviet KGB gave support and some aid to both groups. After the revolution in Ethiopia in 1974, when Ethiopian military capability was sapped by the elimination of so many senior officers and Eritrean guerrilla activity increased, the Dergue was given extra American military aid to combat the activities of both groups. In 1975, two other Eritrean insurgent organizations emerged due to dividing leadership. All told, it was thought there were over twelve thousand active guerrillas, some well armed, trained, and disciplined, but the majority less so, supplied variously by the Soviet Union and some Arab countries. Attempts were made by the Eritrean groups to form liaisons with each other before the anticipated military victory against the Addis Ababa government was achieved, to avoid the Angolan experience of first gaining independence, only to be immediately plunged into civil war. These efforts were all unsuccessful, and the guerrilla groups remained divided, some openly hostile to each other.

In May 1976, the Dergue offered immediate regional autonomy to the Eritrean resistance groups if they would unite; but this was refused as each group now demanded complete independence. The year of 1977 was a good one for the Eritrean guerrillas, who overran practically the whole province, with the exception of a few largely besieged cities.

Once the Ogaden front had stabilized in March 1978, the Dergue turned its attention to pacifying Eritrea, assembling some 60,000 troops for the purpose. This campaign against the guerrillas began in June, and heavy fighting continued until August. Soviet and Cuban personnel stayed in the background, but Cuban troops remained on the Somali front, holding it for the Addis Ababa government so that Ethiopian soldiers could fight in Eritrea.

The Soviets had encouraged the Ethiopian government to campaign into Eritrea under the impression the Eritrean guerrillas would soon be defeated or forced to the conference table. This had not materialized, and despite the use of aircraft, armor, and guns by Ethiopian troops, the fighting was inconclusive. The overriding Soviet aim was to obtain the use of the strategic ports of Massawa and Assab, and when they foresaw a drawn-out guerrilla war developing, the Soviets demanded that the Dergue change its policy to one of reconciliation with the Eritrean resistance groups. In November 1978, the Dergue officially proclaimed that the eighteen-year-long "revolt in Eritrea province" was over. This was an illusion, as the insurgent groups remained intact, either dispersing into small groups or withdrawing to the remoter parts of the province. Any military successes the Ethiopian troops may have had was largely due to insurgent disunity.

The year of 1979 was one of uneasy truce in Eritrea, with the Soviets slowly easing their way into Massawa and Assab. The Soviets had ceased supplying the Eritrean guerrillas—who now obtained arms and aid from Arab countries, mainly through Sudan—while Numeiry continued to provide a sanctuary in his country for Eritrean exiles and refugees.

Djibouti

A brief mention must be made in discussing the Horn of Africa of the small territory of only about 5,800 miles, formerly known as French Somaliland, but which by 1970 had come to be called Djibouti. It had a population of about 220,000 people (1970 estimate), about sixty percent of them being Issas, of Somali stock, and the other forty percent being Afars, who are mainly Christian and do not speak the Somali language. Its capital, also named Djibouti, had developed as a seaport and was for long the only railroad link into the interior of Ethiopia.

This French colony gained its independence on 27 May 1977 as the Republic of Afars and Issas, which joined both the Arab League and the Organization of African Unity. The Afars' mainly Christian minority had vaguely wanted to merge with Ethiopia, fearing victimization by the Issas' Muslim majority, and the Issas vaguely wanted to merge into Somalia for stability. The new government, however, despite being Issa-dominated, remained aloof from either course. The new president, Hassan Gouled Aptidon, also avoided involvement during the fighting between Ethiopian troops and the Eritrean guerrillas, in case a false step might result eventually in his country being occupied. As it was, the closure of the Djibouti–Addis Ababa railroad due to insurgency caused an economic depression in Djibouti.

President Barreh of Somalia tried to tempt the new republic into a defense agreement with his country, but the French had beaten him to it. They arranged to maintain a French garrison in Djibouti of about 4,000 men and retained the use of the naval facilities for their Indian Ocean squadron. The French also formed, armed, and trained a small army of about 2,400 men for the republic. Prior to independence, the French had secret talks with the Somali government, which upset the Afars, who had generally been favored by them; this resulted in demonstrations and some rioting. There was no Soviet imprint on Djibouti in the seventies owing to the French presence.

RHODESIA

In the beginning of 1970, the black insurrection in white-ruled Rhodesia was in progress, with both the Soviets and the Chinese fueling the "freedom fighters." Rhodesia, with a population of about 6.3 million (1970), of which only 274,000 are "white settlers," was technically still a British colony even though the ruling minority had broken away from British sovereignty in 1965 by making a unilateral declaration of independence. An economic blockade was mounted against Rhodesia to try to bring about the capitulation of the "illegal" regime; but it was only partially applied and only partially successful. British policy stated that Rhodesia was to be prepared for independence under a black majority government, but the white settlers, led by the prime minister Ian Smith, objected. On 20 March 1970, the Smith government declared Rhodesia to be an independent republic.

There were two main insurgent groups in 1970. One was the Zimbabwe African People's Union (ZAPU), founded in 1961 and led by Joshua Nkomo. (Zimbabwe is the African name for Rhodesia). ZAPU's purpose was to gain African majority rule through international lobbying, but Nkomo nevertheless sent his guerrilla fighters into Rhodesia. Banned in 1962, ZAPU came under Soviet sponsorship and influence right from its inception. ZAPU had its headquarters in Lusaka, the capital of adjacent Zambia.

The other group was the Zimbabwe African National Union (ZANU), formed in 1963 by dissenting members of ZAPU who wanted to fight a "war of liberation" against the white government. Led by Ndabaningi Sitole, it also had its headquarters in Lusaka. In 1966, it began guerrilla activity inside Rhodesia in a small way. ZANU's main support came from the Chinese, and its guerrilla fighters were sent to Algeria, Ghana, and China for training.

The two groups were continually quarreling with each other. In March 1971, under pressure from the Organization of African Unity and being given a bribe of some $2 million, ZAPU and ZANU were persuaded to form a Joint Military Command; however, this never got off the ground. In September, largely under the threat of withdrawing sanctuary and other facilities, the Zambian government persuaded them to work together in a coalition which became the Front for the Liberation of Zimbabwe (FROLIZI). Both ZAPU and ZANU retained their own separate identities, organizations, and command structures, and their cooperation was more superficial than real. The spring of 1975 saw infighting on tribal lines between the two organizations, which also broke out again in 1978. Until the mid-seventies, there was more quarreling and fighting between ZAPU and ZANU than guerrilla activity by them inside Rhodesia.

Another political resistance group appeared on the scene in 1972: the United African National Council (UANC), led by Bishop Abel Muzorewa, whose object was to obtain independence and black majority rule by peaceful means. When Robert Mugabe was released from detention in Rhodesia, he became, in 1976, the leader of ZANU, ousting Sitole (who formed his own group). The Soviets approached Mugabe with offers of all the military aid he wanted on condition his ZANU broke with the Chinese, but he did not completely trust them.

After the Portuguese revolution in 1974 and the granting of independence to Mozambique, the insurrection situation in Rhodesia changed. In July 1975, the Tanzanian government withdrew facilities it had previously given to the Mozambique FRELIMO insurgent group and gave them to the black Zimbabwe freedom fighters. Full advantage of this was taken by Mugabe; and as Chinese support withered away, he replaced it with what he could get from the USSR. Within eighteen months, he had over twelve thousand ZANU guerrillas in training camps in Tanzania and Mozambique. Not to be outdone, Nkomo visited Moscow in May 1976 to obtain an increase in Soviet-supplied arms for his smaller ZAPU guerrilla force training in Zambia.

In response to American and British pressure, in October 1976, the Patriotic Front was established, which included ZAPU, ZANU, and other smaller groups. Led by Robert Mugabe, it provided a liaison for these various groups, who were still in confrontation with each other. Until 1976, guerrilla activity had primarily been undertaken by Nkomo's ZAPU fighters, but commencing in February 1977, Mugabe's ZANU came into action in a big way, overshadowing his rivals. Mugabe, a Marxist, wanted to establish a black socialist state in Rhodesia, modeled on that of Angola.

Two guerrilla armies took shape and operated independently of each other. They became known as the Zimbabwe African National Liberation Army (ZANLA), led by Mugabe; and the Zimbabwe People's Revolutionary Army (ZIPRA), led by Nkomo. ZANLA mainly operated from Tanzania and Mozambique, and ZIRPA from Zambia. Nkomo visited Cuba in July 1977 and again in August, arranging for a number of his guerrillas to be trained in Angola by the Cubans. By the end of 1977, Mugabe's ZANLA had about seven thousand guerrillas operating inside Rhodesia, while Nkomo's ZIPRA seemed to maintain a steady average of only about two thousand. Throughout, Nkomo was reluctant to commit large numbers of his guerrillas to action in Rhodesia.

During 1978, Soviet weapons in quantity were sent to both black guerrilla armies, which expanded rapidly. By the end of that year, Nkomo's ZIPRA had increased considerably, with about seven thousand men in training in Zambia, another six thousand trained guerrillas waiting to go into action, and some three thousand operating inside Rhodesia. Mugabe's ZANLA reached greater numbers. Guerrilla activity was stepped up inside Rhodesia, and the casualty rate among whites and government security forces began to mount ominously.

The year 1979 was one of bitter guerrilla warfare on the Vietnam pattern of viciousness, with ever increasing numbers of shootings, explosions, and terrorist activities. In September 1978, a Rhodesian passenger aircraft flying near the Kariba Dam in the north of the country had been brought down by a SAM-7 missile; another aircraft was brought down with loss of life in February 1979 by the same means. The exodus of white settlers exceeded 1,000 a month. Groups of freedom fighters now roamed over large areas of the countryside and drove many whites to abandon remote farms. The Rhodesian government figures showed that between 1972, when the insurgency became significant, and the end of 1978, 12,039 people had been killed in the guerrilla fighting; the security forces lost 774 men.

Britain tried hard to bring about a peaceful solution, and elections were held in Rhodesia in April 1979. Bishop Muzorewa's UANC party won a majority of the vote, but his leadership was unacceptable to Mugabe and Nkomo, whose followers had boycotted the election. The deadly guerrilla war continued in intensity, with the Soviets supplying the black freedom fighters with the means to pursue it, and with the white government increasingly on the defensive, its security forces facing about thirty thousand guerrillas.

Suddenly, in December 1979, the miracle occurred: the British organized the Lancaster House Conference in London and persuaded the principal Zimbabwe leaders to attend. A peace settlement was agreed to, and on 28 December a cease-fire came into effect in Rhodesia. By 4 January 1980, over 18,500 black guerrillas had reported to the government monitoring centers; a monitoring force of 1,500 men from British Commonwealth countries was sent to Rhodesia to supervise elections, which voted Robert Mugabe to power as prime minister. He formed a coalition government that included Joshua Nkomo and other leaders. Mugabe declared his policy to be one of nonalignment; he planned to strengthen links with Britain, the EEC, and other world markets. On 5 March 1980, Independence Day, the name of the country was changed to Zimbabwe.

To the chagrin of his Soviet backers and supporters, Mugabe stated that his ZANU party owed nothing to the Soviet Union. It seemed as through the Soviet imprint that showed so clearly on the two main black Rhodesian parties, ZANU and ZAPU, might not be a permanent one after all. The Soviets muttered bitterly about African ingratitude—not for the first time.

NAMIBIA

During the second half of the seventies, the Soviets gained considerable leverage in Namibia (South West Africa) by supporting the South West African People's Organization (SWAPO), an indigenous liberation movement founded by Sam Nujoma in the 1960s. SWAPO was the only black national political organization in the country. Some other smaller ones were mainly recruited on tribal lines. Of Namibia's population of about 750,000 (1966 census), approximately 90,000 were whites, many of whose ancestors had settled there before World War I when the territory was a German colony. The Ovambo tribal group, who lived in the north of Namibia and straddled its frontier with Angola, formed about 60 percent of the African population. Although mainly arid and barren, Namibia has considerable mineral potential, with large deposits of uranium, tin, copper, and diamonds. The capital, Windhoek (Katatura to the Africans), is linked by a railroad to Walvis Bay, the only port of any note.

Helped by the OAU Liberation Committee in 1966, SWAPO established a guerrilla framework but remained small, and barely effective, managing only to obtain a few arms from China, North Vietnam, and North Korea. SWAPO leaders were scattered in exile in Zambia and Tanzania and were divided among themselves. It was not until the Soviet-supported MPLA in Angola gained ascendancy that the Soviets saw SWAPO possibilities and began sending arms and supplies in small amounts. In 1975, SWAPO began to establish training camps in Angola and in Mozambique. In February 1976, the Cubans joined the act and openly declared they would support the "liberation fight in Namibia," meaning SWAPO. Cubans in Angola moved into SWAPO training camps and by the end of the year were training some 2,000 guerrillas.

A few small groups of SWAPO guerrillas began operating on sabotage missions into Namibia.

The League of Nations mandated South West Africa to the government of South Africa after World War I. Its successor, the United Nations, in 1974, called on South Africa to relinquish that mandate. The South African government saw Namibia as an essential buffer state against Soviet-influenced Angola and wanted to ensure that any general election would produce a friendly regime. Its plan was to create a confederation of twelve ethnic groups, or *bantustans* ("homelands"), but SWAPO demanded a united Namibia. In December 1974, SWAPO offered to negotiate with the South African government if that government would recognize SWAPO as the sole representative of the Namibian people and grant immediate independence. Both conditions were rejected, and the following year guerrilla resistance began in earnest.

During 1976 and 1977, the Chinese connection practically disappeared as Cubans trained SWAPO guerrillas and the Soviets worked to gain exclusive influence over this liberation movement. Sam Nujoma implemented the Soviet doctrine of "scientific socialism" as far as he could and allowed both Soviet and Cuban political commissars to operate in his training camps. SWAPO guerrillas at this stage were neither effective nor well disciplined, and Nujoma had leadership problems.

Gradually the tempo of guerrilla warfare increased as more and more small SWAPO armed groups clashed with the South African security forces inside Namibia which, by the end of 1978, numbered about twenty thousand. Guerrilla and terrorist attacks increased in volume, roads and the railroads were repeatedly sabotaged, and fuel trucks had to have a military escort to travel across the country. The South African security forces were increased to about thirty thousand and adopted the policy of "hot pursuit" into Angola after guerrillas who had raided Namibia.

In April 1977, talks began between the South African government and the so-called Western Five—the United States, Britain, France, West Germany, and Canada—to try to find a "settlement plan" for an independent Namibia. General elections were suggested, to be supervised by the United Nations, but the South Africans objected, as this would inevitably bring to power an unfriendly SWAPO government, which might export black dissidents southwards into their own country.

In April the following year, however, the South African government accepted the plan in principle, subject to "certain clarifications," but remained reluctant to implement it. Haggling continued until the end of the decade over such details as U.N. supervision of the respective SWAPO and South African military locations. President Neto of Angola had proposed a demilitarized zone on either side of the Namibia-Angola border, and this produced more discussion and argument. The Afrikander political party, a hard-line white-supremacy one, further complicated the issue.

Although the volume of guerrilla activity inside Namibia steadily increased, South African security forces were generally able to contain it. The decade ended indecisively in Namibia, with the South African government stubbornly and effectively stalling on the independence issue with SWAPO only slowly developing its guerrilla potential, and with ever-increasing Soviet involvement. The Soviet imprint rested on SWAPO; but fielding barely 400 active freedom fighters inside Namibia, SWAPO seemed to be a long way from gaining control of that country.

OTHER SOVIET TENTACLES
IN AFRICA

As Chinese involvement in Africa, especially east Africa, declined in the seventies, the Soviets tried to step in whenever they could, but only had limited success. Apart from Guinea, Senegal, and the Democratic Republic of Congo, the Soviets did not gain much influence in former French colonies, although their tentacles left traces on most parts of the continent. For example, the national armories of the following states had a few Soviet aircraft, tanks, weapons, or vehicles, usually elderly ones: Congo, Guinea, Mali, Nigeria, Senegal, Tanzania, Uganda, and Zambia (apart from those previously specifically mentioned). Soviet "salesmen" had been distributing their "samples." Soviet aid in one form or another was also given to the Central African Republic, Ghana, Guinea, Mali, Mauritania, Nigeria, Senegal, Uganda, and Zaire. Sometimes the Soviets came unstuck: for example, on 8 September 1978, Ghana (once the main KGB base in Black Africa) expelled the Soviet envoys for inciting unrest in trade unions and the universities.

In Uganda, on 25 January 1971, President Milton Obote was overthrown by Gen. Idi Amin, the chief of staff he was about to dismiss. Amin formed a government and quickly made himself president. The Soviets rushed in to supply him with arms and other aid, and with them went Soviet personnel. Amin made an arrangement with Colonel Gaddafi of Libya for Libyans to train his men in the use of some of the new Soviet equipment, which soon included twenty-five tanks (including T–55s), 120 BTRs, and thirty aircraft (including MiG-21s). In January

1973, Libya offered 300 places in its training establishments for Ugandan service men.

Amin developed into a cruel and ruthless dictator who committed many crimes against his own people. He became well known for his part in the famous hijacking of the Israeli aircraft that put down at Entebbe Airport, Uganda, on 28 June 1976. Relations between Uganda and adjacent Tanzania were bad, as the latter country harbored Ugandan political exiles hostile to Amin. The border between the two countries was closed in April 1977. Fighting across the frontier began in November 1978 and developed into an invasion by Tanzanian troops and armed Ugandan exiles. Kampala, the Uganda capital, fell to the invaders on 11 April 1979; a few days later, Amin fled the country with the remnants of his army and the small Libyan contingent that had been sent to help him. He was eventually given sanctuary in Saudi Arabia. The Soviet imprint that had rested on Uganda for almost the whole of the decade was removed.

During the seventies the Soviet imprint flickered over the Democratic Republic of Congo, which had a communist-oriented government. This black republic, of some 130,000 square miles, and a population of about 2.1 million (1970 estimate), lies just to the north of the Congo River estuary, the river itself forming the joint frontier with Zaire for many miles. The Congo government had cooperated fully with the Soviets since 1975 in providing staging posts—at the airport at Brazzaville, the capital, and at the port of Pointe-Noire—for the transit of thousands of Cuban mercenary troops from Cuba to Angola, and then across Africa to Ethiopia. This had been necessary as the Zaire government was then supporting UNITA, which was hostile to the Soviet-backed MPLA. In March 1977, the armed forces ousted President Mairen Ngouabi, who was replaced by Col. Yhombi Opango. Two years later, in March 1979, Opango was in turn ousted by the pro-Soviet faction of the army, who installed Colonel Nguessou as president.

During the early seventies Nigeria recovered from its civil war and became the largest Black African oil-exporting country, but the Soviets failed to capitalize on their arms supplies that had helped the federal government successfully bring the war to a close. The head of state, Yakubu Gowon, tended to be pro-Western and would have little to do with the Soviets. Not until he was overthrown on 29 July 1975 and replaced by Gen. Murtala Mohammed did the Soviets again begin to make headway in Nigeria. In February 1976, Mohammed was killed in a coup; he was succeeded by Gen. Olusegun Obasanjo, who was pro-Soviet. Soviet arms in small quantities, including MiG-21 aircraft, again began to arrive in Nigeria. The Nigerian chief of staff, General Danjuma, went to Moscow; a return visit was made to Nigeria by a Soviet general in November 1977. Agreements were signed for more Soviet arms and for Nigerian officers to attend courses of instruction in the USSR. The Soviet imprint was being planted on Nigeria.

Soviet diplomatic weapons were sometimes more effective than was generally realized. In 1974, a West German concern appeared, known as OTRAG, meaning Orbital Transport and Rocket Company, whose purpose was to construct and fire rockets capable of putting small satellites into orbit. The object was to offer them for sale to Third World nations who wanted their own surveillance satellites to watch their own frontiers and adjacent hostile countries, and who were denied such means by the United States, the Soviet Union, and China.

OTRAG obtained a lease of some 40,000 square miles in a remote area of Zaire for use as a testing and launching ground. In the course of the following two or three years, at least four successful rocket launches were made. This did not please the Kremlin, and Brezhnev openly condemned OTRAG and the governments of West Germany and Zaire. Diplomatic and other pressures were applied by the Soviets, which eventually forced the Zaire government to cancel the OTRAG contract in April 1979. OTRAG was then invited to operate in Libya, and in 1979 negotiated a contract with Saudi Arabia to supply 3,832 ground-to-ground missiles of two types: one with a range of about 1,200 miles, and the other with a range of 200 miles.

Usually the Soviets gave considerable thought and research to their African economic and trade projects, but occasionally they slipped up and were made to look foolish. In the early seventies the Soviets saw an opportunity to break into Zanzibar island, part of Tanzania, then in the Chinese sphere of influence. It was agreed that in exchange for its crop of cloves, Zanzibar's main stable export, the Soviets would establish a tuna fishing and processing industry for Zanzibar. The Soviets sent their fishing vessels, but it was soon found that the tuna could move faster than the Soviet ships, and so the project flopped.

7 Soviet Imprints on Southern Asia

*The Soviet leaders tried to persuade me that India should teach
Pakistan a lesson . . . and tried to incite me to attack Pakistan.*
— Morarji Desai, Prime Minister of India (1977–79),
4 December 1980

URING THE SEVENTIES the Soviets worked to
impose their imprint on Afghanistan, Iran, Pakistan,
and India, their four main target priorities in
Southern Asia. Afghanistan, already a client state, came under full
Soviet military occupation in the last days of the decade. Under the pro-
Western shah, Iran was solidly in the Western camp, but subversive
forces gradually undermined his position, and he left his country for the
last time in January 1979. The Islamic revolution, led by Ayatollah
Khomeini, took over, in which the Soviet KGB played a significant part.
Pakistan, in an uneasy federation of four diverse provinces with severe
economic troubles, lived under the apprehensive shadow that one day the
USSR and India would gang up to dismember the country and divide its
provinces between them. Sri Lanka (Ceylon) is also mentioned because
although it was not a Soviet priority target, surprisingly enough, it
should have been, owing to its vital strategic position and left-wing
governments. The Sri Lankan government demonstrated how conventional forces can defeat communist guerrillas in the field.

AFGHANISTAN

In 1970, the Soviet imprint already rested on the mountainous,
landlocked Afghanistan, which had become tied to the USSR economically and militarily. Ruled despotically by King Mohammed Zahir
Khan, Afghanistan was less a developing country than a backward one.
It had never been colonized by a European power, and in the nineteenth
century had remained a backwater buffer state between Czarist Russian
expansion towards the Indian Ocean and British expansion from their
Indian empire.

133

The U.N. population estimate of 1969 was 16.5 million. The Afghan way of life has hardly changed since Alexander the Great and his army passed through that country on their way to India so many centuries ago, except for conversion to Islam. It was a closed, tribal society, rent by tribal and family feuds. Only a few hundred thousand Afghans, living in the half-dozen major cities, could today be regarded as being de-tribalized and stepping timidly into the twentieth century.

Bordered on the north by the USSR, on the southwest by Iran, and on the southeast by Pakistan, a thin sliver of Afghan territory reached to touch China in the east. Afghanistan emerged with the trappings of a modern nation-state in 1921, and although Lenin was the first to recognize its sovereignty, the Soviets did not impinge on the Afghan scene until World War II, when the country declared itself neutral. Under threat of Soviet invasion, the Afghans ejected all Axis nationals but refused to join the Allied side.

The partitioning of the Indian subcontinent by the British in 1947 brought into being the two separate states of India and Pakistan. West Pakistan accepted existing British-negotiated treaties, which established the disputed Durand Line as the de facto common frontier with Afghani-stan. This line cut through the Pathan ethnic region, leaving some four million Pathans in Pakistan and almost as many in Afghanistan. The Pathans had long wanted autonomy in a Pushtunistan state,[1] which was given indirect support by the Afghan government under the assumption it would include Pakistan's North West Frontier Province, which would then come under Afghan sovereignty. Pakistan's hostility threw Afghanistan into the arms of the USSR. Previous to 1947, the bulk of Afghanistan's trade had been with British India through the famous Khyber Pass; there had also been some trade with Iran, but little with the USSR in the north.

It was not until 1957 that the Soviets managed to obtain their first foothold in Afghanistan, agreeing to supply weapons and equipment, to reorganize the small army and air force, and to accept selected Afghans as students and for military training. By 1970, the Afghan armed forces were completely equipped with Soviet material. The army, about 80,000 strong, consisted basically of an armored division (with some T-34 and T-55 tanks), two infantry divisions, and about twenty motorized and infantry units. A very unpopular form of selective con-scription was in force. The Afghan air force possessed about one hundred Soviet combat aircraft, and half a dozen helicopters. The Soviet military training mission consisted of about one hundred officers.

---

[1] Pushtan is the common language of the Pathans in western Afghanistan.

An attempt was made in the early 1930s to introduce some Western reforms, but these were violently resisted. When the king was assassinated in 1933, the reform program was suspended until after World War II. In the sixties, the Americans competed with the Soviets for influence in Afghanistan and embarked on a strategic road-building program, among other projects. Previously, all-weather roads were practically nonexistent, goods having to be transported mainly by pack animals. A somewhat circular route linked Kabul, the capital, with the main cities of Kandahar and Herut. This "ring road" had junctions with roads leading from Kabul through the Khyber Pass; and from Kandahar to Quetta, in Pakistan; and from Herut into Iran. The Americans improved this age-old route system. The Soviets constructed a road from Kabul through Mazar-i-Sharif and north to the USSR border. The Soviets also helped the Afghans produce natural gas in the north of the country and constructed a pipeline to convey it to the USSR.

In 1964, under Soviet persuasion, a pretense was made at introducing a constitutional monarchy, but King Mohammed Zahir Khan still retained feudal powers. A formal constitution was introduced the following year, which created a legal code and allowed political parties to operate. The first political party in Afghanistan formed in 1965 and was known as the People's Democratic Party; as the Soviets gave advice, it evolved on a communist pattern. Two of the founder-members were Nur Mohammed Taraki and Babrak Karmal.

At the beginning of the seventies, Afghanistan was in a sad economic plight. The decade began with a three-year famine in which it was estimated that over 80,000 people died. The prime minister, Abdul Zahir Khan, an obvious scapegoat, was dismissed by the king in December 1972, and he went off to Moscow to seek political comfort. In July 1973, while out of the country, King Mohammed Zahir Khan was overthrown by an army coup led by Gen. Mohammed Daoud Khan. The coup had been organized by the Soviets: while still prime minister, Abdul Zahir Khan had visited Kosygin in Moscow, in March 1972, when the plot to put Daoud (the Soviet nominee) on the throne was hatched. The Soviets denied any implication in this coup, which was generally reported to be a bloodless one, although eight people had been killed. Daoud became president and additionally prime minister on 18 July, the day after the coup. On the 19th, Daoud's regime was recognized by both the USSR and India. Daoud stated that his objects were to end corruption and to organize a system of democracy. The constitution was set aside, and he ruled by decree. An attempted countercoup was quashed in September, as was a similar one in December.

The coup of 1973 caused a split in the People's Democratic Party

(PDP), which by this time was a thinly disguised Communist Party. The Soviets told the PDP to give full support to the new president. Nur Mohammed Taraki, the secretary general, refused; but a breakaway section of the PDP, led by Babrak Karmal, agreed and cooperated with Daoud, who nonetheless proscribed the Party. The dissenting main body of the PDP came to be known as the Kalk ("The Masses") and the breakaway faction as the Parcham ("Flag"). Intense bitterness developed between these two opposing factions. The Parcham was unofficially tolerated by Daoud, and the proscribed Kalk wing survived underground, although many of its members were imprisoned and a few executed.

With their nominee in power, the Soviets pressed their case and sent more weapons and equipment for the Afghan armed forces, together with more Soviet advisers and technicians. In June 1974 and again in January 1975, Daoud visited Moscow, where he signed a number of the usual Soviet economic and other agreements, including one for the Soviets to construct an oil refinery. In June, Daoud nationalized the banks "to curb the black market" that had developed in the cities and towns.

By April 1977, the Soviets were cooperating in producing oil and natural gas. Afghanistan had become a client-state that practically depended on the USSR economically and militarily. By this time, disillusioned with Asia over the Vietnam experience, the Americans had given up seriously struggling against the Soviets for influence in Afghanistan.

Under Soviet guidance in February 1977, a new constitution was introduced and Daoud formally became president of the Republic of Afghanistan. The Soviets pressured Daoud to bring together the two opposing factions of the People's Democratic Party; and although the two wings did make a reconciliaton, Daoud would not allow the PDP to operate openly and legally. The disgruntled PDP began to stir up trouble for Daoud and schemed to remove him. On 17 November 1977, it launched an unsuccessful coup in Kabul, in which Ali Ahmed Khoram, the planning minister, was killed.

The Soviet imprint on Afghanistan was deepening, but all was not going quite as well as the Kremlin leaders would have liked. Daoud was becoming too independent: he did not always follow Soviet suggestions with sufficient servility and promptness, and he sought other foreign contacts. In particular, the Soviets disliked his continued repression of the PDP, which they thought they had managed to unite again and were fashioning into an instrument through which they might gain absolute control over Afghanistan.

Afghan relations with Pakistan remained strained, mainly over the Pushtunistan issue. On 5 March 1978, Daoud made an unsuccessful visit to that country. Rejecting Pakistan's suggestion that Afghanistan join with Iran, Pakistan, and Turkey in a Regional Cooperation Development Agreement, he angrily declared that his country would remain a strict neutral, conveniently overlooking the tightening Soviet grip.

Early in April 1978, Daoud again visited Moscow. Even though he concluded another agreement on economic cooperation, the Soviets were clearly displeased when he refused to sign a bilateral defense treaty. Daoud's relations with the PDP worsened when, on 17 April, Mir Akhbar Khaiber, a Parcham leader, was assassinated in Kabul and Daoud blamed the PDP both for the killing and the anti-American sentiment that followed. Nur Mohammed Taraki, Babrak Karmal, and Hafizullah Amin were arrested but later released due to Soviet pressure.

On 27 April, with full Soviet involvement and assisstance, an Afghan army coup led by Nur Mohammed Taraki, the secretary general of the PDP and leader of the Kalk wing, was mounted in Kabul. Daoud and his family were killed. All who took part in the coup had been trained and indoctrinated in the USSR, and Soviet tanks and aircraft were used. Taraki's regime was recognized by the Soviet government the following day.

Taraki became chairman of the National Revolutionary Council of the Democratic Republic of Afghanistan, and also prime minister; he later adopted the title of president. Babrak Karmal, leader of the Parcham wing, became the deputy chairman at the insistence of the Soviets, who wanted a united PDP. Many Parcham members had lost their lives or freedom under Daoud's rule, though, and extreme bitterness remained between the two opposing wings. The Soviets insisted the two men work together, but owing to distrust, intrigue, and hatred, the Parcham and Kalk wings of the PDP were again soon at each other's throats, fighting in the streets as well as the council chamber. These factional skirmishes led to assassinations, which in turn invited reprisals.

In July 1978, Taraki dismissed Karmal from the National Revolutionary Council and appointed him ambassador to Moscow. On 10 August, Karmal returned from the USSR to Kabul, suddenly and without permission; in a shootout with the security forces at the airport as he arrived, four of his aides were killed. Karmal was arrested but soon released, again due to Soviet intervention, and withdrew to Moscow.

Part of the price for Soviet support in the Taraki coup had been the complete Sovietization of the Afghan armed forces; and by August, over 2,500 Soviet personnel had arrived in Afghanistan. Soviet officers were paired with senior Afghan ones in the typical Soviet commissar manner, right down to regimental command level. Afghan army strength remained about the 80,000 mark, but more weapons arrived from the USSR.

On 17 August 1978, an alleged conspiracy to oust Taraki was uncovered in Kabul. Gen. Abdul Kader, the defense minister, was arrested and accused of being the ringleader. The main cause of the military discontent on this occasion was that the pride and feelings of the fiercely xenophobic Afghan officer corps had been hurt by the influx of Soviet officers and their assumption of responsibility. At last, on 5 December 1978, the Soviets succeeded in obtaining their long sought after friendship and cooperation treaty with Afghanistan, but they still could not persuade Taraki to conclude a bilateral defense agreement.

On 14 February 1979, the U.S. ambassador to Afghanistan, Adolph Dubs, was taken hostage by four men and held in a hotel in Kabul. Security forces stormed the building and killed all four terrorists, but unfortunately Dubs died of wounds received in the incident. The police were criticized for premature action. Muslim extremists, then usually referred to slightly erroneously as the "Muslim Brotherhood" by the western media, were blamed for this terrorist exploit.

The year of 1979 was one of anarchy in Afghanistan. The upheaval increased in the spring, when street fighting and terrorist incidents between the rival wings of the PDP rose to a crescendo and criminals and opportunists took full advantage of the lawless situation. Several people were assassinated, many disappeared, and the prisons began to fill with political detainees as Taraki cracked down heavily in an attempt to restore law and order in the main cities and towns.

A countryside rebellion that had been simmering during the winter, again vaguely ascribed to the Muslim Brotherhood, erupted in the spring, commencing in areas east of Kabul and along the road to the Khyber Pass. By the end of summer this insurgency was widespread, and the insurgents were calling themselves Mujahideen, meaning "Fighters in the Holy War." Soon the Mujahideen claimed to control twenty-one of the country's twenty-six provinces. Desertion from the army became a rising problem, and in October an army mutiny of some proportion was put down with loss of life. Soviet personnel flew aircraft and helicopters against the Mujahideen due to shortages of Afghan pilots.

Even with more Soviet arms and vehicles and the help of Soviet personnel, Taraki seemed unable to suppress the insurrection: he had hopelessly lost control, and his brutality was beginning to appall even the Soviets. The Kremlin arranged for his removal from power. On 14 September 1979, Hafizullah Amin of the Parcham wing of the PDP was put in his place as president of Afghanistan by the Soviets. It is usually alleged that Taraki was killed in a palace coup, but the date and manner of his death are still obscure. The Hafizullah regime later said that Taraki resigned due to ill health on the 16th (two days after the coup) and died on 9 October. Hafizullah Amin estimated that during Taraki's sixteen months in power, he had caused the deaths of between 10,000 and 12,000 people, mostly his political enemies, many of whom were in the Parcham wing of the PDP. Some authorities put the figure even higher, but there is no way of checking the accuracy of such statements.

For the purpose of the Hafizullah Amin coup, the Soviets had moved ten companies of combat troops into Kabul, and after the coup these Soviet subunits remained in the capital. Amin seemed to be no more capable of bringing order out of Afghan chaos than his predecessor, or to be able to contain the Mujahideen tribal insurgency still in progress. Still more Soviet arms were rushed to the Afghan army, now slightly reduced in strength owing to desertion and new conscripts not responding to their call-up summons. By the fall, the Afghans had over 200 T-34, 500 T-54 and T-55 tanks, about 400 BTRs, 900 guns and mortars, 170 Soviet combat aircraft, and about twenty helicopters.

Disappointed and dissatisfied with Amin's performance and his inability to bring the internal situation under control, Soviet leaders summoned him to Moscow on 4 November, ostensibly to discuss the Muslim insurrection. Actually, it was to ask for an account of his stewardship generally, and to persuade him to agree to have Soviet troops stationed on Afghan soil. Amin refused to go to Moscow.

On 13 December 1979, the U.S. government made a formal protest to the USSR, complaining of the sudden concentration of Soviet troops near the Afghan frontier. The U.S. again protested to the USSR on the 23rd, complaining that it was threatening the sovereignty of Afghanistan by dispatching 1,500 Soviet troops to Kabul and protesting the concentration of "three divisions" near the Afghan border. This was an underestimate, as nearly twice that number were already in Afghanistan with the Afghan armed forces, and five Soviet divisions were lining up to move into that country.

The Soviets struck on 25 December 1979. Their military invasion was spearheaded by an initial airlift of about 3,000 airborne troops, who landed suddenly at the Kabul airport. In a coup manufactured by the

Soviets, Amin was killed and replaced by another Soviet nominee. The new Soviet-installed Afghan president was Babrak Karmal, leader of the Parcham wing of the PDP, who had conveniently been sheltering in Moscow, where he was briefed and conditioned for this puppet role.

In answer to international criticism, the Soviets claimed they had been asked to intervene in Afghanistan by its "legal government," headed by Karmal, under the terms of the 1978 Friendship and Cooperation Treaty. As Karmal had accompanied the leading airborne elements of the Soviet invasion, this fiction was widely disbelieved.

The reaction of the United States to this Soviet invasion of Afghanistan was one of surprise and shock. Carter said it was a "blatant violation of accepted international rules of behavior." This was true, but the Soviets never let fine principles deflect them from their ultimate goals. By the end of the year, over 25,000 Soviet troops were in Afghanistan, settling on the cities, airfields, camps, and the strategic road system, with more troops, aircraft, tanks, guns, and vehicles arriving daily.

The Soviet invasion of Afghanistan took the whole world by surprise: it was a brilliant piece of brinkmanship for which the Soviets should be awarded full marks. The Soviets had correctly calculated that the American president would not receive Western European backing for any effective action that would bring the risk of war with the USSR. After their Vietnam experience, the American people would not want American armed forces bogged down in a similar situation in Afghanistan. Also, 1980 was an election year, and Carter could not hope to be reelected if he drew his country into a shooting war.

Had Carter, with the full backing of his European NATO allies, ordered a Red Alert as Nixon had done in 1973 (without NATO allied support) and had NATO forces begun to mobilize, the probabilities are that the Soviets would have backed away and thinned out their troops in Afghanistan quickly, as they did not want an open confrontation with the United States that could escalate into a World War III. The Kremlin leaders respect strength and resolution and take advantage of weakness and hesitation. Soviet calculations and brinkmanship paid off better than the Kremlin leaders had dared to hope.

The Soviets had long been planning such a move and had been simply waiting for the opportunity. To the Soviets, Afghanistan was a crossroads for the next move towards world hegemony. From Afghanistan the Soviets can either expand south into Pakistan towards the Indian Ocean, or west into Iran towards the Persian Gulf. They will do so whenever circumstances are favorable and the moment opportune.

IRAN

At the beginning of the seventies it seemed that the one stable state in the potentially unstable Persian Gulf region, from which the British were fast withdrawing, was that of Iran, which successive U.S. administrations had supported in the hope that it would continue to develop as a pro-Western bastion and a solid outpost of anticommunism. Iran was a member of the Central Treaty Organization (CENTO), a defensive grouping designed as an "upper tier" against Soviet encroachment southwards. Britain, Turkey, Iran, and Pakistan were members, and the United States an associate; but as CENTO had no international force structure or national forces allocated to it, unfortunately it was toothless and ineffective. Nonetheless, it gave a veneer of false confidence to the West and was an irritant to the USSR.

Iran is a very large country, of some 628,000 square miles, with a population estimated to have risen to over 28 million in 1970, and by the end of the decade to about 36 million. The majority of the people are of Farsi stock, that is Persian, who are Muslims of the minority Islamic Shiite sect. (Most Muslims are of the majority Sunni sect.) Persians and Arabs have been historical enemies.

Iran occupies a vital strategic position on the east side of the Persian Gulf, controlling the northern side of the Straits of Hormuz, through which was carried as much as 60 percent of U.S. oil imports, about 70 percent of the oil requirements of Western Europe, and 90 percent of those of Japan (1976). On the east Iran borders Pakistan; on the northeast, Afghanistan; while to the north it has a common land frontier with the USSR of about 1,000 miles; and to its northwest is hostile Iraq.

In 1970, Iran was ruled autocratically by Mohammed Reza Shah Pahlavi, who with American CIA assistance had been brought back from enforced exile and restored to his Peacock Throne in August 1953. At first the shah worked sincerely to develop his country and introduce much needed reform. In 1963, he launched his so-called White Revolution that included land reform, but his attempts at introducing some degree of Westernization met with hard resistance from the mullahs. In 1970 Iran had about 8,000 mosques with about 180,000 mullahs who, in view of the high illiteracy rate, especially in rural areas, held immense power over the people.

Although the youthful shah had begun with good intentions, he gradually became more dictatorial and impatient of obstruction, and the Majlis (parliament) simply became his rubber stamp. The shah's attitude caused protest movements to arise, which were harshly repressed, and soon many people were imprisoned for just expressing contrary political views. Political parties were progressively banned, overseas Iranian students and political exiles mounted demonstrations against the shah in foreign capitals, and rumors of torture of political prisoners became rife. The notorious SAVAK (Sazeman Attalat Va Amniyate Keskvar), the shah's secret security service, was especially blamed for repression and torture.

Traditionally suspicious of Russian nineteenth-century expansion, Iran had at last concluded a friendship treaty with the Soviets in 1921. During World War II, Soviet troops occupied the northern half of Iran (then still known as Persia), and British troops the southern half, to prevent that country from falling into Axis hands or aiding the enemy. The Soviets made themselves unpopular with the Persian central government in Teheran, the capital, by their open support for the Communist Tudeh Party, and for establishing two "independent republics" in two ethnic regions, both on communist lines, early in 1946. One was that of the Kurds, based in the northern city of Mahabad, and the other was that of the Azerbaijanis, based in Tabriz. The Soviets were reluctant to quit Iran, but when they finally did, Teheran troops quickly demolished both these "independent republics" by the end of the year.

After World War II the Soviets maintained contact with Iran on a pragmatic basis, and there was a certain amount of trade between the two countries. Although ostensibly the attitude of the Kremlin was also cool but correct towards the shah, its KGB was burrowing underground in Iran and fomenting subversion. For example, the shah's government in May 1975 claimed that "200 Marxist-anarchist groups" existed in the country and admitted it held about 3,000 of their members in prison. On 2 June 1976, the Iranian prime minister, Amin Abbas Hoveyda, held a press conference at which he alleged that foreign aid and support were being given to terrorists operating inside Iran, and that they had direct links with the Soviet KGB; with the Popular Front for the Liberation of Palestine, the Palestinian terrorist group that extended training facilities to them; and with Colonel Gaddafi of Libya, who provided funds.

Political parties had all been proscribed by Iran in 1970, but in 1975 the government-subsidized Rastakhiz Party was permitted. But it fell apart and was dissolved in October 1978 when government funding ceased. Urban violence began in 1971, but for a while it was contained at a low level by the efficient but brutal SAVAK and other security forces. Weapons in the hands of the terrorists were mainly of Soviet origin, although there were some Chinese and Western ones, too, the latter usually stolen from Iranian armories. During 1976, for example, the government announced that 101 terrorists had either been executed or killed in clashes with the security forces, and that the shah had amnestied "1,903 political prisoners" that year (although it was admitted another 3,000 remained in detention accused of "terrorist crimes").

By this time, with considerable KGB assistance, political unrest had developed in the universities in Teheran. Students organized and spearheaded demonstrations against political repression, but it was not until 11 May 1978 that the first major, openly anti-shahist mass demonstration occurred in the capital. On 16 September, a SAVAK report quoted in the Majlis alleged the "Communists have a nineteen-point plan for violent unrest in Iran."

Pre–World War II government feeling in Iran had been strongly anti-Soviet, and in 1933, the Anticommunist Act was passed. It was not until October 1941 that the Tudeh Party (The Masses) was founded as a legal political party by Iranian Communists released from prison as a result of the Soviet military presence. At first the Tudeh avoided all mention of communism and denied all connection with the USSR, but in fact it was a Communist Party. Flourishing in the days of the joint Soviet-British occupation of Iran, the Tudeh lost influence in the 1950s and 1960s until, with others, it was eventually proscribed.

Supported by the KGB, the Tudeh Party remained active underground, being the largest, best organized, most efficient of the several subversive organizations, although its leaders were in exile in the USSR. The Tudeh Party broadcast propaganda against the shah via its Radio Iran Courier, from a station in East Germany.

A number of the political parties of the ethnic minorities seeking autonomy or independence openly called themselves communists. The largest was the Azerbaijani Communist Party, and another was the Turkoman Communist Party; the Kurds had half a dozen left-wing parties, two of which called themselves Communist.

In 1971, the National Iranian Front (NIF) was formed as an umbrella organization; it was comprised basically of the Iranian Liberation Movement and the Marxist People's Mujahideen but included other anti-shahist groups, both left-wing and Islamic extremist. This was infiltrated by the KGB; members of some groups had direct contact with the KGB, received money from Libya, or were trained by Palestinian groups in South Yemen.

Beginning in 1972, the NIF was persuaded by its left-wing members to describe all its members as "Islamic Marxists" in an effort to appeal to both left-wing and Islamic organizations alike: Marxists were short on Islamic grass-roots support. This coalition was not a success, and agreements broke down in 1974 when the NIF ejected the People's Mujahideen, after which the NIF components splintered into many small groups. Those of the left-wing or with secular aims continued to call themselves Islamic Marxists, and this expression came largely to be used as a collective expression for terrorists of all sorts. Later, the shah blamed the Islamic Marxists as one of the main causes of his downfall. The two most effective terrorist bodies on the troubled Iranian scene were the KGB-sponsored Mujahideen e-Kalk, an Islamic extremist organization, and the Fedayeen e-Kalk, a left-wing secular one. Both were violently opposed to each other, and both were supported by KGB money.

Opposition to the shah now came from three main sources: the Muslim extremists, who were opposed to Westernization, and who wanted an Islamic state; the middle class, or technical class, who wanted a secular liberal democracy; and the left-wing groups that wanted a social democracy on the communist pattern. From mid-1977 onwards these three disparate groups collaborated—or at least there was some liaison between them—with the common aim of removing the shah. A Soviet espionage network was active inside Iran, as evidenced in December 1977 when Gen. Ahmed Moqarebi, director of military planning, was arrested and executed for passing information to the USSR. At the same time, twenty-six other Iranian officers were arrested and secretly tried for similar offenses.

The general ground swell of the anti-shah movement was fired by Ayatollah Khomeini from his exile in adjacent Iraq. His speeches, recorded on cassette tapes and smuggled into Iran, inflamed and incited the people. It was not until October 1978 that the shah was able to persuade the Iraqi government to expel Khomeini, who went to Paris and continued urging the removal of the shah. During 1978, anti-shah demonstrations, strikes, riots, and terrorism increased in volume, causing the Iranian security forces to gradually lose control of the situation. President Carter tried to impose his human rights principles on the shah and to persuade him to release political prisoners. Small batches were reluctantly freed—for example, on 26 October 1978 (his birthday), the shah released just over 1,000—but a far greater number remained in detention. Those released immediately rejoined the anti-shah mass movement as activists.

By the beginning of 1979, the shah's position had become untenable. On 5 January, the leaders of the United States, Britain, France, and West Germany met on the French West Indian island of Guadaloupe to discuss the situation. Chancellor Schmidt of West Germany and Prime Minister Callaghan of Britain were both in favor of giving continued support to the shah; but Carter revealed he had been taking Khomeini's victory for granted since November 1978. Carter then sent Gen. Huyser, deputy commander of NATO in Europe, on his controversial mission to Iran to persuade the military not to mount a coup, but to let the Khomeini revolution take its course, an action that finally pulled the rug from under the shah.

The shah departed from Iran on 15 January 1979. On 1 February, Khomeini arrived in that country from exile. The Islamic revolution is dated from the 12th; and on 1 April, the Islamic Republic of Iran was proclaimed. Iran withdrew from CENTO and brought its expeditionary force back from Oman.

In February 1979, central authority broke down in Iran. The secret twenty-five-man Islamic Revolutionary Council, headed by Khomeini, issued vague directives which were variously interpreted and enforced by the many local "revolutionary committees," many self-appointed, that sprang up to dominate and wreak vengeance. It is almost an understatement to say that for the remainder of the year the country lacked firm central authority and muddled through in a bloody and chaotic way. The army had been persuaded to stay in barracks, and the Islamic Revolutionary Courts arrested generals and other senior officers, who were either imprisoned or executed; many others fled. The armed services were virtually beheaded.

Political parties were free to operate openly, and about one hundred of them appeared to quarrel and fight with each other. Armories had been broken into and plenty of weapons were available to them. The The Mujahideen e-Kalk, guarding Khomeini, bitterly fought the Fedayeen e-Kalk on the streets until their common paymaster, the KGB, stepped in and enforced a truce. On 5 March, Khomeini organized his Revolutionary Guards, or Pasdars, who eventually numbered over 170,000; a multipurpose security force, their task was to establish and maintain order and to enforce his edicts. In the spring, on the periphery of the country, the Kurds, Azerbaijanis, and Turkomans spasmodically fought against the Pasdars, as Khomeini had rejected all their demands for independence or autonomy.

The Kremlin planned to destabilize and regionalize Iran by persuading the ethnic groups to break free from the central government. It intended, if possible, to establish independent Kurdish, Azerbaijani, and

Turkoman states to form a buffer belt across northern Iran that would contain over 12 million people. Khomeini was strongly anti-Soviet because his religious views conflicted with Soviet atheism and because of Soviet meddling in Iran's internal affairs. He saw the hidden Soviet hand behind the many terrorist groups that roamed the streets of Teheran, and he realized the Soviet aim was to "Balkanize" his country. As a Shiite Muslim, Khomeini called on his fellow Shiites in Iraq to rise in revolt against their Sunni minority government. This displeased the USSR, which was backing the Iraqi regime and did not want any Khomeini-instigated Shiite militancy to weaken its authority.

After a while, Khomeini's criticism turned away from the USSR and toward the United States, which became the "Great Satan." Eventually, on 4 November 1979, the U.S. embassy in Teheran was attacked and its personnel captured, thus beginning the long and tragic American hostage situation.

By August 1979, all left-wing political and secular parties had been banned, and only those with Islamic aims were permitted to operate openly. The one exception was the Tudeh Party, which had over one thousand active members, all with considerable revolutionary expertise, and which had firmly supported Khomeini from the start. The KGB instructed the Tudeh Party to work inside the Khomeini "circle" and to prepare to take full advantage of the anticipated power struggle when the seventy-eight-year-old ayatollah died—a day which many in Iran thought would not be long in coming. The Tudeh developed close links with several of Khomeini's aides and with the pro-Khomeini Mujahideen e-Kalk. Several members of the Tudeh Party and the Mujahideen held dual appointments in the leadership of both organizations.

As the seventies drew to a close, the Soviet Radio Baku station continued to pour out propaganda against Khomeini, urging Iranians to "keep your AK-47s ready for the prolonged struggle." There had been no Soviet AK-47s in the shah's armory; the many now possessed by terrorists had been smuggled into the country under KGB supervision. The Soviet imprint on Iran consisted mainly of its effective espionage network, its manipulation of the Tudeh Party, and KGB control of Marxist terrorist groups such as the Fedayeen e-Kalk.

PAKISTAN

When British India was partitioned in 1947, basically on religious divisions of Muslims and Hindu majority population regions, Pakistan emerged as an independent state. It became a republic in 1956. The partition of the Indian sub-continent involved bloodshed, massive transfers of populations, millions of homeless refugees, and a minor war over the Himalayan province of Kashmir, claimed by both Pakistan and India. Pundit Jawaharlal Nehru, the first Indian prime minister, had hoped to obtain the whole of British India intact; but the Muslim leader, Mohammed Ali Jinnah, succeeded in obtaining a separate Muslim state for the Muslim majority regions.

Pakistan was divided in two parts, each a thousand miles away from the other across Indian territory over which Pakistanis could not travel freely. The larger part was known as West Pakistan, which consisted of four major provinces, all ethnically different: Baluchistan, adjacent to Iran and Afghanistan; Sind, in the south, adjacent to India; the Punjab, also adjacent to India; and the North West Frontier Province, adjacent to Afghanistan. The main port was Karachi, and the inland capital was Islamabad. East Pakistan consisted of parts of the Indian provinces of Bengal and Assam.

In 1970, there was hardly a trace of a Soviet imprint on Pakistan, although a few small Soviet loans and some economic aid had been given, together with the usual Soviet "salesman's samples" of arms in the form of a few tanks and aircraft. These were counterbalanced by some Chinese tanks. The armed forces numbered about 325,000 men, and the paramilitary about 225,000. The army, mainly equipped with old British and American weaponry, was formed into fourteen divisions; the air force had about 270 combat aircraft, mainly British and American; and the navy had one submarine and about twenty surface ships, mostly British.

Pakistan was pro-Western in attitude, was a member of both CENTO and SEATO (South East Asia Treaty Organization), but was in confrontation with Afghanistan, partly because of a disputed frontier, and partly because the Afghan government supported the Pathan call for an independent Pushtunistan, which would incorporate the North West Frontier Province inhabited by Pathans. The real enemy was India, with whom Pakistan had already fought two wars. The first was over the Himalayan province of Kashmir, which had a Muslim population but a Hindu ruling dynasty; on partition, the maharajah had opted to join India rather than Muslim Pakistan. An inconclusive war ensued and continued until U.N. observers arrived to police the so-called cease-fire line that ran across the center of the province. India formally annexed Kashmir in 1957.

In 1965, Pakistan and India fought another inconclusive war from April to September. The Soviets became involved in the cease-fire negotiations, masterminded by Prime Minister Kosygin; in January 1966, at Tashkent, in southern USSR, they sponsored an agreement between the two countries to renounce the use of force against each other. When the 1965 war began, the U.S. administration placed an embargo on arms for Pakistan and India, even though Pakistan was a member of CENTO and SEATO (India was not a member of either).

The main West Pakistan internal problem was the National Awami Party, founded in 1955, which called for autonomy for the provinces of both Baluchistan and the North West Frontier Province. With Soviet encouragement, the Afghan government gave sanctuary to exiled Baluchi and Pathan liberation movement personalities, both movements being formally recognized by Moscow. There were about four million Pathans in the North West Frontier Province, who were largely left to their own devices, never having been completely "pacified" by the British, under the guise of having semiautonomous "tribal territory."

In December 1970 and January 1971, the first general election was held in both parts of Pakistan. In West Pakistan it was won by the Pakistan People's Party, led by Zulfikar Bhutto; and in East Pakistan by the Awami League, led by Sheikh Mujibur Rahman, whose political demand was that of autonomy. Bhutto became the prime minister.

On 26 March 1971, Sheikh Rahman declared East Pakistan to be an independent state called Bangladesh. West Pakistani troops were sent to East Pakistan to enforce sovereignty; a civil war began and dragged on. Encouraged by confirmation that the USSR would support India under their friendship treaty, Indian troops invaded East Pakistan on 21 October 1971, and so the third war between Pakistan and India began. On 6 December, India recognized Bangladesh as an independent state.

Bhutto rushed off to Peking, hoping to obtain a similar comforting assurance from China, although there was no formal treaty between the two countries. China and the USSR were in confrontation with each other, and he hoped China might support Pakistan; but he was disappointed. A cease-fire between Pakistani and Indian ground forces in East Pakistan came into effect on 17 December. The Pakistani troops had been soundly defeated by the Indians this time. Bangladesh formally became an independent republic on 17 April 1972.

On 20 December 1971, President Yahya Kahn had resigned. Bhutto became president in his stead, and also martial law administrator. In January 1972, Bhutto took West Pakistan (now known simply as Pakistan) out of the British Commonwealth because of British support for India during this war. He remained president until a new constitution was introduced in 1973, when he again became prime minister. Diplomatic relations between Pakistan and India were not resumed until July 1976.

The U.S. administration imposed an arms embargo against Pakistan when the third war with India began, which although relaxed slightly in 1973 was not lifted until February 1975. In March 1974, Bhutto visited Iran and obtained a loan of $580 million, but the cool, aloof shah did not hit it off with the flamboyant Bhutto. Saudi Arabia and certain other Muslim countries gave money to help keep Pakistan afloat financially. Embargoed by the West generally and having difficulty in obtaining arms elsewhere, Bhutto again visited China in May 1974. Although he did not obtain many weapons, he did get an agreement from the Chinese to construct a road between these two countries (none existed at all) over the mountainous Himalayan mass, often called the "Roof of the World," along the thin sliver of Pakistan territory that extended to touch China in a five-mile common frontier. This project came to be called the Karakoram Highway.

In October 1974, after India had exploded a small nuclear device (in May 1974), Bhutto traveled to Moscow to seek compensatory aid. The Kremlin leaders viewed him coldly, however, arousing Bhutto's suspicions that the USSR would like to gang up with India to conquer and divide Pakistan's provinces. In March 1975, Bhutto visited President Daoud of Afghanistan in Kabul; this offended the Soviets, who did not want to see good relations between these two countries. On the other hand, the Afghan government did not want to see a strong united Pakistan developing, and was still giving sanctuary to Baluchi and Pathan political exiles, as well as forwarding Soviet arms and supplies into the Baluchistan province, which was in a state of insurrection. Ignored by the West, cold-shouldered by the USSR, and given the brush-off by Afghanistan, Bhutto was forced to look to the Chinese for help.

Even though the American arms embargo was lifted, weapons and supplies were slow to arrive in Pakistan, so on 5 April 1976, Bhutto, who had gained covert French cooperation, announced a plan to establish a "collaborative arms industry" with financial support from certain Muslim states and with French technical assistance.

Part of Bhutto's concern with arms sprang from Baluchi insurrections. In 1947, the Communist Party of India had called for an independent state of Baluchistan. Instead, the Baluchis opted, mainly on religious grounds, to become part of Pakistan. Since then, they had become discontented and restive, complaining their province was just a "colony of the Punjab" (the Punjab being the province from which the majority of administrators came). A Baluchistan People's Liberation

Movement (BPLM) had sprung into existence in the province, supported and encouraged by the Soviets.

The Baluchistan province had an area of about 134,000 square miles, largely mountains and desert; but on its Makran coast, bordering the Indian Ocean, was the port of Gwadar, only 330 miles from the Afghan southern border. Other small ports, such as Jiwani, Pasni, Ormara and Soniani, some of which had been used during World War II, could also be developed. These ports were like glittering prizes to the Kremlin and its expanding global navy. The Soviet peace strategy was to encourage the Baluchis to fight for independence; then, when they achieved it, the Soviets hoped in turn that the Baluchis (and the Afghans) would grant them land access to the Indian Ocean.

Baluchi insurrections in the sixties had necessitated military counter-measures into the province, but none were completely successful. When he came to power in 1971, Bhutto wanted to launch a strong military campaign into Baluchistan to completely crush the insurgents. The Paki-stani chief of staff would not agree and so resigned, to be replaced by Gen. Mohammed Zia ul-Haq. Zia declared martial law in Baluchistan. Bhutto tried to obtain the cooperation of the National Awami Party over the Baluchi issue, but again failed.

In January 1973, disturbances again erupted in Baluchistan when a plan for a new federal constitution was presented. Bhutto launched the first of a series of military operations to reduce the Baluchi insurgents, who eventually were able to put over 20,000 armed guerrillas in the field; the struggle lasted for four long years and was again inconclusive. The Soviet imprint now appeared over the Baluchistan province, as Soviet arms and supplies reached the BPLM insurgents through Afghanistan, and its leaders and guerrilla fighters were trained in camps in that country. Heavy censorship blacked out details of the Baluchi insurrec-tion, but it is known that over 45,000 federal troops were involved by 1977; that both Pakistani troops and BPLM guerrillas suffered heavy casualties; that many Baluchis were detained, and a few executed; and that thousands of others fled into adjacent Afghanistan. Bhutto laid a heavy hand on the Baluchi insurrection.

In March 1977, Bhutto's Pakistan People's Party again won the general election, but widespread allegations of vote-rigging and bribery led to riots and disturbances. In July, the armed forces, led by General Zia, seized power and declared martial law. Zia became the chief martial law administrator, then also assumed the presidency in September 1978. Bhutto was sentenced to death on 3 February 1979 and executed on 4 April, despite pleas to Zia for clemency from many international and national leaders, including Brezhnev.

Zia immediately stopped the counterinsurgency campaign in Baluchistan, announced an amnesty, and released Baluchi prisoners. The Baluchistan province remained quiet from July 1977 until the end of the decade, but suspicion and distrust remained between the BPLM, still illegal, and the Islamabad government. In April 1978, when Taraki came to power in Afghanistan, the BPLM leaders sent him a message of congratulations, as did other exiled Baluchi groups. The Soviet imprint faintly rested on the Baluchistan province still. On 29 July 1978, the Afghan government expressed a wish that the "self-determination of Baluchistan and Pushtunistan" should be resolved through negotiations. This upset Zia, who stated that both Baluchistan and the North West Frontier Province had freely opted to join Pakistan, and that it was none of the Afghan government's business.

China had become a "friend of convenience" to Pakistan, and the Karakoram Highway project forged ahead. The road was formally opened in March 1978. This was a setback for the Soviet peace strategy: should there be an armed clash between Pakistan and Afghanistan, and should the Chinese want to intervene on the Pakistan side or even send arms to counter or forestall the Soviets (as they had done the Americans in Korea in 1950), hordes of Chinese soldiers, tanks, guns, and vehicles could quickly flood along the Karakoram Highway into Pakistan. The Soviets had no wish to tangle with the Chinese—at least not yet for a while—but the existence of the Karakoram Highway endangered the probable Soviet-Indian plan to divide Pakistan between them, or to use Indian forces as proxy troops to fight Soviet battles in the region.

After the Taraki coup in Afghanistan, the U.S. administration once again took an interest in Pakistan, and some arms, including F-5 aircraft, were promised. In March 1979, Pakistan withdrew from the CENTO (it had withdrawn from SEATO in 1973), much to the satisfaction of the Kremlin, and could not truly call itself "unaligned." This solidly pro-Western country had been treated as the poor relation in the CENTO setup, especially over arms procurement, by the U.S. administration, and history must question its policy. A militarily strong Pakistan would have been a valuable ally in this part of Southwest Asia, one much more consistently pro-Western and reliable than the mercurial, pro-Soviet India.

In May 1979, the United States again terminated all economic and military aid to Pakistan because it refused to stop work on its nuclear project. In September and again in December, the U.S. administration offered to resume its aid if Pakistan would abandon this project, promising to send some F-16 aircraft instead of the older F-5s. On both occasions Zia refused.

By 1979, Pakistani armed forces amounted to about 428,000 men, which together with about 500,000 reservists meant that the country had almost one million trained servicemen; but these forces were poorly equipped with out-of-date weaponry. A large trained force was asking for modern equipment, but the request was ignored by the U.S. administration. Small quantities of French material had been received, in-including Mirage aircraft, but the country still only had about 250 combat aircraft. Its navy had been increased in ten years by only two second-hand submarines and a few surface ships.

During the second half of the seventies, the generally assumed reason for withholding Western military supplies from Pakistan, apart from Soviet and Indian pressure, even when the Soviet imprint deepened so quickly and heavily on Afghanistan, was the so-called Islamic nuclear bomb. Clearly, a poor, undeveloped Third World country like Pakistan, with so many economic problems, had no business spending money, resources, and energy to produce a military nuclear warhead. But then neither had India, which had exploded one in 1974. Once that had occurred, Bhutto decided that Pakistan must also have a nuclear weapon as a military counterbalance and to deter Indian aggression. The deep hostility between India and Pakistan—over 80 percent of the Pakistani ground forces were deployed against India, for example—was often overlooked by the West.

In early 1976, the French began constructing a nuclear center at Chasna, near Islamabad. Previously, Canada had given nuclear assistance to Pakistan. On 22 March, Bhutto stated that nuclear power for peaceful purposes was urgently needed in Pakistan, and that his government was planning to construct twenty-four nuclear reactors and power plants. Bhutto hastened to add that it was not his intention to manufacture a nuclear bomb, although in fact this was precisely what he was trying to do. Certain Arab countries became interested in this project and secretly produced funds for it. They considered Islamabad sufficiently far away to be safe from any Israeli air attacks; and it would not be easy for the Israeli Mossad (secret service) to operate successfully in a Muslim country to either damage the nuclear reactor or sabotage its apparatus, as had happened in Europe.

When it became obvious that Pakistan was actually working on a nuclear bomb, the U.S. administration sought to pressure that country into abandoning it. In August 1976, Secretary of State Kissinger visited Bhutto and warned him against buying a French reprocessing nuclear plant he was being offered, and against trying to achieve a nuclear military capability. Bhutto brushed Kissinger's warning aside, but American pressure caused the Canadians and French to pull out by the end of the year. This threw Bhutto into the arms of the Chinese, who gave him some nuclear assistance.

When Zia came to power in July 1977, Chinese nuclear coopera- tion suddenly ceased, and the French again returned to Chasna. Libya by this time was showing a distinct interest in the Islamic nuclear bomb and provided funds for the project. The fuel base was changed from plutonium to enriched uranium as it was thought that uranium could be more easily obtainable on international black markets and by other devious means. The world was scoured for uranium and the necessary apparatus. Nuclear installation parts were obtained from West Germany, Britain, France, and Canada, some illicitly and some openly. During 1978, a large consignment of raw uranium was hijacked by Libyan commandos from the Black African state of Niger, a former French colony, and ended up in Pakistan. Niger was the world's third largest exporter of uranium. A West German firm constructed a uranium enrichment plant near Multan, in Pakistan, and by the end of the decade considerable progress had been made on the Islamic nuclear bomb, although the precise stage of its development was not known.

INDIA

India is huge both in size and population, consisting of over 1.26 million square miles, with an estimated population of about 660 million (1979). Within India, the second most populous nation on earth, extremes of poverty and exploitation contrast starkly with wealth and opulence.

Formerly a British possession, India achieved independence in 1947, but some 62 million (1971) Muslims remained in India rather than moving to Pakistan. The huge "impassable" Himalayan mountain barrier in the north had for centuries cushioned India, but it was sud- denly and dramatically penetrated at two points in 1962 by a Chinese invasion force. The Chinese fought a thirty-three day war against the Indians; and then, just as suddenly, they pulled out again. This was a traumatic shock to Prime Minister Nehru, whose policy was one of neutrality and nonalignment. Previously, when pressed to develop his defense forces, he was reputed to have replied, "Defense against what?" After this Chinese invasion, the Indian armed forces were built up to about one million men, all raised by voluntary recruitment.

In 1970, India was led by Prime Minister Indira Gandhi (daughter of the late Pundit Nehru, who headed the majority Congress Party, which came to be called the National Congress Party). Throughout the seventies there were several minor insurrections in the country, mainly in the northeastern regions and adjacent to the border with Burma. These included the Communist-inspired Naxalites, the Mizo National Front, and the Nagaland National Army, all of which demanded autonomy in one form or another. There were also frequent mass demonstrations in the major cities and periodic communal unrest in certain provinces.

A degree of sympathetic liaison had always existed between Nehru and the USSR, perhaps as a reaction against British imperialism, against which he had fought and been imprisoned. This attitude was continued by his daughter, but more cautiously and shrewdly. Both prime ministers firmly maintained that their country was strictly neutral and nonaligned. A general election held in March 1971 resulted in an overwhelming victory for Gandhi's National Congress Party.

Gromyko visited India in August 1971, when a peace, friendship, and cooperation treaty was concluded, under which both countries undertook to come to the aid of the other in the event of a conflict with a third country, and which prohibited each from entering into a military alliance directed against the other. Gandhi hastened to emphasize this was "not a reversal of the Indian traditional nonalignment policy." The following month she visited Moscow to discuss the East Pakistan issue. A comprehensive technical agreement was signed between the Soviet Union and India in September 1972; and in November 1973, both Brezhnev and Gromyko visited India and concluded more minor agreements on the usual pattern.

Communists in India were smaller in number, but active and quarrelsome and compressed into three or four diverse parties and factions. In all, the Communists gained 48 seats (out of 524) in the Lok Sabha (Lower House) in the 1971 election. The Communist Party of India (CPI), sponsored and helped by the Soviets, had a loose liaison with the National Congress Party; at its Ninth Party Congress in October 1971, it claimed a membership of over 230,000. The smaller Communist Party of India (Marxist-Leninist), the CPI(M-L), formed in 1969, had a membership of about 9,000; and it unusually belied its label, as it looked to Peking for its doctrinal guidance, not Moscow. In November 1970, the CPI(M-L) expelled its secretary general, Charu Mazumdar, for "pursuing a Trotskyist adventurist line," after which the party splintered.

These several Communist factions struggled against each other, often fighting violently on the streets of the cities. Generally, the Kremlin viewed these quarreling organizations with suspicion and disfavor, its only exception being to support the CPI, which was allied with Gandhi's National Congress Party.

Accompanied by Gromyko, Brezhnev visited India in November 1973 to persuade Gandhi to become the USSR's partner in a "Soviet-Indian Collective Security Agreement." She refused, insisting that India remain nonaligned. She suggested an "Indian Ocean Zone of Peace," but this was not quite what the Kremlin leaders had in mind. As bait, the Soviets sent a few OSA missile craft to India, and later some aircraft; but Brezhnev did not seem to be able to persuade the politically astute and agile prime minister to walk into the Soviet spider's web. The shah of Iran visited India in October 1974, his object being to persuade Gandhi to collaborate in a new grouping of Indian Ocean countries, to be formed initially on the basis of economic cooperation, and later to develop into a defensive security pact led by Iran. Gandhi did not take to the shah or his suggestion.

Suddenly, on 18 May 1974, the Indian government startled the world by exploding underground a small military nuclear device at Dakran, in the Rajasthan province, using Canadian nonweapon grade nuclear fuel. It was perhaps a prestige act designed mainly to overawe Pakistan. The government stated that it would not explode another one, but the fact remained that India, with acute problems of feeding its population, had become the sixth military nuclear power in the world.

The Soviets did not relax their efforts to implant their imprint on India. In February 1975, Marshal Grechko, the Soviet defense minister, accompanied by Marshal Pavel Kutakhov, commander of the Soviet Air Force, and Admiral Gorshkov, commander of the Soviet Navy, visited that country. That month the U.S. administration had lifted the arms embargo placed on both India and Pakistan during their Bangladesh war. The Soviets wanted to forestall the Americans and supply Soviet arms in quantity to India, but they had less than partial success.

Gandhi went to Moscow in June 1976 and was there when the news was released that she had arranged for ambassadors to be exchanged with China. Brezhnev was not pleased. Gandhi blandly stated that full diplomatic recognition of China was not intended to upset normal good relations with the USSR. The Kremlin leaders found her a difficult lady to deal with. Gandhi had brought a shopping list of nuclear apparatus and fuel and certain sophisticated weapons, but she was not prepared to pay the Soviet price, which was to accept Soviet military advisers and technicians and other curbs. In December 1976, the Soviets agreed to sell 200 tons of heavy water for use in the Indian nuclear program: that was all. By this time India had eight Soviet submarines, eight OSA missile craft, about seventy SU-7 aircraft, and 220 MiG-21s; the bulk of the remainder of Indian military equipment and weaponry came from Western sources.

Meanwhile, Gandhi became more and more impatient and dictatorial in dealing with parliamentary opposition and general criticism. In 1975, she introduced a state of emergency in India, which enabled her to rule by decree. Soon many political parties and organizations were banned, including all Communist ones except the Moscow-backed CPI, which steadfastly supported her National Congress Party. Eventually, Gandhi was convicted of electoral offenses, but the conviction was set aside by the Supreme Court.

When the National Congress Party was swept from power in the elections of March 1977, victory went to the newly-formed Janata Party, led by eighty-one-year-old Morarji Desai, who became prime minister. The CPI admitted it had made a mistake in allying itself with the National Congress Party. The several other Communist parties, all again legalized, continued to bicker among themselves.

One of Desai's first statements on foreign policy, in March 1977, was to declare that India would not "be properly nonaligned." When Gromyko visited India the following month to test the attitude of Desai towards the USSR, he found it to be cool. Although a couple of small technical agreements were concluded, he made no headway with the new Indian prime minister.

Desai had made a preelection pledge to abrogate the Soviet-Indian Friendship Treaty; but once in office, he found it better to retain that link with the USSR. Indeed, in October 1977, he visited Moscow. The joint declaration at the termination of his talks with the Brezhnev Trio emphasized "close USSR-Indian relations." However, Desai was not happy with the Soviets, and some time afterwards (at a public meeting in Delhi, on 4 December 1980) stated, "The Soviet leaders tried to persuade me that India should teach Pakistan a lesson," and alleged the Soviets continually tried to incite him to attack Pakistan.

Much as an afterthought to the seventies, elections were again held in India in January 1980. Gandhi and her National Congress Party were swept back into power once again. Communists gained forty-six seats in all. Commenting on the Soviet invasion of Afghanistan, Minister

Gandhi stated that "what happened in Afghanistan is an internal matter of that country," adding that she did not approve of "one-sided condemnation." She had nailed her colors to the Soviet mast.

SRI LANKA (CEYLON)

Lying in the Indian Ocean just off the southern tip of India, the small island of Ceylon, a former British colony, became self-governing in 1948, remaining a member of the British Commonwealth. Its governments were increasingly left-wing in character and flirted with both Moscow and Peking, getting more response from China, which provided aids and loans. By 1970, Kremlin leaders regarded Ceylon as being vaguely in the Chinese sphere of influence. Ceylon had great strategic value: once a British naval base, it had considerable facilities, especially at the port of Trincomalee on the east coast. British withdrawal had left a Great Power naval vacuum in the Indian Ocean.

In the general election of May 1970, the Sri Lanka Freedom Party, led by Sirimavo Bandaranaike (whose husband, Prime Minister Solomon Bandaranaike, had been assassinated in 1959), came to power, dominating a three-party left-wing coalition known as the United Front. One coalition member was the Lanka Sama Samaja (Ceylon Equal Society Party); formed in 1935 as a broadly based Marxist organization, it embraced Trotskyism in 1940. In 1964, it was expelled from the Fourth Trotskyist International for its alliance with the Sri Lanka Freedom Party. It was allocated three ministerial posts in the Bandaranaike Cabinet. The other coalition member was the Moscow-oriented Communist Party, which was given one Cabinet post. Of the 150 contested seats in the House of Representatives, Bandaranaike's party gained 90 seats, the Trotskyists 19, and the Communist Party 6.

On the domestic front, Bandaranaike had promised a program of nationalization of foreign-owned tea and rubber estates, and agrarian reform, while her foreign policy was to continue to keep Ceylon independent and unaligned. In June, the Ceylon government extended full diplomatic recognition to both the Democratic Government of Vietnam and that of North Korea. In October, it closed down the American-sponsored Asia Foundation, alleging that it was a "subversive imperialist agency."

Delay in implementing the promised nationalization and agrarian reforms, coupled with rising prices, economic difficulties, and the high rate of unemployment, especially among university graduates, resulted in an outbreak of demonstrations against the government that burst into a full-scale insurgency, beginning in March 1971. This was largely instigated and aided by the North Koreans. On 5 March, terrorist incidents occurred in Colombo, the capital, and quickly spread to other cities. On the 6th, the U.S. embassy in Colombo was attacked by bomb-throwing insurgents.

The insurgent organization was the People's Liberation Front (Janatha Vimukthi Peramuna, or JVP), led by Rohan Wijeweera, who had been a student in Moscow and then spent some time in North Korea. He was demanding the "immediate implementation of socialism." Members of the JVP were mainly university students and un-employed graduates, and it was organized on the communist cell-structure pattern. The JVP frequently referred to itself as the Che Guevara Movement, which left its ultimate aims in little doubt. Although some estimates were considerably higher, it was thought that eventually the JVP had at least 25,000 active members and sympathizers, many of whom were armed.

After the discovery of a large cache of arms, explosives, and bomb-making ingredients at the University of Ceylon, on 23 March 1971, the government declared a state of emergency and introduced the death penalty for arson, looting, damage by explosions, and "trespass." Censorship was imposed and detention without trial was freely used. The authorities stated they had uncovered a plot to overthrow the government. The small army combined with the police to fight this insurgency threat. The JVP guerrillas seized many police stations throughout the country, and the revolt spread islandwide. The armed forces then consisted of about 12,500 men poorly equipped to cope with such an emergency, so foreign aid was sought and selectively accepted from certain countries.[2] For example, the United States provided six helicopters, and the USSR six MiG-17 aircraft.

Driven from the cities, the JVP insurgents tried to emulate the guerrilla tactics expounded by Mao Tse-tung, basing themselves in the remoter sectors of central and southern Ceylon. For about a month they controlled large rural areas in the interior. By mid-April, the forces estimated there were still about 4,000 armed JVP insurgents at large, scattered in some 1,200 square miles of forested hills, rubber plantations, and coconut groves. Identifying the mainspring behind

[2]By 1976, the armed forces of Sri Lanka had increased in strength to about 13,600 men, and their equipment included ten Soviet BTR-152s, six MiG aircraft, and six Chinese patrol craft; otherwise the weaponry came from Western sources.

this communist revolt, the government closed down the North Korean embassy in Colombo on 15 April and deported the ambassador and all personnel.

Severed from active North Korean assistance, the JVP insurgents did less well. Government security forces progressively and successfully harried them, until on 23 April, Bandaranaike claimed that the army was in full control of the situation. She appealed to the Communist insurgents to surrender. On 1 May, a four-day amnesty began when aircraft dropped over half a million leaflets, entitled "A Notice to Misguided Youth," over the guerrilla centers of resistance. On the 5th, the government stated that 3,188 rebels had surrendered to the security forces; other surrenders followed, including that of Rohan Wijeweera, the leader of the JVP revolt.

The intellectual leadership of the JVP had failed to rouse insurgency among the peasants and workers in the interior of Ceylon. Conventional troops not all that well equipped or conditioned for the purpose had defeated armed Communist guerrillas in the field. This example of how a Communist rural guerrilla campaign against a central government can be crushed by conventional means deserves publicity, praise, and serious attention.

In May 1972, a republican constitution was adopted in Ceylon, and the name of the country changed to Sri Lanka, meaning "Resplendent Island." Bandaranaike had difficulty controlling her Communist allies within the United Front coalition, and on one occasion, in September 1973, had to expel them for criticizing her own Sri Lanka Freedom Party; but she took them back in June 1974. Bandaranaike's government did not get around to nationalizing foreign-owned plantations until October 1975, after which unrest on the island again slowly mounted. February 1977 was a significant month: apart from the end of the state of emergency, there was a series of strikes and unrest at the universities; the Communists and Trotskyists withdrew from the United Coalition; and the insurgent JVP once again became a legal party.

In a general election held in July 1977, Bandaranaike's Sri Lanka Freedom Party suffered defeat, and neither the Communists nor the Trotskyists won any seats at all. Victory was gained by the more moderate United National Party, led by Junius Jayawardene, who became prime minister. He implemented an executive presidential system of government and in February 1978 became the first president of Sri Lanka.

Small and remote from the centers of Soviet and Western powers, Sri Lanka seemed content with its isolation, hoping to be overlooked in any regional superpower struggle for zones of influence. Few jet-setting political leaders on their tours of world capitals even bothered to visit Sri Lanka. One exception was the Australian prime minister, Gough Whitlam, who visited Bandaranaike in December 1974; he stated that his government firmly opposed any increase in either United States or Soviet naval strengths in the Indian Ocean and rejected the idea of any escalation of force there. One other was the roving Cambodian foreign minister of the Pol Pot regime, Ieng Sary, who visited Sri Lanka in March 1977, but he had little to say and was coolly received.

The unspoken Sri Lankan objective seems to be to retain its neutral and unaligned status unobtrusively and to avoid being caught up in the East-West conflict. Somewhat surprisingly, in the seventies Sri Lanka was not a priority Soviet target, and the decade ended without any discernable Soviet imprint being imposed on that island.

8　The Soviet Imprint on Southeast Asia

The Presidential Palace in Saigon was not entered by a barefoot guerrilla but by a North Vietnamese tank with an enormous cannon.
—William E. Colby, in *Honorable Men: My Life in the CIA*
(New York: Simon and Schuster, 1970)

AMERICAN MILITARY INVOLVEMENT in Vietnam, Cambodia, and Laos from the mid-sixties to the mid-seventies has been extensively written about, often with a partisan pen, which tends to depict the American government at best as being foolish and naive, and at worst imperialistic and criminal. History will, I am sure, view American involvement in Vietnam in a far different light. American intervention in Vietnam was as necessary in 1965 as it had been in Korea in 1950 to show Western determination to halt the creeping tide of world communism. The fact that it was not successful and the reasons why are different issues. Here it is sufficient to consider the massive Soviet material support for Communist forces in Southeast Asia in the seventies, Soviet rivalry with China, the Soviet use of Vietnamese troops as proxy forces, and the Chinese punishment of Vietnam.

Before World War II, the region of Southeast Asia that comprised Tongking, Annam, Cochin China, Laos, and Cambodia was part of the French colonial empire; and during the war it was occupied by the Japanese. After World War II, the French tried to regain their former position and status as colonial masters but ran into opposition. Believing the statements of the principal Western leaders, the peoples of this region expected to be automatically granted independence, which the French refused to grant. This rejection drove many moderate leaders and the majority of the people into the camp of Ho Chi Minh, the veteran Communist leader who, ejected from Hanoi by the French, took to the mountainous, jungle-clad countryside in Tongking to launch a

161

guerrilla campaign against the French.[1] His Viet Minh guerrilla army, led by Gen. Vo Nguyen Giap, a former schoolteacher, outmaneuvered French conventional forces, eventually inflicting a massive defeat on them at Dien Bien Phu in 1954, after which the French withdrew from their former Southeast Asian colonial empire.

In 1955, the thin strip of territory called Annam was divided along the Seventeenth Parallel. Its northern part, together with Tongking, became known as North Vietnam; and its southern part, together with Cochin China, became South Vietnam. A narrow demilitarized zone separated the two states. Both Cambodia and Laos, adjoining states, were also granted independence. Under the leadership of Ho Chi Minh, with Soviet and Chinese help, North Vietnam quickly developed into a Communist state. Prime Minister (soon President) Ngo Dinh Diem, with considerable economic aid from the United States, attempted to turn South Vietnam into a liberal democracy on the Western pattern, but from the outset he had to contend with Communist guerrilla activity in the countryside that continually increased in volume.

By 1960, Ho Chi Minh had put his Communist state together and was able to turn his attention southwards towards South Vietnam. His intention was to unite the two Vietnams under his Communist leadership. A supply route was developed through the remote, sparsely inhabited, dense jungle areas in Laos and Cambodia, just adjacent to the South Vietnam border, which became known as the Ho Chi Minh Trail and along which the North Vietnamese government sent arms, supplies, and guerrilla fighters into South Vietnam. These Communist guerrillas, the Viet Cong, broke down law and order by terrorist activity, initially by mainly eliminating government-appointed village headmen, and soon dominated large areas in the less accessible parts of the country.

The South Vietnamese government found itself in an increasingly adverse internal security situation. In March 1965, American military involvement began.

By 1970, a fierce guerrilla war had developed between the combined American and South Vietnamese forces and the opposing Communist ones. The Kremlin was actively pursuing its policy of intervening in so-called revolutionary wars by sending quantities of arms to local Communist or left-wing movements. The Soviets considered these to be "low risk" conflicts, meaning the Soviet Union as such would not be brought

---

[1] See Edgar O'Ballance, *The Indo-China War, 1945–54: A Study in Guerrilla Warfare* (London: Faber and Faber, 1964).

into abrupt confrontation with the United States but could skulk in the shadows and officially disclaim any responsibility.

That year the new Soviet MiG-23 aircraft appeared in North Vietnam. In January, the U.S. Pentagon estimated there were about 240,000 armed Communist regulars and guerrillas in South Vietnam; large numbers of both in Laos and Cambodia; and that Soviet and Chinese supplies to them were in full flow along the Ho Chi Minh Trail. South Vietnam was led by President Nguyen Van Thieu, who had been elected to office in October 1967. The Paris Peace Talks, begun haltingly in January 1969, stumbled ineffectively along, while the intensity and bitterness of the war increased.

By this time, Soviet infantry-type arms were beginning to replace Chinese ones; the Soviet AK-47 automatic rifle was replacing the much less efficient Chinese "burp-gun." The acceptance of Soviet arms meant that the Communist guerrillas using them had to rely exclusively on the USSR for ammunition; they could not use either Chinese or captured Western types. The Chinese had previously supplied the bulk of the Viet Cong and North Vietnamese infantry arms; but now the Soviet Union was competing with the Chinese for influence. The Soviets had always supplied the more advanced, sophisticated weaponry such as MiG aircraft, SAMs, ZSU antiaircraft guns, tanks, and naval patrol craft. In 1970, there were over 40,000 Soviet military personnel in North Vietnam.

The opposing force levels were high in 1970. North Vietnam had over 432,000 men in the regular armed forces, which possessed at least 6,000 antiaircraft guns, including many ZSUs; fifty SAM-2 launchers, together with detecting and tracking radars; over 400 tanks and armored vehicles; and over 130 Soviet aircraft. In addition, its paramilitary and militia forces amounted to about 450,000 men and women. The regular armed forces of South Vietnam totaled just over 500,000; in addition, there were almost two million people in the paramilitary forces. The South Vietnamese air force had over 370 U.S. combat aircraft.

In October 1971, Podgorny visited North Vietnam to conclude military and economic agreements. To counter American bombing of North Vietnam, more SAM-2s and their attendant radars were sent; within a year, the country had forty-six battalions, each with six SAM-2 launchers. The number of Soviet military advisers and technicians doubled to about 80,000. The Soviet problem was that at least two-thirds of the essential advanced military material had to be shipped by way of the Cape of Good Hope to Haiphong, the main port of North Vietnam, partly because the Suez Canal was closed (from 1967 to 1975), but mainly because the Chinese disrupted the transportation of Soviet material being sent across China by rail—the obvious route. The supply of arms and material to the Communist armies fighting in South Vietnam, Laos, and Cambodia became a contentious issue and caused acrimonious controversy between the Soviets and the Chinese, as each struggled to obtain paramount influence in that region of Southeast Asia.

Within the North Vietnamese Politburo there arose a pro-Chinese and a pro-Soviet faction. Ho Chi Minh silently straddled the fence, playing one Communist power off against the other. General Giap, who had visited Moscow, was pro-Soviet, as was the North Vietnamese prime minister, Pham Van Dong. This division within the North Vietnamese Politburo was reflected in the leadership of the National Liberation Front, fighting inside South Vietnam, whose pro-Soviet faction wanted to negotiate with the South Vietnamese government to end the war, and whose pro-Chinese faction rejected such negotiations and insisted on continuing protracted guerrilla war. Although Ho Chi Minh had no intention of allowing his country to become a Chinese satellite—it had happened previously in history and left a bitter taste and bitter thoughts —the emphasis within his Politburo came to be pro-Soviet.

The Soviets did not like being played off against the Chinese by the North Vietnamese. During 1963, the Soviet Union temporarily suspended all shipments of military material to North Vietnam in an attempt to bring Ho Chi Minh to the Soviet heel; but this proved to be counterproductive. The Chinese simply took the opportunity to increase their shipments. Ho Chi Minh refused to accept the Order of Lenin, as he did not want to offend the Chinese, saying tactfully that he would wait until the war against the United States had been won.

As a face-saver, North Vietnamese representatives technically took charge of the Soviet material when it reached the Chinese frontier; but even then it took weeks to reach the North Vietnamese border. Soviet military material in transit across China was often pilfered by the Red Guards and harassed by many "inspections" and other deliberate delays. In short, weapons sent from the Soviet Union by sea and those sent across China usually took about the same time to reach their destination; this seemed to average about two months. Chou En-lai, the Chinese prime minister, made counter allegations that the Soviets were undermining North Vietnamese unity against the main Communist enemy, the United States.

At long last, on 27 January 1973, the Paris Agreements were signed by representatives of the United States, South Vietnam, North Vietnam, and the PRG of South Vietnam. By the end of March, the last U.S.

combat troops had been withdrawn from South Vietnam. The Communists had no intention of honoring this agreement, and they hurriedly prepared to seize full control of South Vietnam by force and to oust the Thieu government. A sizable number of Communist PRG troops, usually estimated as being in excess of 300,000, remained inside South Vietnam after the Paris Agreements had been concluded. During 1974, the Ho Chi Minh Trail, previously a maze of jungle tracks along which guerrillas slowly marched southwards, taking up to four months to reach their final destination inside South Vietnam, was improved, and all-weather roads and bridges were constructed, enabling truck convoys to move Communist soldiers and supplies much faster. Inside South Vietnam, the swelling Communist guerrilla armies exerted increasing pressure at many points against the ARVN.

The combined general offensive of North Vietnamese and PRG armies began in March 1975. Saigon, the capital of South Vietnam, fell on 30 April. On 2 July 1976, the two Vietnams were formally united and declared to be the Socialist Republic of Vietnam. With its capital at Hanoi and with a population of almost 50 million people, it became the third most populous Communist state in the world. In September, the SEATO organization was dissolved: the fall of South Vietnam had been its death blow.

After the Paris Agreements of 1973, the so-called Nixon Doctrine for Southeast Asia evolved. The United States would not intervene in cases of "internal subversion," but in the case of "external subversion," a nation could ask for American help. However, the responsibility of ensuring that the non-Communist states of Southeast Asia did not fall to the Communists was to be devolved onto "pillars" like Japan, Europe, and the Southeast Asian countries themselves. The unfortunate drawback to this Nixon Doctrine was that none of the "pillars" mentioned had any influence on the Soviet target countries. When President Ford came to office, his policy was that the United States would guarantee the sovereignty and territorial integrity of the non-Communist nations in Southeast Asia. Unfortunately, by this time the United States did not have sufficient credibility in this region to convince the target countries they could rely on the United States for protection.

Secretary of State Henry Kissinger had been involved in the formulation of these two doctrines, uttered at a time of American military misfortunes, and he was distrusted by most Southeast Asian states. They felt he had sold the South Vietnamese down the river over the Paris Agreements. Some argued that these two American doctrines generally gave the Communists more opportunity and scope for aggression; others consoled themselves with the hope that the Communists were too divided among themselves to be effectively aggressive enough to spread their power and influence into unaligned states or those sympathetic to the West.

In Laos, a country with an area of about 90,000 square miles and a population of about three million, the Communist Pathet Lao guerrilla army, backed by North Vietnamese troops, had long been engaged in what was virtually a three-sided military struggle for power; they fought against the right-wing government forces and those of the "neutralists." In February 1973, a "Stand Still Agreement" between the three had been concluded. Early in 1975, more North Vietnamese soldiers moved into Laos to launch an offensive in conjunction with the Pathet Lao. By May, the country was under full communist control.

In Cambodia, after the Paris Agreements in 1973, there remained at least 25,000 regular North Vietnamese troops, mainly in the "sanctuary" areas near the South Vietnamese border. As the Ho Chi Minh Trail improved, more poured in. Cambodia had become the scene of proxy fighting between the army of Lon Nol, who had ousted Prince Norodom Sihanouk in 1970 and was backed by the United States, and the Communist Khmer Rouge coalition, nominally led by the absentee Prince Sihanouk, which was supported by the Chinese. Prince Sihanouk, who spent his time in either China or North Korea, had made an uneasy alliance with the Khmer Rouge, but was not part of it. The United States provided Lon Nol with some arms and, more importantly, gave him some air support against the Khmer Rouge guerrillas.

The USSR, which had been backing the Lon Nol government, saw that the situation in Cambodia was not to its liking. The Khmer Rouge were fighting the Americans as Chinese proxy troops. In an attempt to wrest the sponsorship of the Khmer Rouge from the Chinese, in March 1975, coincident with the beginning of the North Vietnamese offensives in South Vietnam and Laos, the Soviets switched sides, abandoned Lon Nol, and recognized the Sihanouk Khmer Rouge faction as the government of Cambodia. However, the Khmer Rouge did not reciprocate; they continued to look to Peking for support, ignoring the beckoning signs from Moscow. The Soviets temporarily lost out in Cambodia.

In April 1975, the Khmer Rouge guerrilla forces, which consisted of several diverse groups, drove Lon Nol from Phnom Penh, the capital of Cambodia. With his army of probably over 20,000 men, he reverted to guerrilla warfare in the countryside, basing himself in the remote Thai border regions. In September, Pol Pot assumed the leadership of the newly installed Khmer Rouge government and renamed his country

Democratic Kampuchea, obtaining recognition from both China and North Korea.

Friction arose between the Communist governments of Vietnam and and Kampuchea, mainly over disputed sections of their common frontier and control of ethnic groups in the border areas. For example, Pol Pot claimed Cochin China, where it was hoped oil would be found in quantity, but which had been incorporated into Vietnam. In mid-1978, border fighting broke out between these two countries and fitfully continued. During the Pol Pot regime (1975-78), the inhabitants were driven from Phnom Penh and other main cities into the countryside to work in the fields as peasants; machinery and all Western goods and appliances, such as telephones, radios, and typewriters were destroyed; factories and many offices were also destroyed; and irrigation systems were deliberately broken down. This brought general devastation and famine to the country. There were also many executions and some massacres.

The United Nations later estimated that 3.4 million Kampucheans (the population was then about 7.7 million) were either killed or died of starvation or lack of medical attention (all hospitals having been gutted) during the Pol Pot government's period in office. This U.N. figure is thought to be a slight exaggeration; the number of dead is usually thought to be in the region of two million. Later, in July 1981, Ieng Sary, Pol Pot's foreign minister, insisted that the Kampuchean death toll was only 20,000 to 30,000, which is far too low an estimate to be credible.

In August 1967, the Philippines, Indonesia, Thailand, Malaysia, and Singapore formed the Association of South East Asian Nations (ASEAN) to promote economic and social cooperation among themselves. This was known as the Bangkok Declaration. These states wanted their region to be a zone of peace, and so refused to form themselves into a defensive alliance or to enter into military treaties with any outside nation. ASEAN especially wanted to avoid being drawn into the conflict between powers seeking spheres of influence; but at a meeting in Singapore in July 1977, ASEAN representatives agreed to seek peaceful contact with the Communist nations in Southeast Asia.

Western leaders wanted ASEAN—whose nations generally were pro-Western and anti-Communist—to develop into a military alliance that perhaps could be extended to include Japan and Australasia. Communist leaders sought to prevent this; for example, in September 1978, Vietnamese Prime Minister Pham Van Dong visited ASEAN states to drum up support for the Vietnamese in their confrontation with China, but he failed to obtain any favorable response, as all the ASEAN states wanted to remain strict neutrals. Later, in November, Chinese Vice

Prime Minister Teng Hsiao-ping visited Thailand, Singapore, and Burma (the latter not an ASEAN member) to persuade their governments to support China against Vietnam. Again, the two ASEAN members declined to become involved in the China-Vietnam confrontation, as did Burma.

After the unification of Vietnam in 1975, the Soviets gave the country massive economic and technical aid, and taking advantage of inherent Vietnamese hostility towards the Chinese, elbowed China aside. The Chinese were also disadvantaged as they had not fully recovered from the devastating effects of their Great Cultural Revolution; their general level of technology, industry, and production could not successfully compete with that of the USSR. Vietnam quickly became a Soviet client state, with thousands of Soviet and East European personnel working on development projects in the country. In July 1977, Vietnam became a member of the United Nations; and in June 1978, it became a full member of COMECON. In July, the Chinese government suspended all forms of economic and other aid to Vietnam, leaving the field clear for the Soviets in this respect. On 3 November 1978, a friendship and cooperation treaty was concluded between the USSR and Vietnam: Vietnam became a Soviet satellite state.

Amazed at the success of their Cuban proxy troops in Angola and the Horn of Africa, and the lack of positive American response, the Kremlin leaders decided to coopt Vietnamese forces into this role to fight for them in Southeast Asia against the Chinese. More Soviet modern military equipment and weapons were sent to Vietnam, and the Soviets stirred up friction with both Kampuchea and China.

On 31 July 1978, the Chinese government assured a visiting Kampuchean delegation to Peking that it would afford Kampuchea aid in the event of a Vietnamese invasion; and in September that year, the Sino-Soviet Friendship Treaty (of 1950) was allowed to lapse. Vietnamese troops began deploying against Kampuchea, and on 1 December, China sent six MiG-19s. (The Kampucheans also had American combat and transport aircraft). On the 27th, advancing on a broad front, Vietnamese divisions invaded Kampuchea, sweeping all opposition before them, to reach and occupy Phnom Penh. Pol Pot's Chinese-backed regime fled the capital, and his 25,000-strong Khmer Rouge army withdrew into the countryside to wage guerrilla warfare against the invaders.

In their advance, the Vietnamese forces had taken with them the leaders of the Kampuchean National United Front, headed by a Soviet puppet, Heng Samrin, a Khmer Rouge defector. On 8 January 1979, Samrin was installed in Phnom Penh as head of the Kampuchean government, which was formally recognized the following day by the USSR. Some 200,000 Vietnamese troops remained in occupation in Kampuchea and were soon involved in combating Pol Pot's Khmer Rouge guerrilla army and other small independent groups of guerrillas that roamed the hostile hinterland. Ho Chi Minh's aim of a united Indochina under Vietnamese domination had come to fruition; although Kampuchea was not completely occupied, Vietnamese troops settled on the cities, towns, and road communications and controlled a major portion of the country. The variation was that the Vietnamese had achieved this at the behest of their puppet-master, the Kremlin.

When Vietnam was unified in 1975, the many private traders in the former South Vietnam territory were allowed to continue in business until the economy had been completely communized. Many of them were mostly Hoa, that is, Chinese whose families in some cases had lived in the country for generations. In all, there were about 1.5 million Hoa in Vietnam, many of whom retained their Chinese citizenship. Relations between the Hoa and the Vietnamese had always been uneasy and suspicious, partly because of ethnic dislike of each other and partly because the Hoa always appeared to be the "haves" and the Vietnamese peasants the "have nots."

Commencing in 1975, numbers of Hoa traders were expelled from Vietnam. This outflow rose to a crescendo during 1978, the unfortunate refugees becoming known as the "boat people" who fled, were ejected, or were tricked into leaving Vietnam in small boats to try to obtain sanctuary in adjacent Southeast Asian countries. Some of the boats were grossly overloaded, and others unseaworthy, and many such craft and their passengers were lost at sea. A number of Hoa returned to China, but there was a reluctance on the part of the Chinese government to accept too many of them, and a corresponding reluctance on the part of the Hoa entrepreneurs to "return" to their now Communist "homeland."

In March 1978, the Vietnamese government banned all private trading operated by the Hoa; by May, it had ejected over 83,000 of them. The ranks of the "boat people" increased considerably: by the spring of 1979, they numbered over 250,000. On 2 July, ASEAN states refused to accept any more. The Chinese government officially protested to Vietnam against this expulsion of the Hoa.

Meanwhile, differences between Vietnam and China surfaced over disputed frontier areas, which under Soviet instigation developed into open friction. The first armed clash on the Vietnam-China border of any magnitude occurred in August 1978; others followed, until casualties in frontier skirmishing were almost of daily occurrence. The Vietnam invasion of Kampuchea in December 1978 and the ousting of the Chinese-backed Pol Pot regime upset the Chinese government. On 7 February 1979, Teng Hsiao-ping, chief of staff of the huge Chinese People's Liberation Army[4] as well as vice prime minister, said, Vietnam must be punished severely, and China is considering taking appropriate action." He was as good as his word. On 17 February 1979, the Chinese launched a massive attack across the 450-mile-long frontier into Tonking province. Penetrating a short way into Vietnam on five axes, they moved on routes that converged on Hanoi, the capital. The initial waves consisted of about 120,000 Chinese infantry troops, but their advance was slow through the jungle-clad hills and valleys in the frontier areas. The Chinese were opposed by the 70,000-strong regular Frontier Security Force, and the 60,000-strong regional armed militia.

Still the defense minister, the veteran General Giap was responsible for the defense of his country. He had only six regular divisions in Vietnam proper, as fifteen were still in Kampuchea and six in Laos. The Chinese hoped to panic him into withdrawing divisions from Kampuchea, which would relieve pressure on Pol Pot's Khmer Rouge guerrillas. The Chinese also hoped that Giap would panic and disperse his available divisions, fanlike, to meet the invaders, and so strip Hanoi and other main Vietnamese cities of regular units, leaving their defense entirely to the local militia.

Giap did not panic, but waited to see where the main Chinese thrust would be made. As anxious days passed, he brought one division back from Kampuchea and ordered another to move from Hanoi towards the combat zones. This Chinese surprise attack caused some alarm in Vietnam, though, and although Giap remained calm, certain precautions were taken, such as mobilizing the militia and reservists and conscripting civilians for certain backup jobs. Concrete pillboxes were constructed in and around Hanoi, and the old one-man street foxholes of the days of the American bombing were cleaned out and made useable again, and more excavated, as the Vietnamese government prepared to put up stiff resistance against the Chinese invaders. The political aspect was not overlooked: Party records and state documents were removed from Hanoi to Hue for safety. Also, Ho Chi Minh's embalmed body was lowered into a steel vault within his mausoleum to preserve it for Communist posterity.

---

[4]The Chinese regular PLA had over 3.6 million soldiers, and its armed militia numbered over seven million (IISS figures).

Of the some 600,000 Chinese troops mustered for this campaign, eventually about 200,000 entered Vietnam. Suddenly, on 5 March, the Chinese government announced that its punitive force was to withdraw, having "taught the Vietnamese a lesson for their crime." By the 15th, the last Chinese soldier was clear of Vietnamese territory, leaving behind parts of six provinces completely devastated. The deepest Chinese penetration was eighteen miles, and the main Chinese prestige gain was to seize the Vietnamese frontier town of Lang Son. The Vietnamese government stated that 320 villages had been razed to the ground.

This twenty-eight-day war between Vietnam and China was inconclusive. The large Chinese invasion force had been held within a few miles of the frontier by the comparatively small Vietnamese Border Security Force and the local part-time militia. There were about 3,000 Soviet personnel with the Vietnamese armed forces, but none in a command or executive position; this number doubled before the end of the year. The most unusual feature of this war was that neither side used any aircraft at all: not even a single reconnaissance or bombing sortie was flown over enemy lines. China had at least 1,000 combat aircraft in southern China,[5] mostly Chinese-assembled MiG-19s, which were almost vintage. Vietnam had about 500 fairly modern Soviet combat aircraft, several helicopters, and twenty regiments of SAMs with modern radar.

Led by the seventy-three-year-old Gen. Hsu Shih-yu, the Chinese army was shown still to be the lumbering infantry it was in Korea in 1950, neither conditioned nor trained for modern warfare, poorly equipped, and lacking motor transport, internal radio communication, and coordination. China admitted it had suffered about 20,000 casualties and it is probable the Vietnamese suffered the same number. On 11 March, the Chinese withdrew all its experts working on Chinese-instigated development projects in Laos, thus leaving that field clear for the Soviets.

There can be little doubt that the Kremlin was firmly supporting, and perhaps guiding, their Vietnamese proxy troops. On 22 February, only five days after the Chinese invasion of Vietnam, it mounted a gigantic airlift of weapons, ammunition, spares, and supplies. It was essential to the Kremlin leaders that Soviet weapons be seen to be superior to Chinese ones in battle. During this Chinese invasion the small Soviet naval task force of some twelve surface ships in Vietnamese waters was joined by the *Admiral Senyavin,* a command cruiser, the flagship of

---

[5] Out of a total of about 4,700 aircraft (IISS figures).

the Soviet Pacific Fleet. On 14 May 1979, Deputy Soviet Foreign Minister Nikolai Firyubin announced that Soviet warships were using the U.S.-built naval facilities at Cam Ranh Bay base. He should have added that Soviet submarines were also using the newly built submarine pens there as well.

By the end of the seventies the Soviet imprint was firmly resting on Vietnam, and, through Vietnam, on Laos and the greater part of Kampuchea. With a poor basic economy, a succession of alternate droughts and bad harvests, and insufficient oil, Vietnam had become a Soviet satellite state—a sort of Asian Cuba—dependent almost completely on Soviet aid. Accordingly, it had been easily pressured into providing Soviet proxy troops to fight against Chinese-backed forces, overtly to gain hegemony over that region in Southeast Asia. American influence had been almost completely excluded from Vietnam, Laos, and Cambodia.

9  The Soviet Global Naval Imprint

Henceforth the flag of the Soviet Navy will float proudly on all the oceans of the world. Sooner or later, the United States will have to understand that it is no longer master of the sea.
—Admiral Gorshkov, commander in chief, Soviet Navy, 1973

QUITE PROPERLY, Soviet warheads and delivery systems were the prime focus of Western strategic attention and anxiety, but developing concurrently at a fast rate alongside them, almost unnoticed and certainly heavily overshadowed by the other four Soviet armed services, was the Soviet Navy. At a time when the navies of the United States and the European NATO allies, such as Britain, were being reduced in strength and scope, that of the USSR was rapidly expanding.

Stalin's idea had been to develop a surface fleet of large ships, but this was abandoned after his death in 1953. Khrushchev realized that in a hot war with the West the vital emphasis would be on ICBMs and submarines rather than on big warships, so he planned to develop a large submarine fleet and also a large merchant marine. After his fall from power in 1964, the Brezhnev-Podgorny-Kosygin triumvirate decided to produce a surface navy of small, modern ship and to introduce more efficient submarines and phase out the older ones. The Brezhnev Trio had been profoundly influenced by the backing away of the Soviet leaders during the Cuban crisis in 1962 and was of the opinion the major contributory factor had been the lack of sufficient Soviet naval capability. The trio was determined this handicap should be eliminated.

The architect and driving force behind the new Soviet Navy was Sergei Georgivitch Gorshkov, who had been appointed commander in chief in 1956. Gorshkov was already working on the Khrushchev idea of a huge merchant marine, and he now set his mind and energies to building what he hoped would become the largest, most modern, and best navy in the world. He developed a personalized navy which became almost his own "empire" within the Soviet administrative system.

173

As head of his service, Gorshkov became a deputy defense minister and later a member of the Central Committee of the Soviet Communist Party, which brought him political power as well as executive command. As his prestige and influence rose he was able to boost the importance of the Soviet Navy in the Soviet peace strategy for world domination. He made sure the navy obtained a full share of the defense budget, a share that increased annually.

A career naval officer, as opposed to a political officer, Gorshkov had entered the navy in 1927 and commanded a variety of ships and squadrons, from mine-sweepers to cruisers, before being appointed commander in chief. Deeply influenced by the American admiral and strategist Alfred Thayer Mahan (1840–1914), who contended that sea power is essential to a nation's prestige and economic well-being, Gorshkov insisted that the navy can play an important role in peacetime to help a country's foreign policy operate from a position of strength. This appealed to the Kremlin leaders' inherent craving for "superiority."

During the Khrushchev regime, Gorshkov submissively stated that the primary role of the Soviet Navy was directed towards land warfare, rather than engaging enemy fleets at sea, and wrote that "attacks from the seaward against enemy objectives has become the basic mission of the Soviet Navy." He deliberately tempered his statements in those days to allay any fears on the part of marshals or senior generals of the other armed services, in case they came to regard the rapidly expanding navy with suspicion and to feel that too large a share of the defense budget was being allocated to it. To give the Politburo confidence his orientation was correct, Gorshkov wrote, "He who controls the sea controls world commerce, and he who controls world commerce, controls the resources of the earth, and the earth itself." To show this was in accord with the long-term Soviet global aim, he added, "The goal of Soviet seapower is to effectively utilize the world ocean in the interests of building world Communism."

Analyzing the danger to the USSR from the U.S. Navy as being from nuclear-powered submarines, seaborne aircraft, and marines, Gorshkov defined Soviet naval missions, in their order of priority, as being strategic offense, maritime security of the Soviet Union, interdiction of sea lines of communication, support of ground forces, and support of state policy in peace and war. He stressed the value of maritime flexibility and the psychological value of "showing the flag."

Gorshkov concentrated on producing surface ships that were smaller than their American counterparts but packed with weaponry and modern in all respects. They had a "multipurpose capability," which meant that each had several types of weapons and was able to deal with almost any threat, either from submarines, surface ships, mines, or from the air. Cramming a large number of weapons systems aboard was done at the expense of crew comfort and fuel capacity, the latter drawback meaning that the ship had to be refueled more often than an American one. Multiplicity of weapons meant that several different types of ammunition and missiles had to be stored on board, which further restricted space.

There was a continual process of improvement in Soviet ship construction and of updating and introducing new weapons. Even after less than ten years at sea, some ships, or their armament, were withdrawn to be replaced by others of more modern design, or with more modern weapons. Nuclear-powered ships came into commission in which a "nuclear core" turned water into steam to drive the ship. As nuclear cores could last for many years without replacement, the conventional refueling problem was replaced by the human problem of stamina and endurance.

In 1974, Gorshkov was supported openly in his global concepts by Defense Minister Grechko, who wrote in the Soviet Communist Party journal that the "Soviet armed forces are not restricted simply to the defense of the Soviet Union, but they may operate in any region of the world where the Kremlin leadership might see Party or Soviet interests at stake, or where the world revolutionary process could be assisted."[1] This moved Soviet naval minds away from coastal waters.

Thus encouraged, Gorshkov felt confident enough to burst into print with his peace strategy concept for the long-term Soviet aim of global domination. In his book the *Maritime Power of a State (Morskaya Moshch Gosudarstva),* published in Moscow in 1976, he made a convincing case for a substantial naval component in the defense framework. A few of his comments are of some significance in showing the Soviet rationale behind his naval expansion program. Gorshkov's main contentions were that "navies will remain a highly effective and indispensable means of armed combat, and be constantly used as an instrument of state policy in peace-time"; that "the navy is capable of operationally supporting state interests beyond its borders"; and that "the Soviet Navy is emerging as a factor for stabilizing the situation in various parts of the world."

Gorshkov affirmed "the expanded role of Soviet naval power in international affairs. In particular, the presence of forces of the Soviet

[1]*Problems of History of the Communist Party of the Soviet Union.*

fleet in neutral waters of the world would make it possible to achieve political goals without armed conflict, merely indicating pressure by their political might and the threat of military actions." In support of his global naval ambitions, he surprisingly quoted an unashamed capitalist, "the well-known British adventurist and pirate, W. Raleigh."

Although Gorshkov emphasized the twin traditional naval roles of battle against enemy sea communications and amphibious landings, he did not talk of intervening in the land battle and so was not a challenge to the predominance of the Soviet ground forces. He did say that "naval forces are becoming the main carriers of nuclear weaponry, which is capable of hitting the enemy in all continents and seas," but tactfully stopped short of adding that the Soviet land-based forces did not have this global capability; that the role of the Soviet ground forces was largely that of home defense; and that they had limited expeditionary capability away from the Euro-Asian land mass. For the sake of Soviet armed forces' solidarity and for his own security of position, Gorshkov did not proclaim naval supremacy too loudly.

A great submarine enthusiast, he wrote, "The main components of the Soviet Navy are the submarines and naval aviation . . . . Our main weapons are our ICBMs with MIRVs." Other interesting comments he made on submarines include:

> Submarines have become the main arm of the forces of modern navies . . . . Scientific-technical progress has introduced submarines as the more advanced platform for modern weaponry . . . . Submarines lend themselves to deployment in depth, as they can take shelter in the water, and can use it for concealment . . . . Nuclear-missile submarines now form the most important single component in the Soviet fleet . . . . Western nuclear-missile submarines are the most serious threat to the Soviet Union . . . . The chief role of the fleet air arm is antisubmarine work . . . Surface vessels are to service our submarines and counteract enemy activity.

The small handful of German U-boats that inflicted such crippling losses on Allied shipping in the Atlantic Ocean in World War II made a deep impression on Soviet leaders. When the war ended, they embarked on a program of producing a large submarine fleet, in which urgency of production outran performance and reliability. These earlier submarines were generally short-range ones, with torpedoes that had to be fired from the surface; and they were "very noisy" underwater. The emphasis in the sixties was on replacing them with nuclear-powered longer-range submarines that could fire torpedoes and antisubmarine missiles underwater; but by 1970, only about 60 out of the 370 Soviet submarines were nuclear-powered, the others being diesel-powered.

In 1962, the Soviets fired their first ballistic missile from an under-water submarine, and thus achieved the breakthrough of a naval "second nuclear strike" capability, which the Americans had done two years previously. Soviet ballistic missile-carrying submarines had priority for nuclear power, and the USSR had about fifty of them by 1970. In the decade of the seventies, in which the American ballistic missile–carrying submarines numbered forty-one, the Soviets increased theirs to about ninety. As older models were withdrawn from service and replaced by modern ones, Soviet attack submarines, so called to distinguish them from those carrying ICBMs, were reduced in number from 496 (in 1969) to about 275 (in 1979). In the same period, American attack submarines were reduced in number from 103 to 80.

In 1970, the new Soviet "Yankee" class missile-carrying submarine —with the SS-N-6 missile, fitted with a single megaton warhead, and having a range of about 1,600 miles—was being brought into service. It was comparable in size and speed with that of the American Polaris. Progressively, other improved Soviet submarines were launched, some with antisubmarine missiles with ranges of up to 300 miles that could be fired while submerged.

In the mid-seventies, the new nuclear-powered "Delta" class Soviet submarine was brought into service. The "Delta III," introduced in 1979, was fitted with the SS-N-8 ballistic missile, with a range of over 4,200 miles, which was multiheaded but not a MIRV. The Delta class submarine was the largest in the world, and eventually the range of its ICBM was greater than those on either the American Polaris or Poseidon submarines.

The "Alpha" class Soviet submarine appeared in 1979. It was reputedly able to dive to a depth of 3,000 feet, this capability being due to the use of titanium in manufacturing the hull. At first it was credited by U.S. naval intelligence as having an underwater speed of thirty-two knots, only slightly faster than American submarines; but a nuclear-powered American aircraft carrier with a top speed of thirty-one knots was outpaced by one it was tracking. One authority, Janes, estimated the Alpha class submarine was capable of an underwater speed of about forty-two knots. At that speed, unless the American attacking vessel was fairly close to its target, the torpedoes would run out of fuel before they could catch up with it. The Soviet submarines had distinct advantages over those in NATO navies.

In July 1977, the Soviets had made a demonstration of naval power by sending about one hundred submarines, mostly nuclear-powered, into the North Atlantic Ocean. This showed that the submarine had become the backbone of the Soviet Navy. In emergency, the Soviet Navy would be able to muster over 200 attack submarines (the remainder being in the process of being "turned round" or repaired) to meet about 150, which would be all the combined NATO navies could put to sea. In the event of a Soviet preemptive attack, 80 percent of the Soviet submarines would already be "on station."

Never really in favor of large battleships, as so many Allied ones had been sunk in World War II, the Soviets referred to American aircraft carriers in the sixties as "floating morgues," alleging they were far too vulnerable to submarine and missile attacks to play any really effective part in war. The Soviet Navy relied on land-based, long-range aircraft for aerial support and protection, which was perhaps quite adequate when Soviet warships and submarines seldom moved far from coastal waters. In 1970, the Naval Air Force possessed about 500 bomber aircraft, mostly supporting the Northern and Baltic fleets, which included 300 TU-16s and 50 TU-20s; and some 500 other aircraft, including helicopters.

American naval tactics were based on a mixed task force, centered on an aircraft carrier, which was considered capable of countering practically any enemy contingency, especially from submarines. The aircraft were especially useful in detecting, tracking, and destroying enemy submarines. When Soviet naval vessels began to push outwards into the global oceans, the need for aerial cover was suddenly realized, and the Soviets began to have second thoughts about "floating morgues." They decided to construct "helicopter carriers"; and by 1970, two 18,000 ton "heli-cruisers" were in service, each carrying a few helicopters.

Next, the Soviets, who had no aircraft carriers at all, decided to construct ten "mini-aircraft carriers." These were in fact cruisers with flight decks. The first, the *Kiev,* went into service in 1975, and the second, the *Minsk,* in March 1977; while the third, the *Kharkov,* was undergoing sea trials in 1979. They were of about 40,000 tons displacement, each carried twenty helicopters and twelve VTOL (Yak 36) aircraft, and were virtually floating arsenals, packed with weapons systems and antisubmarine warfare devices. With only helicopters and VTOL subsonic aircraft on board, however, they lacked the big aerial punch of the American aircraft carriers, which the United States was phasing out.

Although the Soviets were obviously shifting to the carrier-led naval task force concept, by 1979 the Naval Air Force still had over 400 land-based TU-26s. The naval task force lacked a marine element, and in the late seventies, the Soviets began to use their "floating docks" and tenders to carry "naval infantry" contingents, as there was no room available on the warships.

The United States saw the main USSR threat to its navy as being from the Soviet submarine fleet, but this did not cause any real concern until the sixties, when the Soviets were replacing their larger diesel-powered submarines with smaller nuclear-powered ones. The absence of any Soviet aircraft carriers had led U.S. naval experts to deduce that this limited the Soviet radius of capability. In 1970, and even before, U.S. naval intelligence thought the main purpose of the Soviet missile-carrying cruisers and destroyers was to counter U.S. aircraft carrier-led task forces at long range, as they were armed with the SS-N-10 missile, which had a range of about thirty miles.

This information had been deduced from photographs taken of Soviet ships, on which certain objects were interpreted as being launchers for the SS-N-10 missiles. It was not until the mid-seventies that it was discovered that these objects were not launchers, but covers for anti-submarine torpedoes. Another mistaken impression by U.S. intelligence was that most of the Soviet surface warships were to be employed to counter Western submarines, while instead they were designed to attack NATO warships.

The ever-expanding Soviet submarine fleet not only caused anxiety to NATO, but prompted its navies to develop an antisubmarine warfare expertise. The object was to detect, track, and "kill" enemy submarines, and a variety of apparatus and techniques had appeared, the principal one in use being known as SONAR, which could be either passive or active. The Soviets had always taken a great interest in electronic warfare, as evidenced by the number of radomes and antenna on their ships, and they applied this interest to antisubmarine warfare technology.[2]

---

[2] The sea is full of "noises," and sound waves and certain other shock waves travel through water much faster than they do through the air. Seawater conversely considerably reduces, almost to nil, electromagnetic radiation (as from radio or radar signals). Soviet submarines were generally much noisier in the water than American ones, and nuclear-powered submarines were noisier than diesel-powered ones. The passive form of SONAR is to quietly listen for enemy submarines on the move without revealing one's own presence or position; sonobuoys, which float either on or just below the surface, will pick up and relay back to a command center the noises a submarine radiates from its engines and the movement of the hull pushing through the water. (Sonobuoys can be dropped into position from aircraft, put over the side of a ship, or anchored into fixed positions to cover narrow channels through which enemy submarines have to pass. Also, a "dunker" sonobuoy can be dangled from a hovering helicopter.) Submarines each have their own peculiar noise pattern—sort of a "signature tune"—that experts can usually detect and identify. The active SONAR device operates by sending out sound waves that would bounce back off a submarine so its position can be located and its course tracked. The drawbacks to active SONAR are that it gives away the sender's position, and the signal takes twice as long to be processed as it has to travel to the enemy submarine and then back to the sender. Another

In 1973, Gorshkov had boasted that "the flag of the Soviet Navy will float proudly on all the oceans of the world. Sooner or later the United States will have to understand that it is no longer the master of the sea." He made good his boast by organizing OKEAN-75, a massive demonstration of Soviet naval capability in which over two hundred major surface combat ships and submarines, together with hundreds of land-based maritime aircraft, took part. With the aid of satellite communications, the Soviets simulated attacks on "enemy targets" worldwide within seconds of each other, exhibiting to the monitoring NATO ships their ability to coordinate global naval operations. This major exercise included anti-aircraft carrier, anticonvoy, and antisubmarine warfare tactics.

OKEAN-75 was a triumphant milestone in the Soviet naval expansion plan, showing the world at large that the USSR was now a global naval power to be reckoned with. One authority, Janes, calculated that the average age of Soviet ships involved in this exercise was about seven years, while that of U.S. Navy ships in service at the same time was about nineteen years. Of OKEAN-75, British Admiral of the Fleet Sir Peter Hill-Norton said, "The United States has never previously faced a global threat to its sea-lane communications from such a mix of subsurface, surface and maritime naval forces. This is a strategic change of kind, not of degree."

The Soviet merchant marine is an arm of the Soviet Navy, its officers are trained as naval officers, and its merchant ships are blatantly used in a reconnaissance and surveillance role. For example, Soviet fishing trawlers, of which there may be as many as 4,000 operating round the world, are all electronic intelligence ships in thin disguise, abristle with antennae and weighed down with electronic equipment, which shadow NATO ships on exercises, follow them on routine patrols, and search out new ports and anchorages.

Profit is a secondary motive, although not an unimportant one, for the Soviet merchant marine, and strategic and diplomatic requirements were, and still are, a first priority. As and when required, Soviet merchant ships are used to rush arms and equipment to client states; to carry troops and supplies for proxy wars at short notice, as in Angola and Ethiopia; to provide follow-up sealifts for foreign intervention; to supply warships and submarines at sea; and for any other strategic, diplomatic, or espionage purpose.

---

detection device is an instrument in a ship that measures the change in magnetic field caused by the metal hull of a submarine passing below. There are others, equally ingenious.

About 1,600 of the Soviet merchant ships were small, general-purpose ones, and construction was in progress in the seventies of a class of new container type and dry-cargo ships. These general-purpose ships, being of shallow draft, were ideal for offloading and taking on cargo at ports with limited facilities, shallow berths, and anchorages, such as many Third World countries possessed.

By 1975, the Soviets possessed about 464 tanker ships, being about 60 percent of the world's total (the United States at that time having only 250). This was a significant factor in the ongoing Soviet peace strategy, as Soviet oil for Warsaw Pact countries, and indeed for any "European front" in the event of a war with NATO, would be transported by land. The Soviets did not strictly need any oceangoing tankers for their own use at all, but they utilized them partly to transport oil to their client states, and partly to obtain hard Western currency. To the Soviets, their oil-tankers were a blackmail trade weapon. The Soviet objective was to carry foreign oil on the high seas at rates lower than the commercially motivated Western companies could offer, and so drive Western tankers out of business, whereupon the monopoly of transporting oil by sea, with all its trade blackmail connotations, would pass to the USSR.

From the planning stage to launching, ship-building is a lengthy business. The Soviets mastered it adequately and then quickened it to produce a score or so major naval combat units annually to join the Soviet fleets. This steady increase made global expansion possible, in addition to meeting other naval priorities. The Kremlin leaders had two main naval priorities. The first was the defense of the homeland, which meant firm control of all coastal waters and the narrow channels leading to the open seas, and a capability if necessary to fight and defeat any attacking NATO naval force at sea. The Far East Fleet was to dominate the Sea of Japan, and to counter any United States naval threat from the North Pacific. The second priority was to win the anticipated Battle of the North Atlantic, to sever the maritime supply route between America and Western Europe, and also to defeat or neutralize NATO navies. The Soviets anticipated this battle might be fought on the lines of that of World War II. A major portion of Soviet naval resources were allocated to these vital tasks, and only a much smaller proportion was available for global expansion.

In the Soviet global context there were also two main priorities. The first was to dominate the East Mediterranean, which perhaps from the Soviet point of view could almost be regarded as merely an extension of defense of home waters; while the other was to dominate the Cape

Route to the Far East. Other global expansionist probes—such as into the Caribbean, the eastern part of the South Atlantic, Southern and Central American waters, or Australasia and the West Pacific—were of much lesser importance and were pursued largely on an opportunity basis.

In the sixties, the Soviets were short of friendly foreign ports where their warships could refuel, and even elementary facilities and anchorages were sparse. In the seventies this situation improved considerably as they successfully began to accumulate more widely-spaced naval facilities to support their global ambitions. The main USSR objective was to develop the capability to deny the use of the global oceans to NATO warships.

Lack of sufficient and adequate naval facilities meant that Soviet warships had to remain at sea for long periods and undertake very long journeys. The Soviet Navy had the advantage over NATO navies as it was able to keep its warships "on station" much longer; they routinely supplied them at sea—either by naval tenders, supply ships, merchant ships, or trawlers—with the so-called Four Bs—bombs, bullets, beans, and black oil. The Soviets measured their naval presence and capability in terms of the number of ship-days, meaning days when a ship was fully operational and at sea, and they achieved a very much higher ratio than NATO navies could reach.

To some extent, the Soviets reversed the old British maxim that trade follows the flag. In many instances, they initially made trade agreements that would allow their merchant ships to call at foreign ports, after which naval facilities were demanded until they almost became Soviet "naval stations" in the full meaning of that expression. The Soviets concentrated on small, unaligned, often newly-emergent Third World nations with a seaboard. The pattern of Soviet progression often began with the visit by a Soviet freighter or trawler, which was followed by requests for refueling, provisioning, and perhaps docking facilities. As encouragement, Soviet "salesmen's samples," often in the form of old trawlers, were given. Promises and trade agreements were coupled with bribes and threats to obtain further facilities.

Warships are much easier to move around the world than armies or land-based aircraft formations; and Soviet naval forces steaming within sight of or just over the horizon from far-flung small states—either to provide reassurance that promised Soviet support would be given, or to underscore Soviet threats or warning—have a profound psychological effect on peoples of tiny defenseless nations, or on tiny islands in remote corners of oceans. The absence of NATO warships makes this especially true. In short, it was a reversion to the gunboat diplomacy of the nineteenth century. The Soviets seldom lost an opportunity to show the flag in as many places as possible. The detente agreements of 1972, in fact, opened up about forty American ports to Soviet ships.

During the Cold War the U.S. Sixth Fleet had moved into the Mediterranean to give some protection to the southern flank of NATO; and by 1970, its strength was about forty-five warships, four submarines and 300 aircraft. Beginning in 1968, Soviet warships from the Black Sea Fleet moved through the Straits of the Bosphorus and the Dardanelles to form the Mediterranean Squadron, which by 1970 had roughly the same number of surface craft. The main difference was that the Soviet squadron did not have any aircraft carriers, having to rely upon land-based aircraft; but it did have more submarines, usually about a dozen or more. The supply line for this Soviet Mediterranean Squadron was the long one of about one thousand miles reaching back through the straits to the Black Sea bases of Odessa and Sevastopol, where its ships had to return for major repairs. The objective of this Soviet naval force was to neutralize the U.S. Sixth Fleet, and in particular the vessels that carried ballistic missiles that could strike into the heart of USSR territory.

In 1970, the Soviets had some naval facilities in Egypt, at Port Said, Alexandria, and Mersa Matruh; and also in Syria, at Latakia. Soviet aircraft based in Egypt, such as the TU-16s, provided aerial support to the Soviet squadron. When Sadat expelled the Soviet personnel from Egypt in July 1972, he allowed them to retain their naval facilities; but these were finally withdrawn in 1976, when Sadat abrogated the Soviet Friendship Treaty. During the Yom Kippur War of 1973, additional Soviet ships, including electronic intelligence ones, appeared in the east Mediterranean for a short period. When the Lebanese civil war began in 1975, the Soviet Mediterranean Squadron was increased in strength to about ninety warships and submarines. Despite receiving large quantities of Soviet weapons, Gaddafi of Libya refused to allow the Soviets any naval facilities, as did both Lebanon and Tunisia; but the USSR did obtain some facilities at the Algerian port of Mers el-Kebir.

Despite the paucity of naval facilities in the Mediterranean, the Soviets continued to maintain their naval squadron there without too much difficulty, and their refueling-at-sea techniques made their 1,000-mile supply line more of a hindrance than a handicap, which they could cope with adequately on a long-term basis. One disturbing fact came to light in September 1979, when the Greek government, which had withdrawn from the NATO military framework in 1974, permitted the USSR to repair ships of the Soviet Mediterranean Squadron at the Syros Island shipyard. During an eighteen-month period, at least twelve Soviet ships were repaired there, including four warships which only had to symbolically remove their guns when they entered Greek waters. This Greek facility enabled Soviet auxiliary vessels, and apparently warships, too, to remain on station in the Mediterranean rather than having to return to Black Sea docks for repairs.

In the global context, the main Soviet anxiety was the dearth of naval facilities available to them on the Cape Route. At the beginning of 1970, there was not a single naval base with major repair docks open to Soviet warships between their western ports and their Far East Fleet base at Vladivostok, a sailing distance of between 8,000 and 10,000 miles. Soviet ships had to use the long Cape Route to deliver arms and supplies to North Vietnam for distribution to Communist armies fighting in Southeast Asia; and during the first part of the seventies, they had to be refueled at sea on the 6,000- to 7,000-mile journey.

Although the Soviets had made only small gains in obtaining naval facilities on the Cape Route in the sixties, this situation was considerably improved in the second half of the seventies due to the decolonization of the Portuguese African possessions; the withdrawal of the British Navy from east of Suez, which left the Indian Ocean comparatively devoid of NATO naval power; and the lack of positive response from the United States and Western maritime nations to Soviet penetration.

The closure of the Suez Canal in 1967 meant that ships of many maritime countries had to use the Cape Route from Europe—by way of the South Atlantic, round the Cape of Good Hope, and into the Indian Ocean—to reach the Middle East, the Persian Gulf, India, Southeast Asia, and beyond. This route became one of the most crowded in the world, used by over 24,000 major oceangoing vessels annually (1970). Uncertainty as to the future of the Suez Canal led certain maritime countries to set up long-term plans to construct larger ships that could carry larger cargoes to compensate for the longer journey—anything between 3,000 and 4,000 miles longer, depending on the port of departure and destination. Oil tankers, for example, became gigantic in size, and far too big to get through the Suez Canal if it ever opened again.

Much of the coastline of the continent of Africa was barred to Soviet warships, especially the Portuguese and Spanish colonies: Portugal was a member of NATO, and Franco's Spain was anticommunist. The Republic of South Africa, which has a 2,000-mile-long coastline and several ports and naval bases, was the vital southern pivot of the African landmass, and was anti-Soviet in attitude.

Although Soviet aid had been given to several seaboard countries on the western side of Africa, such as Mauritania, Ghana, and Zaire, these countries hesitated to allow the Soviets to use their naval facilities. And generally, these facilities did not amount to much. The Soviets had poured arms into Nigeria to enable its federal government to win its civil war, but it showed no particular gratitude, and it was not until 1976 that Soviet warships were visiting Nigeria on a regular basis.

In 1970, an agreement was made for a few Soviet warships to be on station at the port of Conakry, the capital of Guinea; and in 1973, a small detachment of Soviet Naval Infantry (marines) was stationed there. Later, in 1975, the Soviets enlarged the runway on the airfield at Conakry and was allowed the use of it for its long-range maritime reconnaissance aircraft, which enabled them to monitor a wide area of the Atlantic Ocean.

A similar gain was made when the Marxist government of Congo, a former French colony (whose flag was a red one with the hammer and sickle symbol in its center), granted the Soviets naval facilities at Pointe-Noire and use of the airfield at Brazzaville, the capital. This port and airfield were used extensively by the Soviets to ferry supplies and transport Cuban troops southwards to help the MPLA army in Angola. When MPLA forces seized Luanda, the Angolan capital, the Soviets were allowed to use its fairly extensive docks.

In 1970, the eastern side of the African continent offered little to the Soviet Navy, as generally during the sixties, the Chinese had gained influence there at the expense of the Soviets. Soviet warships made occasional visits to some East African ports such as Mombassa, but only on sufferance, as local governments were playing the Soviets off against the Chinese to obtain aid without strings. It was not until March 1977, when the newly liberated state of Mozambique rejected China in favor of the USSR, that the Soviets gained the use of the considerable naval facilities at Nacala and Beira, which dominated the important Mozambique Channel. On the east side of the Mozambique Channel was the island state of Madagascar, where the Soviets had obtained limited naval facilities.

In November 1970, the Soviets were granted certain "harbor facilities" on the island state of Mauritius, a former British colony, some 550 miles east of Madagascar, in the Indian Ocean. These rights enabled fourteen Soviet fishing trawlers a year to dock at Mauritius; and the right to use the airfield allowed them to bring in relief crews. In return, the Soviets provided Mauritius with a few old fishing trawlers at low cost. In the seventies, an average of a hundred Soviet ships of all types annually called at Mauritius. North of Mauritius lie the Seychelles, a group of small islands (total land area only 171 square miles), a former British colony, which became independent in 1976. An American satellite tracking station had been established on one of the islands. A Marxist coup occurred in June 1977, after which Soviet ships began to make frequent visits to Mahe, the main island.

In the northwest corner of the Indian Ocean where it touches the Middle East land bridge, a Marxist government seized power after the British withdrawal in South Yemen, which then virtually became a Soviet client state. The Soviets were given full use of the extensive docks, harbor installations, and the port of Aden, which controlled the southern entrance to the Red Sea. Also, the Soviets were given the use of the uninhabited island of Socotra, which lies astride the Red Sea sealane that was South Yemeni territory. Socotra was used by the Soviet naval infantry and other personnel for acclimatization and assault-landing training. The island had an airstrip but no naval facilities; but by 1979, reports indicated that Socotra was being turned into a large Soviet naval and air base, from which Soviet maritime long-range reconnaissance aircraft started their missions over the Indian Ocean and the Middle East. In 1970, the Soviets also had minor naval facilities at the Sudanese Red Sea port of Port Sudan, but lost them the following year when a Communist coup against President Numeiry failed. The Soviets had also obtained naval facilities in the Red Sea at the North Yemeni port of Hodeida, but these were extremely primitive.

The big Soviet naval gain in this region resulted from the Soviet-Somali Friendship Treaty of 1974, which enabled the USSR to construct huge naval installations and facilities at the Somali port of Berbera; these included deep-water berths for twenty ships, a floating repair dock, and an airfield from which long-range reconnaissance aircraft could operate. On 1 May 1977, President Barreh of Somalia sent a cable to Brezhnev, saying, "Russian aid is inscribed in gold letters in our history." Perhaps he should have said "black letters": a few weeks afterwards, the Soviets switched their allegiance and support from Somalia to its enemy, Ethiopia. The Kremlin leaders obviously reckoned the Eritrean Red Sea ports were of greater strategic value to them than Berbera. Berbera was completely evacuated by the Soviets, and the large floating dock was towed away to Socotra. Somalia sought aid from the United States, but Carter refused and so lost an opportunity to walk into a new Soviet-built naval base: a great omission. By 1979, the president of drought-plagued Somalia was abjectly forced to allow the Soviets to creep back quietly into the Berbera base again.

Farther east, protruding massively into the Indian Ocean, was India, whose governments had always been sympathetic to the USSR and had allowed the Soviets to use certain facilities at the Indian naval base of Visakhapatnam. The Soviets also gained some facilities at the former British base at Trincomalee, on the island of Sri Lanka. Neither India nor Sri Lanka would allow vessels carrying nuclear weapons into their waters. During the Indo-Pakistan war of 1971, a Soviet naval task force consisting of seventeen warships sailed into the Bay of Bengal to establish a presence and to monitor the course of the war. The USSR gave considerable military and economic aid to India in this conflict, but Prime Minister Gandhi hesitated to extend further naval facilities to the Soviet Navy.

The British Navy quit Singapore in March 1976, leaving behind a very extensive dock-harbor-port complex. A tiny island state at the southern tip of Malaysia, Singapore controlled the Strait of Malacca between Malaysia and Sumatra—the western entrance to the South China Sea. Lee Kuan Yew, the prime minister, offered the Soviets use of the naval facilities on a commercial basis, excluding only warships and submarines. The Soviets quickly accepted.

During 1970, only about ten Soviet surface warships were on station in the huge Indian Ocean, visiting ports and generally showing the flag; but by 1979, this number had increased to over thirty. A NATO report (dated 24 December 1973) stated that the Soviet naval presence in the Indian Ocean had risen from "1,000 ship-days" in 1970 to "9,000 ship-days" in 1973; and one source (IISS) estimated that it exceeded "18,000 ship-days" by 1979.

In Southeast Asia, the one big Soviet success of the late seventies was to turn Vietnam into a client state and Vietnamese troops into Soviet proxy ones. The Vietnam-USSR Friendship Treaty gave the Soviet Navy the full use of the extensive naval installations constructed by the United States at Cam Ranh Bay, which contained large repair facilities. The Soviets assembled a submarine squadron to be based in the new submarine pens at Cam Ranh Bay, while Soviet long-range maritime reconnaissance aircraft began operating from former USAF bases at Tan Son Nhut and Bien Hoa. The Soviets also obtained more naval facilities at Danang, and also at the Kampuchean port of Kampon Son (Sihanoukville). Victorious Vietnamese proxy troops had brought a large sector of Southeast Asian coastline under Soviet influence. In February 1979, a Soviet task force of about fourteen warships sailed into Vietnamese waters to remain there on station.

As opportunity permitted, the Soviets penetrated even farther eastwards into the Pacific Ocean, looking for opportunity targets. For example, in 1976 they were offering to construct an airport on the island of Tonga in exchange for the usual "fishing fleet" facilities; and in 1979 they were negotiating for similar rights on the Australian island of Tasmania.

In summary, during the second half of the seventies the Soviet imprint had deepened on the long Cape Route, on a string of major naval facilities from Conakry, Pointe-Noire, Luanda, Beira, Nacala, Socotra, Visakhapatnam, and Singapore to Cam Ranh Bay, and on a dozen or more others with lesser facilities.

The Soviets lacked sufficient naval resources to probe into the Western hemisphere in strength but gave what attention they could to Cuba, their client state and source of proxy troops. By 1979, Cuba possessed two old Soviet submarines, with two or more on order, and about eighty small Soviet patrol craft of different types. In the sixties the Soviets had consolidated their hold on Cuba and had constructed a large naval complex at Cienfuegos, on its southern coast, which included deep-water anchorage, three large docks, major naval repair facilities, and a communications center. Soviet naval visits were frequent, and joint Soviet-Cuban naval exercises were held in the Gulf of Mexico. From 1972, five Soviet submarines were permanently on station to monitor American naval activity. The Soviet naval imprint was deeply in Cuba, but less so in South and Central America.

10  Some Thoughts for the Eighties

No NATO weapons, conventional or nuclear, will ever be used in Europe except in response to attack.
— President Reagan: 18 November 1981

THE EIGHTIES BEGAN with a Presidential Election in the United States. Many causes and issues tended to hang fire as the nation waited to see whether President Carter would win a second term in the White House, or whether there would be a new President, with new policies. The Kremlin leadership was hoping that Jimmy Carter would remain in office to continue his debilitating, appeasing strategic policies that were so advantageous to the Soviets. A new president, Ronald Reagan, took his place on 20 January 1981.

In foreign affairs the new Administration's program was based on "Four Pillars"—restoration of economic and military strength; the re-invigoration of United States alliances and friendships; the commitment to peaceful change in the world; and that the superpower relationship should be based on greater Soviet restraint and reciprocity. The Reagan Administration made a realistic appraisal of the Soviet threat and global ambitions, and decided the United States could only negotiate successfully with the Soviets from a position of real strength, as any other approach would be treated with contempt.

To repair neglected defenses the largest military budget ever handled by the Pentagon, of some $222 billion, was presented to the nation. One objective was to modernize the United States strategic nuclear forces by producing one hundred MX intercontinental ballistic missiles, each with ten warheads to break Moscow's monopoly on large, accurate missiles, and to give the Soviets an incentive to cut back on their ICBMs. Another was to produce one hundred B-1 long-range bomber aircraft to replace the aging B-52s, the first squadron to be operational by 1986; and another was to develop the advanced technology bomber, a project that had come to be known as "Stealth," as it was designed to elude enemy radar detection. Later, on 9 August 1981, President Reagan authorized the production of the neutron bomb. This change of American direction caused the Soviet leadership some anxiety. The somewhat discredited linkage policy, in which progress in one area was dependent upon cooperation in another, which President Carter had tried to revive when the Soviets invaded Afghanistan, was abandoned by President Reagan.

The Reagan Administration continued the two-track policy, which was both to introduce the TNF, Theater Nuclear Force, into Western Europe, and at the same time seek arms control and arms reductions. This was accepted by the NATO Foreign Ministers, meeting at Gleneagles (Scotland) in October 1981. Already, under its 1979 declaration, the United States had withdrawn 1,000 nuclear warheads from Western Europe while the Soviets had been deploying their mobile S-20s, introducing improved nuclear-carrying aircraft, and bringing new medium-range nuclear missiles into service. However, the TNF project, aimed at positioning 572 Pershing IIs and cruise missiles in Europe beginning in 1983, had run into a problem of European reluctance. For example, the governments of Belgium and Holland, both of which were facing elections, had yet officially to agree to accept their quota of these weapons.

On 23 February 1981, President Brezhnev presented his report and policy speech to the 26th Congress of the Soviet Communist Party in Moscow. The 74-year old leader put forward his so-called Peace Plan, claiming that "Our common aspiration is to do everything possible to relieve the peoples of the danger of a nuclear war, and to preserve world peace." Accusing the United States of "adventurism and readiness to gamble with the vital interests of humanity in the name of narrow and selfish goals," he called for a summit meeting with President Reagan, and for an "active dialogue" that would "embrace a wide range of issues."

Brezhnev rejected the suggestion that the Soviets had any military superiority, claiming there was "approximate parity," and that the "military and strategic equilibrium prevailing between the United States and the USSR, and the Warsaw Pact and NATO, was objectively a safeguard to world peace." He offered to discuss arms limitations, and suggested a moratorium on the deployment of the United States and Soviet "medium-range nuclear weapons in Europe," meaning a freeze at existing levels while negotiations were in progress. He also said that the proposed area for "confidence-building measures" might extend as far eastward as the Urals, and called for a conference on the Middle East, now "that the Camp David process has failed."

President Reagan indicated that he was ready to resume strategic arms limitation talks, but that there were many other urgent, serious matters to be resolved, such as the flow of Soviet arms through Cuba to Central America. The moratorium suggestion was rejected as it would abort the TNF project, and leave the Soviets with overwhelming superiority in medium-range missiles in Europe. It was then estimated that the Soviets had 250 SS-20s, 340 SS-4s, and 40 SS-5s deployed, some two-thirds of which were facing NATO. These weapons were regarded by the Soviets as medium-range ones, having ranges from 625 miles to 2,800 miles. The United States Administration could not agree that there was even "approximate" strategic parity between the two superpowers.

During the early months of the Reagan Administration some blundering statements were made by the President and his Secretaries of State and Defense on strategic matters which provided fuel for Soviet propaganda, and gave anxiety to the NATO allies. The impression given was that in some circumstances the United States might make the first nuclear strike in war, and might be contemplating fighting a nuclear war in Europe only. Haig's unfortunate remark that it "might be necessary to fire a nuclear warning shot for demonstrative purposes," alarmed the allies.

Eventually, to clear the air and to combat Soviet propaganda, at the Cancun (Mexico) Conference, on 21 October, President Reagan openly denounced the Soviet leadership for trying to drive a wedge between the United States and its European allies, and called the Soviet suggestion that America was considering fighting a nuclear war at Europe's expense a "downright lie." On 18 November, he went further and stated that "no NATO weapons, conventional or nuclear, will ever be used in Europe except in response to an attack."

Antiwar and antinuclear weapons protest groups in Western European countries had periodically swelled into activity, which then gradually subsided again, as they proved largely ineffective. In Britain, the much publicized annual protest march from Aldermaston (where nuclear weapons were manufactured) to London, had never prevented successive British Governments quietly, and sometimes secretly, continuing with their nuclear weapons program and, for example, producing the Chevaline nuclear warhead.

During 1980 and 1981, these groups became hyper-active, and suddenly mushroomed into a massive "peace movement" that gathered momentum and swept through Western Europe gathering young and restless people as recruits. This alarmed governments in Western Europe, but delighted the Kremlin leadership, which gave these demonstrations and activities priority coverage on their own television screens and in their media.[1] The various peace movement groups were united against the introduction of the TNF into Europe, and most also wanted to remove any nuclear weapons already there, their reasons varying from ecological and religious, to political and dissident.

In Italy, a country with plenty of internal problems, the Movement for Peace and Disarmament was slow to take off, and did not really get going until August 1981, when it was revealed that 112 cruise missiles its government had promised to take, were to be positioned in Sicily. In October, over 200,000 people in Rome demonstrated against them, and in November, another 200,000 marched through Florence in protest.

In Britain, the main protest movement was the Campaign for Nuclear Disarmament which had been organizing the Aldermaston Marches since the early fifties. Within two years their membership rose from about 3,000 to over 250,000. It was stated in the House of Lords (Upper House of Parliament), on 25 November, that there were "nine card-carrying Communists" among the organizers and the Earl of Kimberley said that "leading Communists use the CND platform to attack the United States' militarism, while praising the so-called Soviet peace-making initiative."

In West Germany over 300 new peace groups appeared which joined with the some 500 existing youth protest groups of one sort or another. Many of these came together under the coordinating umbrella of the European Nuclear Disarmament movement, whose platform was a "Nuclear-free Europe from Poland to Portugal," which moved its headquarters and operations-center to London. Other peace and anti-nuclear weapons movements sprang up in France, Switzerland and Spain, and it was claimed that many East Germans crossed the border to demonstrate on the streets of West Berlin.

Although probably well over 90 percent of the peace movement members were young people, there was a sprinkling in their ranks of older individuals from all walks of life. One group, which surfaced in November 1981, consisted of a retired admiral, and six retired generals from NATO countries (France, Greece, Italy, Netherlands, Norway and Portugal), who said they had banded together to lend "expertise to the campaign for arms control." They sent a memorandum to SHAPE, in Belgium, calling on the Alliance to remove all nuclear

---

[1] After President Carter cancelled the production of the Neutron Bomb in 1979, President Brezhnev personally decorated Aleksander Romanov, the former Soviet Ambassador to Holland, for his success "in marshalling the resistance of the people of the Netherlands" against the Neutron Bomb.

weapons from the arsenals of Western European nations, and "to end their vassalage to the United States." The memorandum also called on the British and French governments to dismantle their nuclear weapons, and claimed that "political prejudice and factual inaccuracy within the Alliance has created an exaggerated perception of the Soviet threat."

During 1981, massive demonstrations and meetings were held in several major Western European cities, and a number of spectacular mass marches took place, all well recorded by television cameras. One demonstration was by 400,000 people in Amsterdam, and another, also of 400,000 people, took place in Madrid, both in November. Previously, commencing in July, peace movement demonstrators marched from Copenhagen, their numbers being swelled en route by detachments from several nations, to arrive for a massive rally in Paris on the 6th October — Hiroshima Day. These mass peace protest meetings, demonstrations and marches caused anxiety to both the American, and Western European governments, and might well have led Brezhnev to think that NATO would soon disintegrate in Western Europe.

Brezhnev tried a propaganda ploy which he hoped would hasten NATO's dissolution. On 7 November, Marshal Ustinov, the Soviet Defense Minister, stated that "it is absurd to believe that the Soviet Union might contemplate a nuclear first strike strategy." This was just what the peace movement members wanted to hear, and it could hardly have been a more timely political statement. If Ustinov's statement was correct, Soviet military books will have to be rewritten.

Uncharacteristically, to bolster the European peace movement, President Brezhnev, who was due to visit West Germany on 22 November, outlined his views on the American TNF project, and made what was virtually a unilateral disarmament offer to the United States, in interview form for a West German magazine.[2] He confirmed for the first time that the SS-20 had three warheads, and claimed that the medium-range nuclear missiles in Europe were roughly equally balanced, "approximate parity" being his frequent expression. He said that the proposed TNF missiles would create a marked American superiority in this field that would force the Soviets to deploy more SS-20s.

President Brezhnev made his offer to withdraw his medium-range nuclear missiles back to the Urals (from where they could still hit all major Western European cities), and to have a moratorium on such missiles while talks on their reduction were in progress, which would still have left the Soviets with their six-to-one superiority ratio. Brezhnev

[2] *Der Spiegel,* of 1 November 1981.

stated he was willing to reach agreement on major reductions of nuclear arsenals on both sides, proposed an end to nuclear arms production, and declared he wanted peace with the United States. He also stated that the Soviets had 975 "missiles and aircraft" in Europe, but claimed that NATO had 986 "missiles and aircraft." Nuclear arithmetic was becoming confusing.

On 18 November, President Reagan, at the National Press Club, Washington, outlined his "Zero Option," an idea that had been previously put to him by Chancellor Schmidt of West Germany, which basically was that if the Soviets would dismantle their SS-20s, SS-4s and SS-5s, he would cancel the proposed American TNF for Europe. He suggested that talks be opened between the United States and the USSR to take over from where the SALT ones had foundered, and that they should be known as START, meaning "Strategic Arms Reduction Talks." He agreed that talks on "military confidence-building measures" should continue, and the Geneva Conference should go ahead. The U.S. President called for a reduction of conventional forces in Europe, which he referred to as seeking "equality at lower levels of conventional forces," and noted that the Soviets had more divisions in East Germany than the whole Allied invasion force had on D Day in Europe. He also called on the USSR to accept Western proposals to lessen the risks of a surprise attack, and the chances of war arising out of uncertainty and miscalculation; and to accept a conference on disarmament in Europe.

Dr. Luns, the NATO Secretary General, hailed these Zero Option proposals as an "historic initiative," and challenged the Soviets to make substantial reductions in their own nuclear armories. The Zero Option proposals were well received by all NATO European governments, even those of Belgium and Holland which still had to decide whether or not to accept the TNF. Moreover, it severely blunted the aims of the European peace movement.

President Brezhnev was very angry, as he had been both upstaged and outflanked. He clearly thought the European peace movement was running in his favor. President Reagan seemed suddenly to have shed the Soviet-inspired image of a trigger-happy war-monger, and to assume one as the champion of peace and arms reduction, which image Brezhnev himself sought. On the 22nd, President Ceausescu of Rumania, who had previously called for a nuclear-free Balkan zone, openly expressed approval of Reagan's Zero Option, officially mustering his people for marches and demonstrations, culminating in a rally of 300,000 in Bucharest.

Brezhnev, who had hoped to visit West Germany in the guise of a messenger of peace, was greeted at Bonn, on the 22nd, by about 50,000 demonstrators hostile to the Soviet Union, chanting anti-war slogans, and also by some 5,000 Afghan protestors, shouting "Russians out of Afghanistan." Chancellor Schmidt was having some trouble with an extremist section of his own Social Democratic Party which was against acceptance of the TNF. Schmidt, who was in favor of the TNF, warned Brezhnev not to overestimate the value of the West European peace movement as a means of achieving unilateral disarmament, and said that if no agreement was reached on the reduction of medium-range nuclear missiles at the Geneva Conference by the fall of 1983, he would go ahead and accept the TNF.

Schmidt was not able to convince Brezhnev that the Americans were sincere in wanting an agreement on arms control and reduction. Schmidt said that "the Soviet leadership cannot correctly evaluate the intentions of the American leadership." This was mirror-imaging in reverse. The Russians, who were being forced to the negotiating table by American resolution, could not believe that the Americans would not do just as they would in such circumstances. Reagan had turned the tables on the Soviets. Chancellor Schmidt did claim that he had persuaded the ruffled Brezhnev to agree to participate in the Geneva Talks.

The Geneva Talks on medium-range nuclear missiles opened on 30 November. It was agreed their sessions should not be open to the media so that matters could be discussed freely. It was anticipated the conference would be a lengthy one, as the Soviets wanted to discuss British and French nuclear weapons, and it was not absolutely clear whether the Americans were going to insist on the dismantling of all the SS-20s, or just a proportion, and would agree to a few remaining to face China. Long arguments were ahead, especially over arithmetic, as the United States claimed it had only 560 "aircraft" in Europe, but that the Soviets had 3,825 "missiles and aircraft," while on the other hand the Soviets still insisted they had only 975 "missiles and aircraft" in Europe.

NATO European problems continued to crop up, one of which was the Norwegian proposal, originally mooted by President Kekkonen of Finland, under Soviet pressure, for a Scandinavian "nuclear-free zone," to consist of Norway, Denmark, Sweden and Finland, in which there would be no nuclear weapons positioned at all. This would have been advantageous to the Soviets, who had a missile-packed area on the Kola Peninsula, adjacent to Finland, from where SS–20s could reach any part of Western Europe. There was no mention by the Soviets that they might include their Kola Peninsula in this proposed nuclear-free zone. The United States was against such nuclear-free zones as they cut across American efforts to reach agreements with the Soviets on reducing the numbers of missiles in Europe. Denmark and Sweden would not agree, and when a general election in Norway, in September 1981, brought a more moderate government to power, the whole idea was dropped.

This might have been one up for President Reagan in Europe, but he was soon one down again, as the general election in Greece, in October, brought the Socialist leader, Andreas Papandreou, to power as Prime Minister. His pre-election pledges had been to take Greece out of the NATO military framework again, to remove all U.S. nuclear weapons from Greek soil, and to close down all U.S. bases. Greece was in dispute with Turkey, and he was upset by the continuing amounts of American aid, military and economic, going to that country. Prime Minister Papandreou also called for a "nuclear-free Balkan zone." These problems are still to be solved, and NATO may have to compromise in some way at the expense of Turkey, to retain Greece within NATO. This position in NATO was compensated to some extent by the accession of Spain to the Alliance, its formal application being made in December 1981.

Eastwards across the Iron Curtain the Kremlin leadership was having trouble with Poland, one of its main Warsaw Pact members. The economic situation in that country had been deteriorating for some time, giving rise to unrest that broadened into political discontent that came to a head on 14 August 1980 when a series of strikes began at the Gdansk shipyards and other Baltic ports. Strikes were then illegal in Poland, but the small dissident organization, KOR (Self Defense Committee), which had been formed in 1976 to defend workers victimized by the authorities after the food riots of that year, consistently campaigned for free trade unionism. KOR had brought discontented intellectuals and workers together, and was determined to press for liberal trade union concessions, such as the right to strike. KOR members had been active in organizing these August strikes.

Pressure mounted, and on the 31st, Edward Gierek, the Polish Communist Party leader, made the "Gdansk Agreements" between his government and the strikers, which allowed them to establish trade unions, and gave them the right to strike. This agreement was condemned by the Kremlin leadership, and most other Warsaw Pact governments, as weakness and appeasement, and on the 6th September, Gierek was replaced as Party leader by Stanislaw Kania, who the Soviets hoped would take a harder line.

Strikes continued in the Baltic ports, and spread to other parts of Poland as a spontaneous trade union movement sprang into being, and developed, under the leadership of Lech Walesa. The organization came to be known as "Solidarity" (Solidarnosc), and soon had over 10 million members. On 24 February, the Polish Government granted a Charter of Recognition to Solidarity as a trade union, allowing it to have access to the media, but inserted a clause insisting that it must acknowledge the supremacy of the Communist Party. Solidarity protested against this restriction, and on 10 November, by a Court decision, had this clause deleted. This liberal success was unprecedented in Communist Poland, and emboldened Solidarity to press for more political advantages. It next demanded reform of the Secret Police, and under threat of a nation-wide strike, the Government agreed to discussions.

The demand for political concessions alarmed the Soviet leadership, which saber-rattled in the background while urging the Polish government to take stern measures against this thin wedge of pluralism. Walesa was a moderate leader, who wanted to progress step by step, and not to recklessly cause a head-on clash with the government which might provoke Soviet military intervention under the Brezhnev Doctrine, but as Solidarity expanded, and became a nation-wide force, some of the new leaders wanted to push for more political concessions. The Catholic Church, still a major influence in Poland, supported Solidarity.

In January 1981, unrest spread throughout the universities, and on the 21st, over 10,000 students occupied the Lodz University, demanding political relaxations. In February, General Jaruzelski, who had been the defense minister since 1968, was brought in as Prime Minister, retaining also his Defense portfolio, but he was no more successful in curbing Solidarity than his predecessor. A series of wildcat strikes swept across the country, and during the last six months of 1981, for example, there was a strike of some sort, somewhere in Poland, on every single working day, which further debilitated the failing economy.

While putting all the pressure it could on the Polish Communist Party leadership, the Soviets hesitated to intervene, hoping the adverse situation could be solved domestically to the Communist satisfaction. The Soviet leadership knew that Solidarity members would offer violent resistance, and was not sure whether the Polish armed forces would stand aside and allow Soviet troops to take over the country, as had happened in Czechoslovakia in 1968. Although Poland relied almost completely on Soviet oil, gas, iron ore, and many other essential items to run its economy, the Soviets did not apply sanctions, but kept supplies at, or even above, their normal flow; and also gave other extra aid. The Soviet leadership knew that poverty, repression and desperation are the recruiting agents of political insurrection, and did not want to stir up anything that could not be contained internally.

In October, General Jaruzelski replaced Kania as Party leader, while still retaining his appointments as Prime Minister and Minister of Defense, being given sole charge to bring his country safely back under Communist domination. The Polish armed forces still had considerable prestige, and the Soviets were hoping a Polish general would save the situation for them.

A new dimension was introduced in December when, on the 2nd of that month, a week-long sit-in by 340 cadets at the Warsaw Fire Academy was resolved when troops and police, using their new riot equipment and tactics for the first time, stormed the building and evicted the cadets. The Fire Service cadets had been demanding "civilianization" to obtain student freedoms and benefits which were not available to the military. This incident ranged Solidarity openly against the Polish armed forces.

As 1981 ended, the struggle between the Polish Government and Solidarity intensified. A thirst for political freedom had seized many in Poland, and the Government is at a loss as to how to cope, and contain it. Concessions had only led to further demands, but repressive measures could spark off all-out revolt, something Brezhnev seeks to avoid, now he is wearing his lambskin clothing. If Poland gains pluralism, which does not seem impossible, it would mean a probable course of neutralism. From a military point of view then, the keystone to the Warsaw Pact strategy in Europe would be removed. This thought should be another incentive for President Brezhnev to be more reasonable and conciliatory in the arms limitation talks.

The wolf's skin can sometimes be glimpsed through the sheepskin clothing, as happened on 27 October 1981, when a Soviet W Class submarine ran aground in Swedish territorial waters near the naval base of Karlskrona, in the Gulf of Finland. The Soviet excuse was that this had been due to faulty navigational equipment, but the Swedes claimed that the boat was on an espionage mission in a restricted area at a time when they were testing out a new torpedo; and moreover that the Soviet submarine was carrying nuclear-tipped torpedoes. It was, in fact, renewing sea-bed sensors for future nuclear torpedo and nuclear mine-laying guidance, as any Soviet operational plan for the Baltic must include neutralization of the Swedish navy, and denial of the Baltic to NATO navies. The Swedes made good propaganda use of this Soviet mishap, interrogating the captain, and holding the vessel in their waters for ten days, to the acute embarrassment of the Kremlin leadership.

The Swedes alleged the Soviets made frequent submarine espionage missions against their coastline areas.

Turning to the Middle East, the most significant events of 1981, were the assassination of President Sadat, the success of the U.S. Rapid Deployment Joint Task Force on Exercise Bright Star, and the failure of the Arab Summit Fez meeting. First of all, in Israel, the Middle East catalyst, the general election of July 1981 returned Menahem Begin to power by the tiny majority of two, to head a coalition movement which had to make considerable concessions to its politial partners. Much hung on whether the Israeli Government would keep its word and withdraw completely from the Sinai by April 1982. The United States had hoped, and indeed counted on, a more moderate government coming to power in Israel, which might take a more realistic look at the Palestinian problem, and perhaps, even unofficially, have some contact with a re-shaped Palestine Liberation Organization.

The Israeli policy for its West Bank "Occupied territories," of Judea and Samaria, was the so-called "Jordanian Solution," under which King Hussein of Jordan would resume limited sovereignty over that territory, when its Arab inhabitants would be considered as Jordanian citizens, but in some sort of federation with Israel, in which Israel would retain all defense responsibilities. The Israeli Government said openly that it considers Jordan to be the "Palestine State," and that there is no room for any other. The PLO has gained considerable influence in the West Bank, and used terrorist and intimidation tactics against those Palestinians collaborating officially with the Israeli authorities.

The Israeli Government was still actively involved in Lebanon, to its north, supporting Major Haddad's Christian "Free Lebanon" strip of buffer territory along its northern frontier; supplying the Christian militia with arms and ammunition; and perhaps taking part in covert activities that included terrorism. The Israeli "Lebanese Solution" meant the removal from that country of both the Syrian Arab Deterrent Force that had been in occupation of large parts of the country since 1976, and the Palestinian guerrillas, alleged by the Israelis to number about 7,000; and then to make "peace" with a Christian-dominated Lebanon, as a "second stage" of the Camp David Peace process. In July 1981, fighting between the Palestinians and the Israelis lasted for a fortnight, in which northern Israelis towns and settlements were bombarded by ground-based weapons, and Israeli aircraft and artillery replied by bombarding Palestinian-occupied areas of southern Lebanon.

A controversial incident occurred on the 7th June 1981, when Israeli aircraft bombed the Iraqi nuclear reactor near Baghdad, which was reportedly progressing well with its project to produce a nuclear warhead. Prime Minister Begin later admitted that the so-called "Missile Crisis," when some Syrian SAM-6s were moved into Lebanese territory in April to counter Israeli aerial activity, had been manufactured as a cover. In the first six months of 1981, the Israelis had brought down fourteen Syrian aircraft.

In Lebanon the civil war situation still simmered on with frequent clashes between the many competing factions, over 45 separate militias, and armed groups having been identified.

In Egypt, President Sadat was slowly and patiently pushing through the peace process with Israel. However, in 1980 he began to run into domestic opposition to his policies. There was a revival of Muslim extremist groups. Men took to wearing Islamic-style beards, and women to covering themselves with the shapeless chadour, or a veil, especially at the universities and educational campuses. This movement was aimed against Sadat's peace agreement with Israel, his secular state, and the Coptic minority in Egypt which probably numbered about eight million. These Muslim extremists, influenced by the Khomeini Shia Revolution in Iran, were trying to force a similar Sunni Muslim one in their own country.

There were four main forces in Egypt. The first was President Sadat and his National Democratic Party, which was in power, but in the wings enviously plotting and planning to seize power, were two others. One was the Muslim Fundamentalists, who wanted an Islamic state and society in Egypt, and the other was composed of Baathists, Communists and Nasserites, who wanted a secular, left-wing controlled state. But neither had the muscle to make a successful coup against Sadat without the support of the fourth power: the armed forces, which so far had backed Sadat. Both Fundamentalists and left-wingers had made attempts to subvert the armed forces to their cause, and reports of plots, dissidence and military purges leaked out from time to time.

During 1981, Fundamentalists stirred up trouble between themselves and the Copts, in the Coptic town of Asyut, and in religious disturbances lasting a fortnight or so, in August, some seventy people were killed. Sadat stepped in and arrested over 1,500, mainly Fundamentalists, but also a few Copts, to show he was even-handed. The following month, President Sadat warned Egypt's half-million students, forbade women students to be dressed "like walking tents," and male students to wear the long white galibaya gown and white head-caps, on campuses. Cairo briefly became known as the "city of vanishing beards." However, Sadat was not thorough enough, or had moved too late.

On 6 October 1981, President Sadat was assassinated by members of the Takfir Wal Higra group while watching the annual Armed Forces Day Parade in Cairo. Takfir Wal Higra is a familiar Koranic expression, usually translated as "Flight from Sin and Atonement," illustrating the Prophet Mohammed's flight in A.D. 622, from the then sinful city of Mecca to Medina to start his Islamic society. While all eyes were turned skywards to watch a spectacular fly-past of the Egyptian air force, a truck in the procession stopped outside the dais. Six men in military uniforms jumped out, threw grenades and fired their automatic weapons into the crowded dais, killing Sadat and seven others, and wounding several more. One of the assassins was killed by the security guards, and the others, all wounded, were captured.

The leader was Khalid al-Islam-Bouli, a serving army officer, and his five companions were former regular soldiers, who had obtained weapons, uniforms and a place in the lieutenant's truck. Some 356 people were arrested as suspects in the plot, and a purge of Fundamentalists was made in the armed forces. The assassins and twenty others were brought before a military court in Cairo in November, where although four admitted killing Sadat, they pleaded Not Guilty, claiming that the act was justified under the Shariya (Religious Law) as the President was a "heretic," and as such could be lawfully killed.

The Vice President, Hosni Mubarak, who had commanded the Egyptian air force in the Yom Kippur War of 1973, was elected President, and held the government steady during this crisis. He has a less flamboyant style and personality than Sadat. Mubarak declared his policy was to continue the peace process with Israel, and to maintain a close liaison with the West. He sought reconciliation with moderate Arab states, and made progress with Sudan, Oman and Somalia, hoping that after the failure at Fez, Saudi Arabia would openly range itself on Egypt's side against the Rejection States of the Arab League. If he is successful, a new-look Arab League could be formed, based on Egypt. When the Israelis evacuate the Sinai, Mubarak's policies may become more pro-Palestinian. He is continuing Sadat's "Infitah" (open door) policy, but has modified it to an "Infitah of Production."

After a dismal and discouraging start the United States Rapid Deployment Force project, officially designated the Rapid Deployment Joint Task Force in March 1980, designed primarily to deter Soviet aggression in the Middle East and Persian Gulf area, suddenly became a success. Its first overseas exercise in 1980, in Egypt, was a modest one, involving about 1,400 U.S. military personnel operating in the desert with Egyptian troops.

This was considerably expanded the following year in "Exercise Bright Star 82," a somewhat confusing code-name as this forty-four day joint exercise took place in November and December 1981, in Egypt, Oman, Sudan, and Somalia. In the first stage some 4,000 United States troops, together with as many Egyptian ones, trained together in Egypt; a large paratroop descent was staged; and six U.S. B-52 aircraft made the 7,500-mile journey from the United States, refuelling in mid-air, to each drop twenty-seven 500-lb. bombs, and return to base.

A thousand United States Marines made a thirty-hour beach landing exercise in Oman, near Salallah, while U.S. military personnel carried out a joint exercise in Sudan and Somalia. The fact that these three countries openly cooperated with the United States in joint exercises, although small ones, was a good sign for the future. The Bright Star joint exercises in the Middle East should obviously become an annual feature, and more moderate Arab countries, such as Saudi Arabia, Jordan, and the Gulf States, should be encouraged to participate.

In general, moderate Arab States know the Soviet threat is the paramount one, but none dare openly say so, as they have to plug the Israeli threat first, and, in theory at least, support the Palestinian cause. None could accept foreign troops or bases on their soil permanently, which would be equated with "colonialism," a stigma too much for Arabs to bear, but they know what a glittering economic and strategic prize they present to the Soviets. They also know they cannot defend themselves against Soviet-inspired dissidence or proxy troops, and so are increasingly willing to accept American military protection, provided it is presented in an oblique guise.

Feeling somewhat pushed aside by the success of Bright Star, and American success with certain Arab States, the Israeli Government endeavored to seek closer strategic ties with the United States, which so far had been wary of entering into any written defense agreement with Israel. In December, the Israeli Defense Minister visited Washington, and returned with a vaguely worded agreement for joint United States-Israel military exercises, and for the American strategic use of the two new U.S.-built airfields in the Negev, but this was met with confused Israeli criticism. Close Israeli-American strategic cooperation will mitigate against the Bright Star concept, and will deter Arab States from continued cooperation with it, so the United States will have to walk an uneasy tightrope on this issue.

The other significant event in the Middle East in 1981, was the rejection of the Saudi Arabian eight-point peace plan, the Fadh Plan, by the Arab States at the Summit meeting at Fez, in November, which, among other things indirectly indicated a recognition of Israel. This was the first Arab peace initiative since the establishment of the State of Israel in 1948. The Fez Summit Meeting had been called by King Hassan, of Morocco, but both Presidents Assad of Syria and Saddam Hussein of Iraq, and seven other Heads of Arab countries stayed away, and so the meeting had to be abandoned. This was a big prestige blow for Saudi Arabia, and may cause that country to re-align itself with Egypt, and re-think how to distribute its subsidies to certain Arab states. Both the United States and the Soviets were in favor of the Fadh Plan, the Soviets seeing it as a means of creeping back into Middle East negotiations.

The Saudis successfully negotiated the purchase of four American AWACS aircraft, despite intensive pressure from the pro-Israeli lobby in Washington. The pro-Israeli argument was that the Saudi regime was unstable and that such valuable and sophisticated aircraft might fall into either Soviet hands, or be seized in some Khomeini-type revolution, but the counter-argument was that it would be some time before the AWACS would be delivered, and more years before they were fully under Saudi control, owing to the need to train Saudi personnel to operate them. The Saudis had already been lent four AWACS aircraft to monitor the Iraq-Iran battle area. Had this U.S.-Saudi deal fallen through, the Saudis could have purchased the British "Nimrod" aircraft, which the U.S. Secretary of Defense admitted were "92 percent as good as the U.S. AWACS." Internal security had been tightened up in Saudi Arabia, but the possibility of a young officer-type coup in the future cannot be ruled out.

President Assad of Syria was in deep trouble, virtually fighting a civil war against the Muslim Brotherhood, known in this country as the Islamic Fighters for Freedom, which he alleged operated from safe bases in northern Jordan. The Syrian government used the weapons of execution, detention without trial, and other dubious methods, including suspected Death Squads; while the Islamic Fighters responded with car-bombs, explosions and assassinations.

In October 1980, President Assad concluded a standard Friendship and Cooperation Treaty with the USSR when he visited Moscow, and has since received more Soviet weapons and equipment, together with more Soviet military personnel. Soviet military advisers in Syria became targets for terrorists, and several were killed by deliberate "car accidents," but official silence hung over that black area. In August 1981, an explosion outside the Soviet Embassy in Damascus occurred as

Russian children were leaving school, officially killing three children, but other reports state the dead numbered about thirty.

The economy of Syria was in a precarious state, and the government was again at loggerheads with adjacent Iraq. For many months the Saudis had kept the economy afloat with large subsidies, but since the Fez rejection it is probable these have ceased, and perhaps went to support the opposition Islamic Fighters instead. President Assad was reluctant to release his hold on Lebanon, knowing that if he withdrew his Arab Deterrent Force, the Palestinian guerrillas would be exposed and vulnerable to both Christian and Israeli attacks, and he would lose what little influence he thinks he exerts in the Lebanese situation.

King Hussein of Jordan, was generally in favor of the Israeli "Jordanian Solution" because he would regain limited sovereignty over the West Bank, but hesitated to declare himself. He had sat on the fence for so long that he was deliberately ignored by the Carter Administration. In November 1981, he confirmed he was buying SAM-7 missiles from the USSR, claiming they were half the price of the U.S. HAWKs he had previously bought, and had no political strings attached. The conditions imposed by the U.S. for the sale of the HAWKs were that they must be in fixed positions facing away from Israel. SAM-7s were man–mobile. King Hussein's best course for long–term survival is to give facilities to the U.S. Rapid Deployment Joint Task Force, and to participate in Exercise Bright Star.

In Libya, Colonel Gaddafi continued to finance and support a wide variety of liberation movements and terrorist groups. His oil exports declined from about two million barrels a day in 1979, down to 700,000 in 1981, mainly due to maintaining a high price on the world market, which meant he no longer had huge sums of surplus cash to dispense to dubious causes world-wide, and would even have to borrow money to finance his many development schemes, including his $62.2 billion Second Five Year Plan (1981-85).

Gaddafi had African aspirations and wanted to unite the Muslim African countries into a Sahelian Empire under his leadership. The Presidents of Mali, Niger, Senegal and Somalia all accused him of working to overthrow them, and his diplomatic representatives were expelled from several African countries, notably from Ghana in 1980, and about fourteen African countries severed diplomatic relations with Libya. Gaddafi was sending arms to the Somali Salvation Front, established in 1979, which was engaging the Somali army in a guerrilla campaign in Ogaden province, and also to the POLISARIO, still fighting against the Moroccan army for part of former Spanish Sahara, claimed by King Hassan; and was behind the attempted coup in Gambia in July 1981.

In July 1980, French troops left Chad, the country to the south of Libya, which has reputed uranium deposits and other mineral wealth. A civil war broke out between President Goukani Weddei, and his former Defense Minister, Hessine Habre, the latter being supported by Sudan. In September, Goukani called on Libyan troops to help him, which in December forced Habre's small army to move to the eastern region of the country near the Sudanese frontier. The Libyan contingent in Chad rose to about 15,000 troops. The OAU decided the Libyans should withdraw and be replaced by a mixed African peace-keeping force under its sponsorship. In November, Libyan troops withdrew from Chad, but OAU replacements were slow to arrive. Gaddafi, who wanted to stage a grand spectacular OAU Summit Meeting in Tripoli in 1982, when he would become its Chairman, did not want any African complications to spoil it.

Concerned that Libyans with professional qualifications left to work abroad, and that many who went abroad to study for them did not return; and also concerned about the numerous groups of exiles plotting his downfall, in February 1980, Gaddafi issued a "come home or be killed" ultimatum to certain individuals. In a ten-week period in the spring of 1981, eleven Libyans were assassinated in London, Athens and Rome, and the American authorities reported that Libyan hit squads were roaming the United States searching for victims, armed with a "hit list" of one hundred names. In October, the American Ambassador to Italy, on a visit to Milan, had to be taken out of the country quickly as a Libyan plot to kill him had been uncovered. In December, it was announced in Washington that Gaddafi had sent a six-man hit squad to kill the U.S. President. President Reagan advised American citizens to leave Libya. It is unlikely that President Reagan will repeat the mistake of the Carter Administration, which vetoed any suggested Egyptian military invasion of Libya.

On 17 August 1981, combat aircraft from the U.S. Sixth Fleet in the Mediterranean clashed with and shot down two Libyan aircraft in the Bay of Serte (Sidra). Gaddafi claimed a 200-mile territorial sovereignty from his Tripoli shore, which included the Bay of Serte, but was not recognized either internationally, nor by the United States. The Carter Administration had instructed U.S. warships and aircraft to keep clear of this disputed area to avoid confrontation, a decision reversed by President Reagan. The Libyans, and indeed many others in the Middle East, looked at the United States with new respect and interest.

It was revealed that the Carter Administration had placed similar restrictions on the U.S. Navy in the area of the Soviet Kola Peninsula, and one wonders what other still confidential strategic decisions, so detrimental to American foreign policy, it had made.

President Numeiry of Sudan had to deal with continued opposition from both the Islamic Fundamentalists and the Communists. Libyan money played a big part in instigating trouble in Sudan, and in November 1980, a Cuban diplomat was deported, accused of interfering with internal matters. In September 1981, President Numeiry dissolved the National Assembly and appointed an Arab military governor of Equitoria province. This may bring about a resurgence of Black African sessionist insurgency in the south. The prospect of free elections again in Sudan is dim.

Sudan had a spill-over of some three-quarters of a million refugees from the adjacent territories of Chad, Eritrea, Ethiopia and Uganda, and had become a sort of confused Ho Chi Minh Trail for the various national insurgency movements in the region. In November 1980, Numeiry signed an agreement with the Ethiopian government aimed at preventing subversive activities across their common border, but it did not work. In August 1981, Gaddafi concluded his treaty with Ethiopia and South Yemen, which threw both Sudan and Somalia into the arms of Egypt.

In September 1980, Iraqi armed forces invaded the Khuzistan province of Iran, and advanced on a broad front some way against negligible opposition, succeeding in eventually taking the oil town of Khoramshahr, and besieging the oil-refinery town of Abadan, both situated on the east side of the wide Shatt al-Arab waterway that separated the two states, which was itself closed to navigation by the war. Surprisingly strong impromptu resistance was put up by the Pasdaran (Revolutionary Guards) and other armed groups, who were soon joined by elements of the shattered regular army which were brought out from the barracks on to the battlefield.

The governments of both Iraq and Iran seemed to be trying to push this inconvenient war to one side, and to ignore it as much as possible. President Saddam Hussein was struggling to preserve a veneer of normality in his country, to push ahead with his development schemes, to continue the annual Baghdad Trade Fair, to contain the northern Kurds, again restless and discontented, and to counter both the Islamic Fundamentalists and Communists on his domestic front. This war has proved that nationalism in the Middle East and the Gulf area is more powerful than religion. It was anticipated by Ayatollah Khomeini that the six million Iraqi Shias would rise up and overthrow the minority Sunni government in Baghdad, which he urged them to do, but this did not happen. The Iraqi Shias showed they were Arabs first, and Shias second; and have rediscovered historic enmities with the Persians.

President Saddam Hussein declared he would accept a cease-fire, but not withdraw from any Iranian territory he had occupied; while the Iranians refused to consider one until he does. President Hussein thought he saw the chance of a quick victory against a defenseless Iran to gain full control of the Shatt, and perhaps also obtain portions of Khuzistan province. But he had miscalculated, and obviously wished he had never started the war. Iraq was short of military manpower, and its political People's Militia carried out many garrison and rear-areas military tasks.

Preoccupied with an internal power struggle, Iran had little time for the war, but once its internal problem is solved, it will concentrate on driving the Iraqis out of the country. In the short term, the military stand-off will continue, but in the long term, as both countries have huge reservoirs of oil underground, and so can obtain credit, the Iranians should win, mainly on the factor of their military strength potential. The Iraqis will not only lose control of the Shatt, but may also have to forfeit parts of their territory. Both Iraq and Iran are constructing other means of transporting their oil abroad: the Iraqis through pipe-lines across Arab countries to the Mediterranean, and another pipe-line is projected through Jordan to the Gulf of Akaba; while the Iranians are running pipe-lines to their southern ports.

Ayatollah Khomeini was largely brought to power in Iran by the well organized Mujahideen, but when he denied them any share of power, they turned against him, and soon were openly fighting on the streets of Teheran and other cities, against the Pasdaran, the Hollbolis, and other Islamic Fundamentalist groups. This developed into virtual civil war, which dates from 20 June 1981, when President Bani-Sadr was impeached by the Majlis.

The Khomeini regime uses execution, detention and perhaps torture, repressive legislation, assassination and Death Squads, against the the Mujahideen and its left-wing allies, such as the Fedayeen, all of which were supported by the Soviet KGB and the Tudeh Party. During the first six months of this civil war, the Government admitted it had executed over 2,000 people, some extremely young. Amnesty International (13 October 1981) stated that from February 1979 until the end of September 1981, over 3,350 people had been executed in Iran.

In November 1981, the "National Resistance Council" was formed by President Bani-Sadr, and Massoud Rajavi, leader of the Mujahideen, both of whom had escaped from Iran. The largest Kurdish Democratic Party, the KDP, also joined this Council, on being promised ultimate Kurdish autonomy within an Iranian Federation. This is a formidable coalition opposition to the Khomeini regime that must stand at least an equal chance of victory in the civil war, remembering that the KGB is backing the Mujahideen. However, once such a coalition gained power it would doubtless splinter over differences of ideological opinion: it is a coalition of convenience, similar to the one that removed the Shah from power.

Khomeini's Shia Revolution has not spread outside the borders of Iran into the Gulf States, as had been expected and feared, as both Sunni opposition and nationalism were too strong. The contest is between Islamic Fundamentalists with ample grassroots support, who want an Islamic state and left-wing groups, with considerable revolutionary expertise and techniques, and KGB backing, who want a secular state. The U.S. would be wise to back Bani-Sadr, and if, and when, the National Resistance Council ultimately crumbles when perhaps power is within grasp, to continue to back him. This is one arena where the Americans should back the winner right from the start.

Turning to Southwest Asia, during 1980, the Soviet army settled on the main town of Afghanistan and the few strategic roads, expecting the puppet Afghan armed forces to cope with local protest and dissidence. The "Mujahideen," as the Afghan resistance fighters became known, lacked central direction and sufficient suitable arms, and spend as much time fighting each other as they did fighting the Soviets and the puppet Afghan army.

Afghan leaders in exile were divided among themselves, individually boastfully claiming unverifiable support from the interior, while in fact having very little effective contact with the Mujahideen proper. Military aid was slow to reach the Mujahideen, who mainly relied upon the small, but steady, trickle of Chinese arms, through the remote and mountainous Wakhan Strip since the Pakistan Government would not allow arms to be sent across its territory. Despite their expressions of support, several countries that might have been expected to send practical aid, held back. The only exception was Egypt, which sent some Soviet weapons, including SAM-7s and anti-tank missiles. Saudi Arabia sent a large sum of money, which was held on deposit in Pakistan until the Afghan exiled leadership united: it is still on deposit. Perhaps two million Afghan refugees have fled into Pakistan, which has the majority of them, and into Iran, and now are in primitive refugee camps being provided with some of the basic necessities of life by the United Nations, and other relief organizations.

Afghanistan has often been referred to optimistically as the "Soviet's Vietnam," but the analogy is not quite adequate. The main differences are lack of blanket jungle cover to conceal guerrilla movement; the general inhospitable terrain making living off the land impractical for long; Soviet control of the air; Soviet brutality in counterinsurgency tactics; and Soviet "psychological operations" of turning one tribe against the other, a relatively easy task which has been effective. Censorship cloaks many dubious Soviet activities, and Western journalists in particular are unwelcome in Afghanistan. President Babrak Karmal, the puppet leader, visited his masters in Moscow several times for briefings. Little reliable news has come out of Afghanistan, and the many rumors are easily magnified and believed.

The puppet Afghan army had shrunk in size to about 40,000 men; the Government had difficulty in enforcing conscription; and morale is low. The army is used by the Soviets against the Mujahideen on the ground to protect towns, to provide escorts for convoys, and to garrison military posts and key points. Unpalatable as this may be to Western ears, despite difficulties, the Soviets are maintaining the Afghan insurrection without too much trouble. The USSR has annexed the strategically valuable Wakhan Strip, thus severing land connection between the Afghan Mujahideen and China. There is little evidence of any intended Soviet withdrawal from Afghanistan, as the stand-off situation is one they can handle adequately for the time being. The insurgent potential of the Mujahideen is obvious, but they need uniting, suitable arms and training, and to be formed into a single guerrilla army with a clear strategic direction.

The U.S. should take a leaf from the Soviet peace strategy book and seriously consider supporting the Afghan Mujahideen. After all, the Soviets supported the Viet Cong very effectively in Vietnam, and are even now supporting Communist insurrection in Central America. At the very minimum this course could become a valuable bargaining counter with the Soviets, and at the maximum might eventually result in the Soviets quitting the country and a pro-Western Afghan Government materializing.

Disillusioned by the close Indian-USSR ties, and Indian prevarication, the Reagan Administration at last turned its attention to Pakistan, recognizing its potential as a bulwark against the spread of Communism in Southwest Asia, and that its disintegration can only be of benefit to Soviet global expansion. The Americans seem to have been forced to choose the winning side. American objections to backing Pakistan came from opposition to its military government, and its alleged nuclear warhead project, but frigid insulation can only exacerbate such a situation. It must surely be better to become involved, and to try to influence and change such policies. There is much less liberal freedom in Saudi Arabia than in Pakistan, but U.S. Administrations have made much of the former, and little of the latter, which smacks somewhat of of material expediency. In October 1981, President Zia stated he was pressing ahead with the formation of a large advisory federal council as a first step towards a new kind of political structure which is to be the basis of a general spread of democracy downwards to the people in the villages. He should surely be encouraged to continue on such a course.

Relations between Pakistan and India continued to be poor. On 4 September 1981, when Pakistan tried to re-enter the British Commonwealth of Nations, its application was blocked by India; and in November, India expelled three Pakistan diplomatic officials, and in return Pakistan expelled four Indian ones. On 19 October, the Pakistan Government offered to conclude a "No War Pact" with India: a month later, the Indian Government reluctantly, and not very convincingly, agreed in principle, but quibbled over details. Pakistan still maintains liaison with China, which supplies some arms, and in November, General Yang Dezhi, the People's Liberation Army Chief of General Staff, spent a week with General Zia, obviously discussing strategic problems and eventualities.

The attitude of the Pakistan Government towards Afghanistan has been rigidly correct. It has refused to acknowledge the Babrak Government; condemns the Soviet invasion; will not allow itself to become a Ho Chi Minh Trail for arms for the Mujahideen; and will not permit military training in its Afghan refugee camps. The Pakistan armed forces desperately need modern tanks, missiles, aircraft and communication equipment, and on 15 September, General Zia accepted a five-year $3.2 billion military and economic package which included forty U.S. F-16 aircraft.

On the other hand, India is practically the only non-Communist country in the world to officially recognize the puppet Afghan Government. In December 1980, President Brezhnev visited Prime Minister Gandhi in India. Later, on 25 August 1981, at Soviet prompting, she put forward proposals for regional talks to be held by the USSR, United States, India, Pakistan and Iran. The object was to introduce Soviet participation in regional affairs. No response came from the United States, Pakistan or Iran.

India is a much larger and stronger military power than Pakistan, and one source[1] claimed that, during the previous five years, India had concluded arms deals to the value of between $10 billion and $12 billion. This tended to overawe Pakistan, but the opening of the Karakoram Highway link with China, and United States support, has reduced the USSR-Indian prospects of carving up that country between them.

Ever pressing to obtain footholds in India, in November 1981, the Soviet Oil Minister visited that country offering to exploit Indian oil resources, particularly in the offshore fields on the eastern and western coasts. The Soviets want to ease out Western oil interests. The following month the Indian Government signed a trade agreement with Poland, valued about $200 million. Mrs. Gandhi is finding it increasingly difficult to keep a credible foot in both the Western and Soviet camps.

In Southeast Asia, Vietnam had become a Soviet client state, dependent almost entirely on that country for economic and military aid and expertise. In July 1980, the Vietnam Government granted oil concessions to the USSR. Over 150,000 Vietnamese troops remained in occupation of Kampuchea, propping up the puppet government of Heng Samrin, which was opposed by three Khmer Rouge guerrilla armies unable to form a coalition, but which carried out low level guerrilla activity against the government and Vietnamese forces in which Soviet military, and other, advisers became casualties.

In July 1980, India recognized the Heng Samrin Government; in September, the Government of Vietnam offered to withdraw its occupation force from Kampuchea if a "Vietnamese controlled and sponsored" demilitarized zone could be established to embrace Laos, Kampuchea and Thailand; and in October, the Pol Pot faction managed to retain the Kampuchean seat at the United Nations. Incidents were frequent along the Thailand-Laos, and the Thailand-Kampuchean, borders. The next domino to teeter is Thailand, as the Vietnamese are instigating insurrection in its eastern jungle provinces. When Thailand has been sufficiently "softened up," and the moment is opportune, the probability is that major Vietnamese incursions will raise the threshold of operations to full-scale guerrilla warfare in these provinces in an attempt to repeat the Viet Cong pattern of subversion and victory. Friction continues along the Vietnam-China border.

In the Pacific Ocean, the Solomon Islands, previously under Australian administration, were granted independence in 1978,

[1] Nur Ahmed Hussain, Director, Pakistan Institute for Strategic Studies, Islamabad, Pakistan.

becoming a tiny sovereign state of only about 160,000 people, in a total island area of about 11,500 square miles. In August 1981, the Solomon Islands Government had rejected a Soviet offer to prospect for oil on its sea-beds. However, the following month, there was a change of government, and the new Prime Minister, Solomon Mamaloni, stated that the anticommunist policies of his predecessor would be abandoned, and he sent off a mission to visit the USSR and other Communist countries to explore the possibilities of closer ties. Perhaps Soviet naval, and other, facilities in the Solomon Islands can soon be anticipated.

Switching now to Africa, several diverse governments, guerrilla armies and movements continued to jostle each other in the Horn of Africa. In Ethiopia, Colonel Mengistu's Marxist Dergue tried to walk the unsteady tightrope between two badly needed allies, Libya and Sudan, and after failing to work with President Numeiry, opted for Libya in August 1981. Cuban troops and many military advisers from Warsaw Pact countries remained in Ethiopia. In June 1980, the Soviets had supplied that country with stocks of nerve gas, but so far Mengistu has hesitated to use it.

During 1980 and 1981, the Dergue launched at least four military campaigns into Eritrea to try to bring that province under its firm control, but all were unsuccessful.

In September, the EPLF movement launched an all-out assault on the Muslim ELF, driving it out from Eritrea into Sudan, where it barely survives. In November, Ethiopian armed forces mounted a major attack on the EPLF guerrilla army, which had to be called off, owing to heavy government casualties. War is again in full progress between the Dergue and the EPLF, while rumors of the use of lethal gas and chemical weapons abound, but have yet to be conclusively proved. In August 1980, the OAU had recognized the disputed Ogaden province as being an integral part of Ethiopia, most of which was still held by Somali troops, but where a Libyan-financed guerrilla movement, the Somali Salvation Front, SOSAF, had been operating with increasing effectiveness against the Somali authorities.

At least 20,000 Cuban troops remained in Angola, propping up the Marxist MPLA Government, and Soviet warships were based on Luanda, to monitor Western shipping in the South Atlantic on the Cape Route, the number on station being increased from three in 1980, to at least ten a year later. The Angolan Government barely controls the eastern half of the country, as the UNITA movement, led still by Jonas Savimbi, dominates a large section of the hinterland. Savimbi's guerrilla army has prevented the Benguela railway from operating between the copper-mining areas of Zambia and Zaire and on the Atlantic coast. In August 1980, UNITA guerrillas blew up several oil tanks in the southern port of Lobita, and in November the following year, destroyed the country's only oil refinery at Luanda, which forced the government to import fuel. This became a restricting factor for the Cuban and Angolan forces operating against UNITA in the east, and against South African military incursions in the south.

Savimbi had been starved of military supplies, but admitted he had obtained about 500 tons of arms from the Chinese in 1980, insisting that none came from the Soviet Union. President Carter had forbidden any member of his administration from having any contact with UNITA, but Ronald Reagan, in his pre-election campaign, stated he was in favor of aiding that movement. It was not until December 1981 that Savimbi went to Washington to talk to the U.S. Administration.

The Reagan Administration has the golden opportunity to make up for the previous administration's miscalculation in option out of the Angolan civil war, and thus allowing by default the Cubans to move in to defeat UNITA and put the Marxist MPLA in power. The South African Government is obviously secretly cooperating with UNITA, and perhaps helping it too, but UNITA needs more help still—and urgently. If American arms and aid are sent to Savimbi's guerrilla forces, it will enable him to increase military pressure against Cuban troops in Angola, and perhaps pave the way for a new Angolan Government sympathetic to the West. Savimbi has no love for the Soviets, who supported the MPLA against him in the civil war. Cuban troops in Africa are Castro's achilles heel: Savimbi, who can prick that vulnerable heel, is the man to back in Angola.

Namibia continued to be an African trouble spot. It was due to become independent by 1983, but talks dragged fruitlessly on, with impatient SWAPO leaders demanding to be allowed to walk in and take the country over. SWAPO is being actively aided by the Angolan Government, which allows it to have bases, training camps, headquarters and sanctuary inside Angola. SWAPO raids and terrorism into Namibia resulted in a number of South African military punitive raids being launched into Angola, which increased in size and frequency. One of the first of these, a contingent some 3,000-strong, in June 1980, claimed to have demolished the SWAPO headquarters, and inflicted many casualties. Other similar operations followed. A large South African punitive operation into Angola occurred in August 1981, and another in November, both of which destroyed bases, camps and captured quantities of weapons and equipment, some Soviet. In the August raid, several Soviet personnel were killed, and one captured. The Angolan Government admitted it had been unable to regain control of large areas of its southern territory.

In Mozambique, the Marxist Government is getting a taste of its own medicine as it is facing a guerrilla insurrection in its northern provinces from a South African-backed resistance movement, which during 1981, was sabotaging road, rail and pipeline links, and bridges, with Zimbabwe to the north along the so-called "Beira-Umtali Corridor." The Soviets occasionally have difficulty in retaining the loyalty of some African regimes they have helped in the past. For example, in January 1981, President Nguessou of the Congo turned to the West for technical aid and expertise he was not able to obtain from the Warsaw Pact countries: he was feeling the pinch of Soviet economic blackmail, and did not like it.

Lastly we come to Latin America, or to be more precise, the Central American states, almost in the American backyard, where the Kremlin leadership was using Cuba as its proxy to export Communist insurgency. After it had triumphed in 1959, Castro's Revolution in Cuba was seized upon by the Soviets who falsely claimed it as their own. Cuba was to be the springboard for exporting Marxist-Leninist revolution to Latin America, but for two decades the Soviets and the Cubans had a distinct lack of lasting success. The most notorious failure was that of Che Guevara, the Argentinian, who had assisted Castro in the Cuban Revolution, then went as an uninvited Communist missionary to Bolivia, only to be hunted down and killed by U.S.-trained Bolivian counter-insurgency personnel in October 1967. A number of Communist-inspired revolutionary groups and factions materialized in Latin American countries, but they were crushed by right–wing governments or coups, especially in Argentina, Bolivia, Chile and Uruguay.

These failures caused the Soviets to modify their expansionist policy to cultivating and assisting almost any non–doctrinaire revolutionary factions, and to encourage them to enter into broad political fronts where they could be infiltrated and subverted. Cuba would remain the catalyst and Soviet proxy. Suddenly, in 1979, the Soviets and the Cubans had a break–through in Nicaragua. By this time, Soviet priorities were first of all to complete the process of gaining full control of Nicaragua, and then to subvert and overthrow the regimes successively of El Salvador, Guatemala, Costa Rica, Honduras and Panama.

Cuba was almost completely dependent upon the USSR, which subsidized its economy by about eight million dollars a day, and provided it with cheap oil and wheat, while taking its sugar crop. Cuba had Soviet arms far in excess of its normal defense needs. The Cuban Government provided training facilities for several Latin American revolutionary groups, and had become a sort of supply depot for "target countries," sending them arms and other subversive necessities. Cuba also "laundered" money for revolutionaries. For example, in September 1980, Iraq sent $500,000 to Nicaragua through Cuba, only to be up-staged in December the following year by the Palestine Liberation Organization which sent $12 million.

Nicaragua, whose main problems were poverty and under-population, had been under the rule of the Samoza family since 1933, which had succeeded in crushing successive coups and revolutionary movements. In 1978, widespread strikes and disturbances erupted in which the FSLN (Frente Sandinista de Liberacion National), known as the Sandinistas, took the prominent part. Named after Augusto Sandino, a revolutionary leader killed in 1934, the FSLN was founded in the early 1960s. In 1974 it gained publicity by seizing hostages in Managua, the capital. Again, in August 1978, the Sandinistas seized hostages, and flew off with them to Panama. By the end of the following month, President Samoza had restored order with his National Guard troops, but by this time over 5,000 people had died violent deaths.

In January 1979, the Sandinistas recommenced insurgent activities which developed into civil war. During the first six months of the year, they and their allies gained control of all the towns in the country, and put a strangle-hold on the capital. In July, President Samoza was forced to resign and leave the country (to be eventually assassinated in Paraguay in September 1980). Some 5,000 of Samoza's National Guard troops withdrew into Honduras. Daniel Ortega came to power as coordinator of the Junta of National Reconstruction, which originally included moderates.

The Ortega Junta was determined to move rapidly towards a Marxist State in Nicaragua, and gradually closed down independent radio stations and newspapers, and arrested businessmen and moderate politicians. About 3,000 Cuban civilians arrived to help reorganize the government service at all levels on Marxist lines, as well as a number of Cuban economists and school teachers. The new Junta decided to build up its armed forces to about 50,000 men: Samoza's army had numbered about 12,500. In 1981, twenty-four Soviet tanks arrived by way of Cuba; Nicaraguan pilots were training in Bulgaria, and MiG-21 aircraft were expected. Nearly 2,000 Cuban advisers and technicians were with the Sandinista armed forces.

The U.S. had suspended all military aid in February 1978 because of Nicaragua's disregard for Human Rights. In October 1980, it agreed to a United States aid package of $75 million, but this was held up by Congress, and in April 1981, the Reagan Administration suspended all aid to Nicaragua, because the Ortega Junta was arming, and training, left-wing Salvadoran guerrillas. In August, the United States announced it would not send any more aid to Nicaragua until the Sandinista's policies changed. The following month the Ortega Junta declared a National State of Economic and Social Emergency. Nicaragua can be regarded as the first "domino" in the Central American pack to fall, as it has become a Cuban proxy that is sending aid and arms to insurgents in El Salvador. At first the governments of both Mexico and Venezuela supported the Sandinistas, but since, both have had second thoughts.

The next Communist target in Central America was El Salvador, where on 15 October 1979, President Humberto was ousted by a military coup, motivated by general protest against continuing political violence and disorder. Power was assumed by a five man "Revolutionary Junta," of two military officers and three civilians; the Christian Democratic Party being the main influence in the new government. The Revolutionary Junta was less successful than Humberto in restoring a semblance of law and order, which deteriorated further. There was a spate of assassinations and political kidnappings, which were countered by harsh government measures, that included the alleged use of Death Squads.

In March 1980, Archbishop Romero, an outspoken critic of the lack of Human Rights in El Salvador, was assassinated; in June and again in August, there were national strikes which involved violence, causing the Government to declare a State of National Emergency; in October, the South African Ambassador (who had been kidnapped in November 1979) was killed by his captors; in December, four American missionaries were murdered, by which time groups of armed insurgents roamed the countryside wantonly killing and committing atrocities.

In May the Moscow-oriented El Salvadoran Communist Party, and the five main armed insurgent groups, came together into an umbrella organization, known as DRU (Unified Revolutionary Directorate), to fight a prolonged guerrilla war on the Vietnam pattern to obtain power. The main insurgent group was the "FPL" (Fuerzas Populares de Liberacion Farabundo Marti). Farabundo Marti was a revolutionary leader killed in 1932. Guerrilla operations had re-commenced with renewed vigor in the countryside and were countered by government troops, the National Guards, and the ORDEN, (Democratic Organisation), a rural militia. In October, DRU was superseded by the FMLN

(Farabundo Marti National Liberation Front) whose declared objective was to "create party unity to form the basis of a People's state after a guerrilla victory."

Some FMLN guerrillas operated from a sanctuary in Honduras. In 1969, El Salvador and Honduras had fought a brief war, known as the "Football War," over the result of a World Cup Match. As a result, El Salvador had occupied sections of Honduran border territory. On the cease-fire this became a demilitarized zone where FMLN guerrillas sheltered. Acceptance of a formal peace treaty between these two countries did not occur until October 1980 when the joint border was reopened and diplomatic negotiations resumed. Alleged massacres by Salvadoran government troops occurred in areas adjacent to the de-militarized zone. By December 1980, the FMLN boasted it had several guerrilla columns, some with artillery, on "four fronts." During 1980, the FMLN linked up with another insurgent group, FDR (Revolutionary Democratic Front) which had been founded in April, and consisted of eighteen unarmed groups including trade unions and academic bodies, all opposed to the government.

The Revolutionary Junta of El Salvador was neither able to control its armed forces, nor defeat the insurgents in the field, or indeed reduce political anarchy in the country. After the murder of the American missionaries, United States aid ceased. This, and other pressures, caused the Revolutionary Junta to reorganize. The two military members were dropped, and Jose Napoleon Duarte was proclaimed President on 13 December 1980. The following month, limited American aid was resumed, which included four helicopters, some M-16 rifles, and military instructional teams.

On 10 January 1981, FMLN members seized a radio station, issued a call to arms against the government, and declared it was launching a major offensive. The government responded by proclaiming martial law. From March until September, government forces made ineffectual counter-offensives against the guerrillas in the countryside. In August, the insurgents commenced staking out "liberated zones," in which they began to establish their own schools, clinics and farms, and by November dominated several provinces, and areas adjacent to the Honduran border. U.S. Secretary of State Haig that month determined the insurgency in El Salvador was at a military stand-off.

The FMLN claimed it had over 5,000 full-time guerrilla fighters, and about 30,000 part-time ones, who were being gradually integrated into the guerrilla army, as well as a number of groups of militia and local defense units. They were being armed mainly with Soviet weaponry arriving through Cuba, and were trained by Cuban personnel. In November 1981, Castro denied a report that he had sent "600 Cuban troops to El Salvador," but admitted he had sent "2,000 civilian volunteers," half of them women, mainly schoolteachers, but evidence pointed to the fact they were more likely to be civilian administrators.

The Salvadoran armed forces had been only about 17,000 strong, and a Pentagon assessment report said that they were little more than a "19th Century gendarmerie." President Duarte stated he required an army of up to 50,000 men to combat the insurgency successfully, and asked for American help. The Reagan Administration, in March 1981, cautiously gave a military grant of $75 million, but hesitated to send arms in quantity, which caused Duarte to rush to Washington, saying that he needed $300 million in order to win his insurgency war. By June, the Salvadoran army had reached a strength of about 20,000, but was still inadequate to cope successfully with the guerrilla opposition. For example, it had only one "rapid reaction" unit, the "Atlactl Brigade," an American-trained one of about 1,000 men, which after months of continuous action, had worn itself out by November. The problems of the Salvadoran army centered around low pay, low prestige, corruption, lack of motivation and lack of good non-commissioned officers.

In August, while on a visit to Mexico, President Mitterrand, who came to power in France in May 1981, signed a statement with President Portillo, declaring that they considered the FMLN should be recognized as a "representative political force" in El Salvador, but this was rejected by most other Latin American countries. Promising elections in October 1982, President Duarte said he would allow the FDR coalition to take part in these elections if its members were prepared to lay down the arms—which many of them had taken up in previous months.

At the OAS meeting in December 1981, at St. Lucia, El Salvador won a diplomatic victory, as OAS member states by a majority backed the Duarte Revolutionary Junta, and its plans for a 1982 election, condemning any action that constituted any "violation of the principle of non-intervention." Most OAS members had the USSR, Cuba and Nicaragua in mind. Mexico, Grenada and Nicaragua voted against this motion. In the two years, 1980 and 1981, over 26,000 people in El Salvador had been killed due to political violence.

The Big Three of the OAS countries, excluding the United States, are Mexico, Argentina and Brazil; the latter two competing with each other to be the first to produce a nuclear warhead. Claiming to have the fourth largest oil reserves in the world, the Mexican Government had become increasingly influential in Latin American councils, and does not like it to be thought that it is tied to Uncle Sam's coattails. Its president,

Portillo, for example, deplored the Reagan decision to produce the neutron bomb. The Mexican Government sees itself as a conciliatory force between the United States and what it considers to be U.S.-backed right-wing OAS states on the one hand, and the left-wing extremist of Cuba and Nicaragua on the other. It wants the United States to include Cuba in American programs to aid the poor nations of the Caribbean region, which the Reagan Administration is naturally loath to do.

General Omar Torrijos, who became Head of State for a time in 1978, remained the most influential man in the country. He had persuaded his government originally to support the Sandinistas in Nicaragua, and Panama was one of the first states to recognize the new Sandinista Government in 1979. Panama had been a transit point for gun-running between Cuba and Nicaragua. Despite his cordial relations with Cuba and support for the Sandinistas, General Torrijos was regarded by the United States as being a stabilizing influence in Central America. Commencing in March 1981, relations between Panama and Cuba began to deteriorate, and General Torrijos, who was killed in a plane crash in August, accused Cuba of being a destabilizing influence in the region.

Cuban relations with other Central American states were poor. In May 1981, after a number of border incidents with Nicaragua, Costa Rica severed diplomatic relations. Costa Rica has probably one of the poorest economies in the region, and was facing financial disaster. When, in April 1980, the Cuban Government had allowed over 100,000 refugees to quit the island, a few thousand of them remained in that country, continually making difficulties.

The Guatemalan government is faced with an insurgency problem with several groups of left-wing guerrillas active in different parts of its countryside. More than 1,000 of these guerrillas have been trained by the Cubans, who are trying to unite the various factions against the government. So far the Reagan Administration has refused military assistance to Guatemala because of allegations its government is using Death Squads and has a singular disregard for human rights. But if it hesitates too long, it may be too late to save this unsteady "domino" from falling. The Guatemalan Government claims Belize, adjacent to it. A former colony of British Honduras, Belize was granted its independence in September 1981, when it became the 156th member of the United Nations. The population of Belize is only about 160,000, and it has a small defense force of only 600 soldiers, so a British military contingent is to remain for the time being. The United States fears that if Belize falls to Guatemala, instability will result in that area.

Honduras has borders with three troubled countries: Guatemala,

El Salvador and Nicaragua, and insurgency from them spills over. Honduras is said to be the most impoverished state in Central America, and the United States fears it may be the next Cuban "target" country. The elections of November 1981 brought a liberal government to power which has to face potential Communist insurgent problems. Members of the Honduran Communist Party fought in the Cuban "International Brigade" during the Nicaraguan civil war, and many are being trained as guerrillas in Cuba.

On mainland South America, Cuba is training insurgents for the left-wing M-19 movement in Colombia, also some 500 members of the "Revolutionary Movement of the Left" of Chile were traincd in Cuba. The Caribbean island of Grenada, a former British colony, gained independence in March 1980. In September 1981, Cuba signed a technical and economic agreement with its government, on the pattern of the usual Soviet one. Cubans are working on constructing an international airport at Grenada, to be operational by 1982, which will be a convenient staging post for aircraft flying from the USSR to Cuba. Occasionally Cuba meets with a rebuff. In Jamaica, for instance, in November 1981, diplomatic relations with Cuba were severed after the Cuban Ambassador had been asked to leave overnight for allegedly interfering in domestic affairs.

The American problem is clear, but the alternatives are painful. The Soviets, through Cuba, are exporting Communist insurgency into Central America, and already Nicaragua is being turned into another springboard to be used against small, vulnerable and unstable "target" states. To do nothing would be to allow by default these "target" states to fall to Communist insurgents one by one. If these states were liberal democracies, it would be simple for the United States to provide military aid in quantity, to help their governments crush guerrilla armies. The snag is that most of them are thinly disguised right-wing military dictatorships that use repressive methods, tend to ignore human rights, and sometimes try to outdo the insurgents at terrorism. If arms and money were poured in to bolster up such regimes, the United States would stand accused of acting contrary to its declared principles, and apart from domestic and allied reprobation, would become the subject of biting and bitter Soviet propaganda.

Secretary Haig has said several times that he wants "to go to the source of the trouble," probably meaning Cuba. He has been reported to have said that "Nicaragua becomes more like Cuba every day," and has indicated he would like to take military action against the Sandinista regime, but Brazil, Mexico and other Latin American countries are against this course. The Brazilian Foreign Minister, Saraiva Guerreiro (7 December 1981) said, "Nicaragua as a sovereign state has the right to buy or receive arms from any country it wants." Mexico is too important for the United States to turn it into a confrontation state, and its government wants the United States to talk directly to Castro to find some agreement less than the military option.

Another possibility is that the United States should mount a sea-blockade around Cuba to prevent imports arriving, but as so many of them arrive in Soviet or Warsaw Pact countries' ships, this might bring about a dangerous confrontation. The U.S. Navy turned this suggestion down on the grounds that it would be extremely expensive and that the United States blockade would syphon off too many warships from other vital strategic areas.

The best compromise course for the United States to take would be to give sufficient military support to Central American countries with a Communist insurgent problem, even though the actions of their governments were dubious, primarily as an incentive to modify their policies. American aid should be conditional on governments accepting human rights responsibilities and adhering to conventional usages of war. It must be better to have some contact, and influence, than to opt out altogether, as happened in Nicaragua, and is the case in Guatemala. Soviet peace strategy should be countered by like means, and all diplomatic, political and economic pressures should be exerted against both Cuba and Nicaragua.

To counteract the Soviet long-term aim of global hegemony and strategic dominance as revealed by a study of covert activities in the seventies, the U.S. should have a strong, sustained foreign policy, geared to strategical requirements. The United States should be working to weave countries that are pro-Western in outlook and inclination into regional defense alliances.

Those who scorned or doubted the controversial domino theory should take another look at Southeast Asia, where progressively Vietnam, Laos and Kampuchea have fallen under Soviet proxy domination; and where the next dominoes to fall may be Thailand, Malaysia and Burma. The ASEAN Alliance should be supported, given teeth, and expanded to include Burma, long a Western outcast, and should develop closer links with the United States, Japan, and Australia. American influence and contact may help to modify the harsh policies of certain regimes. The absence of the United States by default simply leaves doors open for the Soviets to walk in.

In the seventies the Kremlin leadership never gave any hint it would ever respond to goodwill concessions from the United States, or ever had any intention of making any arms limitations or reductions. American strength and resolution have successfully brought a sulky and reluctant President Brezhnev to the conference table at Geneva; not a sudden Soviet change of heart. The Soviets probably will use their usual delaying tactics—dragging out proceedings indefinitely and ineffectually. If no agreement is reached on the reduction of medium-range nuclear weapons by the end of 1982, the United States should consider going ahead with its TNF plans.

Economic aid is a weapon to be used skillfully and shrewdly. The Soviet economy is failing, and if armament priorities were slackened, the Soviet people would be better fed and housed. Americans cannot be expected to pour wheat into hostile Soviet hands that one day may direct nuclear missiles against them. It seems incredible that the United States has been buying some 70 percent of Libyan oil exports, and giving economic aid to that country, when its leader, Colonel Gaddafi, was rumored to have sent hit men to kill the President of the U.S. The linkage policy might be revived, refined and used positively.

The United States hopefully can improve its record of backing governments, liberation movements and political causes. It would do well to support UNITA in Angola; the National Resistance in Mozambique, the Mujahideen in Afghanistan, and President Zia of Pakistan, instead of such countries as Ethiopia and India.

Should the Soviets take military action in Poland, or anywhere else in the world, the United States should be ready with a swift counter move. The American RDJTF project should be further developed, and used to support states in the Gulf area if required, and also other small countries friendly to the United States.

The Soviets should never be allowed to overlook, or push aside, the Helsinki Final Act, to which they agreed, and no opportunity should be missed to spotlight instances of Soviet deprivation of human rights both to the Russian people and the world at large.

Lastly, perhaps while United States resolve and strength can prevent a Third World War between the two superpowers, the dark cloud, "tiny as a man's hand on the horizon," should not be ignored. Several Third World countries are frantically working to produce their own nuclear weapons, and the 21st century may become one of small Third World wars, unless the United States takes the lead in insisting upon more strict observance of the conditions of the Nuclear Non-Proliferation

Treaty to prevent this possibility from happening. Imagine an Idi Amin (formerly of Uganda) or a Colonel Gaddafi, with a nuclear warhead, even a small one. It would be like giving a small boy a catapult on condition he does not use it. The decade of the Seventies was one of Milestones of Miscalculations, but perhaps the signs are that the one ahead can be a better and brighter one.

Bibliography

Chapman-Pincher, H. *Inside Story.* London: Sidgwick and Jackson, 1978.

Clark, Gen. Mark E. *Calculated Risks.* London: Harrap, 1951.
　　From the Danube to the Yalu. London: Harrap, 1954.

Colby, William E. *Honorable Men: My Life in the CIA.* New York: Simon and Schuster, 1978.

Douglass, Joseph D. *Soviet Military Strategy in Europe.* New York: Pergamon Press, 1980.

____. *Soviet Policy in the Third World.* New York: Pergamon Press, 1980.

____. *The Soviet Theater Nuclear Offensive.* Washington, D.C.: U.S. Air Force, 1976.

Heikal, Mohammed. *The Road to Ramadan.* London: Collins, 1975.
　　Sphinx and Commissar. London: Collins, 1978.

International Institute for Strategic Studies (London). *Military Balance* (Annual reports).

____.*Strategic Survey* (Annual reports).

Jane's All the World's Aircraft. London: Sampson Low, Marston and then Jane's Publishing Co. (annually).

Jane's Fighting Ships. London: Sampson Low, Marston and then Jane's Publishing Co. (annually).

Jane's Infantry Weapons. London: Sampson Low, Marston and then Jane's Publishing Co. (annually).

Lee, William T. *The Estimation of Soviet Defense Expenditures: 1955-75.* New York: Praeger, 1977.

Lenin, Vladimir Ilyich. *Collected Works,* 4th ed. Moscow: 1975.

Nixon, Richard. *The Real War.* New York: Warner, 1980.

Sokolovsky, V. D. *Soviet Military Strategy,* 3rd ed. (translated by Harriet Fast Scott). New York: Crane, Russak, 1975.

Thompson, Robert. *Peace Is Not at Hand.* London: Chatto and Windus, 1974.

Works translated by the U.S. Air Force

Byely, B., ed. *Marxism Leninism on War and Army.* 1974.

Druzhinin, V. V., and Kontoroy, D. S. *Decision Making and Automation—Concept, Algorithm, Decision.* 1975.

Grechko, A. A. *The Armed Forces of the Soviet State.* 1977.

Kozol, S. N. *The Officer's Handbook: A Soviet View.* 1977.

Lomov, N. A., ed. *Scientific-Technical Progress and the Revolution in Military Affairs.* 1974.

Savkin, V. E. *Basic Principles of Operational Art and Tactics.* 1974.

Sidorenko, A. A. *The Basic Offensive.* 1973.

Index

ABM systems, 24, 27, 30
ABM Treaty, 24, 30
Abu Dhabi, 96
Aden, 89
Afars, 123–24
Afghanistan, 13, 35, 133–40, 141, 190, 195, 208–9; India and, 134, 156–57, 210; and Iran, 134, 137, 141, 208; Iraq and, 83, 84; and Pakistan, 134, 137, 140, 147, 149, 150, 151, 152, 208, 210; U.S. and, 13, 34, 135, 136, 138, 139, 140, 190, 222
Africa, 5, 9, 103–31, 184–85, 204–5, 212–14. *See also* individual countries
Aini, Muhsin al-, 91
Aircraft carriers, 178
Airport agreement, Soviet-Norwegian, 53
Ajman Dubai, 96
AK-47s, 10–11, 146
AK-74s, 11
Alawite Shiites, 75, 79
al-Bakr, Ahmed Hassan, 80, 82, 83–84
Albania, 43
Alexander the Great, 134
Algeria, 64, 100, 101; and Portuguese Guinea, 106; and Rhodesia, 124; Soviet navy in, 183
Ali, Salem Rubayyi, 90
All-arms strategy, 18
Alpha class submarines, 177
Amin, Hafizullah, 137, 139, 140
Amin, Idi, 129, 130, 223
Amnesty International, 207
Andom, Aman, 118
Andpopov, Yuro, 9

Andreotti, Guilio, 54
Angola, 103, 104, 108–12, 212–13; Cubans and, 104, 111, 112, 126, 130, 168, 185, 212, 213; and Namibia, 127, 128, 129, 213–14; Rhodesia and, 125, 126; and Soviet navy, 180, 185; U.S. and, 111, 213, 222
Annam, 161, 162
Apel, Hans, 58
Aptidon, Hassan Gouled, 123
Arab League, 61, 98–99; Djibouti in, 98, 123; Egypt and, 98–99, 201; and Lebanon, 94, 95; Magreb in, 100; Somalia in, 98, 114; and Yemens, 91, 92–93
Arafat, Yasir, 66, 99–100
Argentina, 214, 218
Armed forces, Afghan, 134, 137–38, 139, 209; Angolan, 112; Chinese, 170–71; El Salvadoran, 218; Ethiopian, 117–18, 121; European NATO, 173, 184, 187; Indian, 153; Irani, 145; Kampuchean, 169; Libyan, 85, 205; Pakistani, 147, 152, 210; in Rhodesia, 125–26; Somali, 114, 115, 116, 117; Soviet, 6, 10, 17, 106, 139–40, 171–72, 173–88; of Sri Lanka, 158; Sudanese, 72; U.S., 16, 49, 173, 174, 173, 205–6, 221; Vietnamese, 163, 165
ASEAN, 167–68, 169, 221
Asia Foundation, 157
Assad, Hafez, 75–76, 77, 78–79, 80, 203, 204
Assam, 147

227